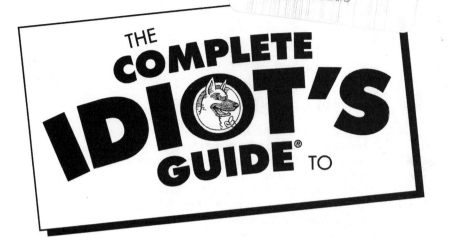

German Shepherd Dogs

by D. Caroline Coile, Ph.D.

Howell Book House   Alpha Books
Divisions of Macmillan General Reference USA
A Pearson Education Macmillan Company
1633 Broadway, New York NY 10019-6785

International Standard Book Number: 1-58245-047-1
Library of Congress Catalog Card Number: 99-19609

01 00 99   8 7 6 5 4 3 2 1

Interpretation of the printing code: The rightmost number of the first series of numbers is the year of the book's printing; the rightmost number of the second series of numbers is the number of the book's printing. For example, a printing code of 99-1 shows that the first printing occurred in 1999.

Printed in the United States of America

Alpha Development Team

Publisher
Kathy Nebenhaus

Editorial Director
Gary M. Krebs

Managing Editor
Bob Shuman

Marketing Brand Manager
Felice Primeau

Acquisitions Editor
Jessica Faust

Development Editors
Phil Kitchel
Amy Zavatto
Georgette Blau

Production Team

Development Editor
Seymour Weiss

Production Editor
Carol Sheehan

Copy Editor
Lisa M. Lord

Cover Designer
Mike Freeland

Photo Editor
Richard H. Fox

Illustrator
Bryan Hendrix

Designer
George McKeon

Indexer
Maro Riofrancos

Layout/Proofreading
Eric Brinkman, David Faust, Sean Monkhouse

Contents at a Glance

Contents

Foreword

no-bil-i-ty. (no bil' i te) n. Grand, stately, splendid, magnificent, and greatness of character.

A German Shepherd Dog exemplifies the definition of nobility and possesses all the characteristics therein.

Whether you are considering your first German Shepherd Dog or have been involved with the breed for decades, your breed of choice is universally regarded as the "King of Canines."

Since World War I, German Shepherd Dogs have served mankind with intelligence, ability, and courage as sentry dogs, Red Cross Dogs, in the military with the K-9 Corps, as messengers, as Guide Dogs, as Service Dogs, as Anti-Drug Dogs and, of course, in all aspects of the entertainment industry as stars of gigantic proportion. But perhaps the most important service to man is the unequaled ability to be a truly loving and loyal family companion. Regardless of the task at hand, you can count on the German Shepherd Dog to do the job well, and do it with style and grace.

This book provides excellent insight into the breed, its history, and its capabilities. If you are interested in a satisfying pet, a herding or obedience dog of remarkable potential, or a prospect for conformation showing, this book will guide you in the right direction in an informative and understandable manner. You will most certainly enjoy your journey into the wonderful world of the German Shepherd Dog.

The history and origins of the breed included in this book will enthrall you as you begin to understand the Shepherd's great character. You will learn what to expect in selecting and preparing for this grand addition to your home. You will begin to understand training and, no doubt, find it to be a splendid experience. If your interest lies in showing, you will find that experience to be both absorbing and exhilarating.

As the owner and breeder of Rin Tin Tin and the author of the historical account of the legendary Rin Tin Tin IV bloodline titled *Rin Tin Tin's Legacy,* I applaud D. Caroline Coile, the author of this book, for her ability to convey important knowledge in an enjoyable manner. Caroline's style of writing will appeal to readers of all ages, and this book will be a "must have" for the library of every German Shepherd Dog owner.

As you read this book, you will no doubt fall in love with the German Shepherd Dog (unless, of course, you already have). Nobility is so important to this universal favorite among dogs that the component is set forth in the breed Standard: "the ideal dog is stamped with a look of quality and nobility—difficult to define but unmistakable when present." We wish you a happy discovery in the pages ahead.

Yo Rinty!

—Miss Daphne Hereford

Owner/breeder of Rin Tin Tin, President of Rin Tin Tin, Inc.

Introduction

At first I worried about the market for this book. After all, a complete idiot would assume he or she already knew all there was to know about dogs and not bother to buy the book. Plus, a complete idiot would be interested in one of those other breeds more suited for complete idiots, instead of a German Shepherd.

Then I realized I was reading the title wrong. It's not a book for complete idiots, but a complete book about German Shepherds (yeah, still for idiots—but not complete ones; don't you feel better now?). This means I don't plan to leave anything out, but I do plan to start with the basics and work from there. With this in mind, I am optimistic about the market for the book because it has been my experience that most dog owners, while they may not actually be idiots, do incredibly idiotic things—but that they really don't want to.

In fact, I would be willing to bet that dog owners are second to none (with the possible exception of car owners) on the idiotic-actions-per-minute scale. This is because most people seem to have the idea that they are born with an innate knowledge about dogs and their care. What they aren't born with they pick up from their neighbor (whose dog just got run over) or their grandparents (whose dog just gnawed on a kid). Dogs have been the focus of bizarre ideas throughout history, and as a result of the folklore surrounding them, they still are plagued with dumb, dangerous, and downright demented doggie dogmas.

Perhaps the greatest testimony to the dog's intelligence and hardiness has been its ability to survive as a species despite being domesticated by a bunch of idiots. The problem is a lot of dogs still fall by the wayside, being killed, overtaken by disease, or abandoned to the pound, because of the idiotic notions of their owners. Even sadder, most of these owners were not idiots, just intelligent people who were never given the right information. Some of them actually had dog care books on their shelves, but the books were filled with either hand-me-down dog lore or such unrealistic scare tactics that they stayed on the shelves. This book was written to make sure you have practical, clear, up-to-date information so you can share a long and healthy partnership with your German Shepherd.

Sharing your life with a German Shepherd means more than just caring for it, though. We get dogs for lots of reasons, but one of the main ones is because they are just plain fun! So besides jamming this book full of information on caring for your dog, I've also crammed in everything I know about enjoying your dog. If you've dreamed of hauling home trophies, all sorts of Shepherd competitions await you. If you've dreamed of being a hero, all sorts of Shepherd community services also await. If you're like most people and simply dream of sharing your life with a devoted partner, I'll give you some ideas about adventures you can both enjoy.

Know Your Shepherd Like a Book

Here's a preview of what to expect in this complete guide.

Part 1: Design of the Ultimate Canine. What is it about German Shepherds that has kept them among the most popular and useful of all breeds throughout the world? Trace the origins and come to understand the forces that shaped the Shepherd of today. Familiarize yourself with the essentials of the German Shepherd physique and mystique, and finally, do some soul searching to decide if you are the right person for this breed.

Part 2: A Good (Ger) Man Is Hard to Find. And a fool and his money are soon parted. The most astute businessperson turns into a babe in the woods when it comes to finding a good dog, and finding a good German Shepherd entails even more caveats. This section will lead you through the process of finding a good source and picking a good dog, with special alerts to rip-offs and danger signals.

Part 3: Puppy Love. You get only one chance to make a first impression. Here you'll get tips to get you through those difficult first days, while saving your sanity, your carpets, and maybe even your pup's life. If you still have money burning a hole in your pocket, you won't when you get through buying all the stuff listed here, but you'll also get advice on what stuff you really need and what you can do without. This section will help you help your pup grow into its full potential.

Part 4: The Good Shepherd. You wouldn't have chosen a German Shepherd if you didn't place great value on intelligence. Your job is to shape that intelligence so your dog develops into a productive member of society rather than a canine delinquent. Dog training methods have undergone a revolution in the past few years, and you can be the first on your block to train your dog the right way. Nonetheless, no matter how good a job you do, your dog is bound to develop a few bothersome behaviors. Look here for the latest scientific ways of dealing with them.

Part 5: A Dog's Life! Eat, drink, sleep, be brushed, washed and poofed, run, swim, play—it's a dog's life, all right. Where do I sign up? Even fun and games have a serious side, and this section guides you through walking, feeding, and grooming your German Shepherd the right way. How you do it can affect your dog's health and happiness.

Part 6: In Sickness and in Health. It's a little scary at first trying to decide what's normal, what's abnormal, and what's an emergency in an animal with a body so different from our own, especially when that animal can't even tell us where it hurts. All dogs need some normal health and veterinary care, and if you choose your veterinarian wisely, you will have a trusted member on your dog's health team to guide you. To make it even more complicated, German Shepherds have their own set of problems to which they are predisposed, problems you seldom see in other breeds. You are the front line of defense when it comes to your dog's health, and this section will supply you with some formidable ammunition.

Part 7: It *Is* How You Play the Game. Finally, the fun stuff! German Shepherds can do just about anything, and they excel in all sorts of canine competitions. Your Adonis can strut in the show ring or your Einstein in Obedience Trials—there's something for just about every Shepherd! Their true forte is in serving others, and here they have proved their mettle as search-and-rescue dogs, protection dogs, Therapy Dogs, and—well, you'll have to read the chapter because the list is too long. Most Shepherd owners prefer simply to share every aspect of their everyday lives with their dogs, and here you will find advice on how to have fun safely.

Part 8: If You're Not Part of the Solution.... Then you're part of the problem. Once you've read this far, you no longer have the excuse of being an idiot, but you will probably realize you are surrounded by idiots when it comes to dogs. Do your part for the future of dogs, and set a good example. You can do even more for the breed by helping German Shepherds in need.

Tidbits

I will be assisted throughout this book by two "coauthors," Al and Shep, who insert their comments throughout. Al tends to be very authoritative—and always right—so pay attention to what "Al Says." Shep is all ears, but most of what he hears is just plain wrong. So consider carefully whatever "Shep Heard"; he probably heard wrong!

Also look for specific "extra" German Shepherd information sprinkled throughout the pages in the "Germane to Shepherds" boxes. Just so I'd look smart, I made sure to include a bunch of words and sayings you might not know, but you can look smart too by learning what they mean and nonchalantly springing them on your friends. The definitions can be found in the "Learnin' German" boxes. And to keep you on your toes, be forewarned that I have included several "Pup-Quiz!" boxes when you least expect them.

Al Says

Look here for little extra kibbles of information thrown in for good measure.

Shep Heard

Check out what Shep heard for the most insidiously incorrect dogma dogging the dog world.

Germane to Shepherds

Here you'll find non-generic extras specific to German Shepherds.

Learnin' German

You, too, can rattle off cool-sounding dog lingo like a pro by checking out the definitions here.

Pup-Quiz!

No cheating—put your books away and get out your pencil. And keep your eyes on your own paper.

About the Author

One of my earliest memories was a close-up view of the inside of a dog's mouth right before it bit me on the eye. As the dog bites amassed throughout the years (some people are slow learners), for some perverse reason I grew to be totally fascinated by dogs. I had to know everything about them, from the inside out. Well, I didn't really want to see them inside out; I prefer mine outside out. I got dogs of my own, which didn't bite me but caused me to start asking questions: "Why won't he come when he's called?" "Do you think he might be deaf, and how would I know?" "Is disobedience hereditary in dogs?" "Can this dog be helped?" Run-of-the-mill dog lore wasn't good enough. I had to turn to scientific literature and research. In the process of finding the answers, I ended up doing dog research myself and getting a doctorate in psychology/neuroscience, with special interests in dog behavior, senses, and genetics. I even stopped getting bitten by dogs.

Meanwhile, I've owned anywhere from none (too few) to 12 (too many) dogs at a time. Some of them have been big-time show dogs (Best in Show and Best in Specialty Show and Pedigree Award winners), and some have miraculously been ranked number one and number two in the country for Obedience. Others have never set foot in any ring but are still Best in Yard winners and number one in vital categories, including puking on manuscripts, digging holes in chairs, pushing people off beds, and grabbing food off counters. We are so proud. This book is dedicated to the dogs that have forced me to learn more and more by never letting me take anything for granted: Baha, Kara, Khyber, Bobby, Khyzi, Sissy, Dixie, Hypatia, Savannah, Kitty, Beany, Jeepers, Junior, Wolfman, Stinky, Luna, and Honey.

When I announced to my friends that I was writing this book, all concurred I was the ideal choice. Finally, it seems they had acknowledged my 10 previously published books on dog care, plus my two masterpieces *"Show Me!"* and *"The Encyclopedia of Dog Breeds,"* as well as my roughly 100 published dog-related articles (some award-winning)—yes, finally it appeared I had won the admiration of my peers. They, however, kept laughing and saying it had something to do with how the title of the book was fitting. Fitting what? I don't get it.

Part 1

Design of the Ultimate Canine

How do you create a legend? Although some owners might contend that German Shepherds were sent to Earth from above, the truth is they are a man-made breed (sort of). They are the result of very special ingredients, however, blended to a precise secret recipe by a master chef. That recipe survives today in the form of the breed Standard. This vision of perfection is that way because it has to be to do the many jobs asked of it. Some people like Poodles and some people like Shepherds. Make sure you really like and know German Shepherds. Don't try to get a German Shepherd and expect it to act like another breed—it's not in its genes. If you really can appreciate the many attributes and needs of this dog made in heaven, you might just have the makings of a match made in heaven.

German Shepherd Genesis

In This Chapter

➤ In the beginning...

➤ How one man shaped a breed

➤ From shepherd to police dog to war dog to actor

➤ Every silver lining has a cloud

A low growl warns of an intruder's presence... A steady pull guides a blind person away from danger... A hurtling form brings down a fleeing criminal... A cold nose reassures a worried mother... A lithe shape searches amid a pile of rubble for buried victims... A warm body huddles close to keep a lost person alive... The best dog in the world joins his special boy on a grand adventure every day and guards at the foot of his bed every night.

Intelligence, loyalty, nobility, sensitivity, courage—the German Shepherd Dog is what we wish more humans were like. It is the dog not only of action-adventure movies, but of real-life heroism. But it wasn't always so. The German Shepherd of today arose from humble beginnings, an unassuming dog with a good work ethic. There were many such dogs in the late 19th century; what eventually made the German Shepherd different was in large part the life's work of a single man. Max von Stephanitz shaped the German Shepherd into the

Learnin' German

In Germany, the German Shepherd Dog (GSD) is known as the **Deutsche Schaferhunde. Alsatian** is a traditional name for the breed in England, but is neither correct nor current. I use Alsatian only occasionally, because just try rhyming something with "German Shepherd Dog" or "Deutsche Schaferhunde"!

breed that would become the most popular and versatile dog in the world. To understand the dog, you must understand its roots.

Alsatian Creation

Dogs have shared a relationship with people throughout the world and recorded history, a relationship based originally on function. Who knows what first possessed a caveman to invite a wolf into his home and thus cause the first case of a dog wetting in the house (or cave, as the case may be). Either cavemen didn't mind this or the dog proved to be so useful that a few sacrifices had to be made.

Those dogs that proved less useful or that were too wild, skittish, or dumb probably ended up in the caveman's pot, while those that proved helpful lived to produce more of the same. Some were better at sounding alarms at intruders, and some were better at chasing down game. Eventually breeds were born by mating the best guards to the best guards and the best hunters to the best hunters. As other animal species became domesticated, dogs that could guard and control them became especially important. It was these early stock-tending dogs that the German Shepherd claims as its forefathers.

Al Says

The first dogs are thought to have been domesticated about 12,000 years ago. Dogs and wolves are considered by many scientists to still be the same species, *Canis lupus*, although sometimes the dog is considered a subspecies, *Canis lupus familiaris*, or a separate species, *Canis familiaris*.

Of course, these early canines weren't really breeds. Few cavemen had AKC (American Kennel Club) papers for their dogs, so pure breeding wasn't terribly important to them. Still, with time, strains of dogs became more and more specialized, so that by the 19th century, the German countryside was home to a group of adept but diverse sheep-herding dogs. Many of the dogs were not large or tough enough to handle some of the bigger, stubborn sheep found in Germany. The custom in Germany was to rely on sheepdogs, not fences, to contain the sheep. Farmers and herdsmen needed a dog that could prevent sheep from wandering into forbidden fields, drive them to new areas, protect them from threats, and act as a sort of mobile fence by patrolling along the unfenced boundaries. These were very different requirements than those for sheepdogs in most other parts of the world. Although many of the German dogs met these challenges admirably, too many did not.

Enter Captain Max Emil Frederick von Stephanitz, born in 1864. Von Stephanitz was a cavalry officer who had some knowledge of functional animal anatomy. He admired the German sheepdogs but envisioned a dog that consistently combined all their best traits. He was not the first person to have such a vision, but he was the first to bring that vision to reality. Although he was determined to create such a breed in the 1890s, he was not in a position to pursue his dream until he married an actress in 1898—an act so unworthy of an officer that he was asked to leave the military.

Shep Heard

...that German Shepherds are part wolf. Shep heard wrong! German Shepherds have no more wolf in them than any other breed of dog. But, of course, all dogs are wolves!

Although he had experimented (somewhat unsuccessfully) with breeding dogs in the 1890s, his luck changed in 1899, when he found the dog that embodied his ideal. He bought the dog, called Hektor Linkrsheim, and immediately changed his name to Horand von Grafrath. Having discovered the dog that would found the breed, von Stephanitz then founded a club devoted to the breed, the *Verein für Deutsche Schaferhunde* (SV), with Horand as the first dog registered.

The SV immediately set about holding annual *Sieger* (national championship) shows, in which von Stephanitz judged and chose the best male (the Sieger) and female (the Siegerin). He based his awards not only on the dogs' merits, but also on their pedigrees and ability to counteract faults prevalent in the breed. Because breeders usually flocked to the Sieger of the year, von Stephanitz was able to steer the breed's development in this way. He could steer it even better by deciding which dogs should be registered or bred. As the SV grew, local branch clubs arose. Local Breed Wardens were appointed who would inspect litters and evaluate breedings. This iron-fisted policy may have seemed tough, but was largely responsible for the breed's rapid rise in quality. That tough operating policy is still in place in Germany today.

War and Police

Von Stephanitz demanded that the dogs be useful first, second, and always. Beauty, while appreciated, was not a top priority. Sound temperament and body, as well as a zest for life and work, were paramount, and he devised Herding and Obedience Trials for testing these qualities. Yet even as the ultimate German sheepherding breed was growing in popularity, German sheepherding was on the decline. Now that von Stephanitz had created the sheepdog of his dreams, it was threatened with large-scale unemployment. Leave it to von Stephanitz to reinvent his precious breed, promoting German Shepherds as police and military dogs. Although the military scoffed at the notion, by placing several dogs with the police force, he demonstrated their courage and ability to deter and apprehend criminals. As their reputation for police work grew, a few were adopted by the military. Those few were so good at their mission that when German troops entered World War I, they did so with the German Shepherd at their side. No other dogs had ever proved so useful or versatile in wartime. Whether searching for wounded soldiers, laying phone lines, or serving as messengers, sentries, or guards, the German Shepherd introduced a new element into warfare.

World War I was a turning point for the breed. Soldiers from abroad returned home with tales of the uncannily intelligent German dogs. Foreign countries saw their usefulness and also adopted them for military and police work. The breed gained immense popularity in the years following the war. With popularity came indiscriminate breeding by unknowledgeable or unscrupulous breeders. Von Stephanitz implemented a system for surveying dogs and then recommending them for breeding or excluding them from it. That survey system, the *Körung*, is still in effect today. Von Stephanitz could save his beloved German Shepherd, but he could not save himself from the breed's success. With the coming of the Nazi regime, Nazi SV members effectively overthrew von Stephanitz. Amid threats of being sent to a concentration camp, he finally gave up control of the SV in 1935. He died a year later, 37 years to the day of the SV's founding. However, he left a legacy of the most incredibly versatile dog ever known.

Germane to Shepherds

About 1,500 GSDs were used by the German army in WWI and about 25,000 in WWII. At the beginning of WWII, 32 dog breeds were acceptable for military service; at the end, the German Shepherd stood alone.

Alsatian Migration

In the early 1900s, purebred-dog mania was sweeping Europe and America. Anything that looked like a pure breed and could be trotted around a show ring was fair game. The German Shepherd was no exception, and the first GSD (then called German Sheepdog) was registered by the American Kennel Club in 1908. Perhaps because they didn't have the eccentric looks or foo-foo ways of some of the more popular breeds, they really didn't make that much of a hit; those early imports had little impact on present GSDs in America. All things German became unsavory during WWI, and the breed lost much of what favor it had found in America. The American Kennel Club changed the breed's name to simply Shepherd Dog in an attempt to protect the breed from patriotic zealots. With the ending of the war in 1918, the American public was quick to forgive the breed its German heritage, and coupled with tales of the dogs' incredible feats of war service, dog lovers were even faster to welcome them into their homes. In fact, wherever soldiers came from, German Shepherds followed them home, spreading throughout the world.

Germane to Shepherds

In England the breed was first known as the Alsatian Wolfdog (despite being of neither Alsatian nor wolf derivation). The "Wolfdog" part of the name was dropped relatively soon, but it was not until 1979 that the name was changed to German Shepherd Dog.

WWI may have sparked the general public's interest in the GSD. It was two dogs, however, that set it ablaze.

Howlywood Stars

Amid the influx of German Shepherds following WWI came a dog that would never distinguish himself in the show ring, but would become the most famous dog in America. Etzel von Öringen was born in 1917, trained for police work in Germany, and brought to America in 1921, where he eventually became the property of an actor/writer and dog trainer team. Retrained and renamed for the movies, "Strongheart" was an instant screen sensation, the first truly famous animal star. If the public was infatuated with the German Shepherd before, they were now head over heels in love!

Such was Strongheart's fame that it seemed he would never be eclipsed. Yet the greatest canine star of all time had already been born and would soon become a household word. During WWI, an American army patrol discovered the lone survivors of a bombed German dog kennel, a mother and her five newborns, and took them back to base. After the war, one member of that patrol, Lee Duncan, returned home with two of the pups, a brother and sister named Rin Tin Tin and Nannette (named after good luck dolls children gave returning soldiers in Europe). Nannette's luck didn't hold, as she soon died of distemper, but Rin Tin Tin (or Rinty to his friends) went with Duncan to Los Angeles.

In 1922 Rinty was entered in a dog show, which he lost, and a jumping competition, which he won with a jump of nearly 12 feet. The jumping event was filmed, and Rinty was a natural on the big screen. He appeared in several film shorts doing various stunts, and Duncan optimistically wrote a script for a feature-length film starring Rinty. As so often happens, it was turned down by studio after studio, until his big break came when Rinty was able to step in and play the part of a wolf, completing in 20 minutes what the studio had not accomplished with a real wolf in days. The grateful studio, a small one named Warner Brothers, decided to feature Rinty in first one film, and then film after film. Rin Tin Tin is credited as the dog who saved Warner Brothers and made the company a household word to this day. Rinty seldom rehearsed, having an uncanny ability to understand what was required of him. Strongheart had been a star; Rin Tin Tin was a superstar!

Rin Tin Tin, the legendary German Shepherd movie hero, captured the public's admiration for and fascination with the breed.

Rinty lived a long life, filming 21 silent movies and 8 "barkies." He made personal appearances all over the country. When he died at age 14, understudies Rin Tin Tin II, III, and IV followed in his pawsteps. Rinty left a treasury of films, but more than that, both he and Strongheart exposed almost every person in America to the wonder of the German Shepherd.

Germane to Shepherds

Yet another famous German Shepherd film and TV star was Bullet, Roy Rogers's dog.

Bullet helps Dale Evans bring in the "bad guys." (Green & Tillisch)

It Was the Best of Times

At the time, it seemed all the GSD had to do was to be seen to be coveted. Shepherds had gone to many parts of the world following WWI. Wherever they went, people wanted more. They spread around the globe and in short order became the single most popular breed in the world. It seemed the only limit to their abilities was the imagination of the people who trained them. During WWII, they were the first dogs to be trained to locate buried victims in British air raids, the precursors of today's search-and-rescue dogs. The GSD's role as a guide dog for the blind began in Germany after WWI, but became greatly expanded after WWII, thus beginning a legacy of helping disabled people live with more independence and dignity. Their presence on police forces throughout the world grew to unsurpassed levels. Just as important, they proved themselves to be dependable and loyal family members. As more and more German Shepherds gained fame through heroic deeds, often literally saving people's lives, more families chose the GSD as their breed.

Serious dog fanciers continued to breed and compete with GSDs, excelling at obedience, tracking, and

Germane to Shepherds

The top-winning AKC show dog of all breeds, of all time, is a female German Shepherd named Champion Altana's Mystique, winner of 275 all-breed Best in Show awards.

conformation competitions. Actually, they didn't just compete; they won. German Shepherds became invincible in the obedience ring and dominated the Working Group, and later the Herding Group, at AKC shows. The German parent club, the SV, became the largest and most powerful breed club in the world. It now has over 100,000 members and 2,133 local clubs governed by 20 *Landesgruppen* (local) branches in Germany. The World Union of German Shepherd Dog Clubs, or WUSV, has over 450,000 members worldwide.

Germane to Shepherds

The GSD was initially classi-fied in the AKC Working Group, but in 1982 the herding breeds, including the GSD, were split off to form their own Herding Group.

It Was the Worst of Times

Whenever something gets popular, people try to make a buck. German Shepherds have been very popular for a long time, and many people have tried to make a lot of money at the dogs' expense. As early as 1920, opportunists had stepped in and begun breeding GSDs as fast as they could. Not every GSD has the temperament, health, or physical qualities that exemplify the breed, so not every GSD needs to be bred. Yet poor-quality dog after poor-quality dog was bred repeatedly, with no regard to the quality of the dogs pro-duced or the lives they had. Dogs with poor temperaments were sold to unsuspecting families, and the German Shepherd gained a reputa-tion as a biter. Dogs with poor health were also sold, with their lov-ing families agonizing over diseases that seemed to plague the breed. The German Shepherd became the poster child for hip dysplasia, and with the public's growing awareness of hereditary problems in pure-bred dogs, the GSD show breeder got the blame. More German Shepherds fell into the wrong hands, often owned by people who thought the meaner they could make them, the better protectors they would be. It doesn't work that way, and German Shepherds were blamed unjustly for the bad habits they had been taught. As numbers grew, prices fell, sometimes to nothing, and more people got GSD pups on a whim, only to abandon them over the slightest problem.

11

Von Stephanitz could probably not have foreseen the popularity and worldwide impact his breed would have throughout the 20th century. But he certainly never imagined that this most noble of dogs could be found peering from a cage at an animal shelter—a breed that would give its life for the people it loved, but was too often the victim of human stupidity and greed.

The Least You Need to Know

➤ German Shepherds arose from generations of courageous, vigilant, intelligent dogs that specialized in tending livestock.

➤ Max von Stephanitz orchestrated the creation of the perfect German sheepdog.

➤ World War I introduced the German Shepherd to the rest of the world, and movie stars Strongheart and Rin Tin Tin made the breed a household word.

➤ The German Shepherd is the most versatile and popular breed in the world, but popularity carries the price of overbreeding and neglect due to greed and ignorance.

Chapter 2

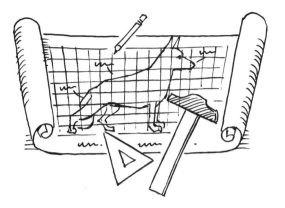

Blueprints and Pawprints

It's no accident that German Shepherds look like German Shepherds. They look like they do because they are built a certain way to do a certain job. Looks aren't everything, however. A good-looking GSD should also exhibit sound conformation and be able to move with efficiency and strength, and needs to have the good sense to be able to direct his good-looking, good-moving self to do some good work. The good Shepherd of today is the result of generations of breeding to an exacting blueprint, a standard of perfection (not just a standard of "good enough") of the idealized German Shepherd.

A Fine Design

In the United States, the accepted breed standard is the one submitted by the German Shepherd Dog Club of America to the American

Kennel Club. Other German Shepherd organizations that are members of the WUSV abide by the SV standard. There are few substantial differences between the AKC and SV standards, however. A good German Shepherd is a good German Shepherd, no matter what standard it is judged by or what country it is in. Following is the complete, official AKC standard for the German Shepherd Dog.

Germane to Shepherds

Secondary sex characteristics in GSDs include a larger build, more powerful head and jaws, and perhaps a slightly thicker coat and cocky attitude in males.

General Appearance: The first impression of a good German Shepherd Dog is that of a strong, agile, well-muscled animal, alert and full of life. It is well balanced, with harmonious development of the forequarter and hindquarter. The dog is longer than tall, deep-bodied, and presents an outline of smooth curves rather than angles. It looks substantial and not spindly, giving the impression, both at rest and in motion, of muscular fitness and nimbleness without any look of clumsiness or soft living. The ideal dog is stamped with a look of quality and nobility difficult to define, but unmistakable when present. Secondary sex characteristics are strongly marked, and every animal gives a definite impression of masculinity or femininity, according to its sex.

Size, Proportion, Substance: The desired *height* for males at the top of the highest point of the shoulder blade is 24 to 26 inches; and for bitches, 22 to 24 inches.

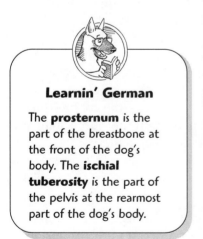

Learnin' German

The **prosternum** is the part of the breastbone at the front of the dog's body. The **ischial tuberosity** is the part of the pelvis at the rearmost part of the dog's body.

The German Shepherd Dog is longer than tall, with the most desirable *proportion* as 10 to $8^{1}/_{2}$. The length is measured from the point of the prosternum or breastbone to the rear edge of the pelvis, the ischial tuberosity. The desirable long proportion is not derived from a long back, but from overall length with relation to height, which is achieved by length of forequarter and length of withers and hindquarter, viewed from the side.

Head: The *head* is noble, cleanly chiseled, strong without coarseness, but above all not fine, and in proportion to the body. The head of the male is distinctly masculine, and that of the bitch distinctly feminine. The *expression* keen, intelligent and composed. *Eyes* of medium size, almond shaped, set a little obliquely and not protruding. The color is as dark as possible. *Ears* are moderately pointed, in proportion to the skull, open toward the front, and carried erect when at attention, the ideal carriage being one in which the center lines of the ears, viewed from the front, are parallel to each other and perpendicular to the ground. A dog with cropped or hanging ears must be *disqualified.*

Al Says

The word "fine" used in a breed standard means "delicate." Coarseness refers to overly large features and bones.

Seen from the front the forehead is only moderately arched, and the skull slopes into the long, wedge-shaped muzzle without abrupt stop. The *muzzle* is long and strong, and its topline is parallel to the topline of the skull. *Nose*—black. A dog with a nose that is not predominantly black must be *disqualified.* The lips are firmly fitted. Jaws are strongly developed. *Teeth*—42 in number—20 upper and 22 lower—are strongly developed and meet in a scissors bite in which part of the inner surface of the upper incisors meet and engage part of the outer surface of the lower incisors. An overshot jaw or a level bite is undesirable. An undershot jaw is a *disqualifying fault.* Complete dentition is to be preferred. Any missing teeth other than first premolars is a *serious fault.*

Neck, Topline, Body: The neck is strong and muscular, clean-cut and relatively long, proportionate in size to the head and without loose folds of skin. When the dog is at attention or excited, the head is raised and the neck carried high; otherwise typical carriage of the head is forward rather than up and but little higher than the top of the shoulders, particularly in motion.

Learnin' German

The **stop** is the transition from the muzzle to the forehead along the head's topline. An **overshot bite** is one in which the incisors (front teeth) of the upper jaw extend beyond those of the lower, leaving a gap between them. In an **undershot bite**, the upper incisors are behind the lower incisors. The first **premolars** are the very small teeth immediately behind the canine teeth.

Topline—The *withers* are higher than and sloping into the level back. The *back* is straight, very strongly developed without sag or roach, and relatively short. The whole structure of the *body* gives an impression of depth and solidity without bulkiness.

Chest—Beginning at the prosternum, it is well filled and carried well down between the legs. It is deep and capacious, never shallow, with ample room for lungs and heart, carried well forward, with the prosternum showing ahead of the shoulder in profile. *Ribs*—well sprung and long, neither barrel-shaped nor too flat, and carried down to a sternum which reaches to the elbows. Correct ribbing allows the elbows to move back freely when the dog is at a trot. Too round causes interference and throws the elbows out; too flat or short causes pinched elbows. Ribbing is carried well back so that the loin is relatively short. *Abdomen*—firmly held and not paunchy. The bottom line is only moderately tucked up in the loin.

Loin—Viewed from the top, broad and strong. Undue length between the last rib and the thigh, when viewed from the side, is undesirable.

Croup—long and gradually sloping. *Tail*—bushy, with the last vertebra extended at least to the hock joint. It is set smoothly into the croup and low rather than high. At rest, the tail hangs in a slight curve like a saber. A slight hook—sometimes carried to one side—is faulty only to the extent that it mars general appearance. When the dog is excited or in motion, the curve is accentuated and the tail raised, but it should never be curled forward beyond a vertical line. Tails too short, or with clumpy ends due to ankylosis, are *serious faults*. A dog with a docked tail must be *disqualified*.

Forequarters: The shoulder blades are long and obliquely angled, laid on flat and not placed forward. The upper arm joins the shoulder blade at about a right angle. Both the upper arm and the shoulder blade are well muscled. The forelegs, viewed from all sides, are straight and the bone oval rather than round. The pasterns are strong and springy and

Learnin' German

The **topline** is the line formed by the silhouette of the neck, withers, back, loin, and croup. A **roach** in the back refers to one that is arched upward like a Greyhound's back. The **bottom line** is the line formed by the silhouette of the chest and abdomen.

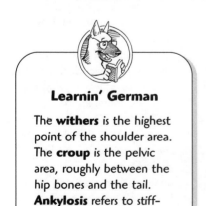

Learnin' German

The **withers** is the highest point of the shoulder area. The **croup** is the pelvic area, roughly between the hip bones and the tail. **Ankylosis** refers to stiffened or fused joints.

angulated at approximately a 25-degree angle from the vertical. Dewclaws on the forelegs may be removed, but are normally left on. The *feet* are short, compact with toes well arched, pads thick and firm, nails short and dark.

Hindquarters: The whole assembly of the thigh, viewed from the side, is broad, with both upper and lower thigh well muscled, forming as nearly as possible a right angle. The upper thigh bone parallels the shoulder blade while the lower thigh bone parallels the upper arm. The metatarsus (the unit between the hock joint and the foot) is short, strong and tightly articulated. The dewclaws, if any, should be removed from the hind legs. Feet as in front.

Learnin' German

The **pasterns** are the "ankles" or "wrists," just above the feet. The **dewclaws** are the poorly attached fifth toes, analogous to the human thumb, growing from the area of the inner pastern.

Coat: The ideal dog has a double coat of medium length. The outer coat should be as dense as possible, hair straight, harsh and lying close to the body. A slightly wavy outer coat, often of wiry texture, is permissible. The head, including the inner ear and foreface, and the legs and paws are covered with short hair, and the neck with longer and thicker hair. The rear of the forelegs and hind legs has somewhat longer hair extending to the pastern and hock, respectively. *Faults* in coat include soft, silky, too long outer coat, woolly, curly, and open coat.

Learnin' German

The **metatarsus** is often simply called the "hock."

Color: The German Shepherd Dog varies in color, and most colors are permissible. Strong rich colors are preferred. Pale, washed-out colors and blues or livers are *serious faults*. A white dog must be *disqualified*.

Gait: A German Shepherd Dog is a trotting dog, and its structure has been developed to meet the requirements of its work. *General Impression*—The gait is outreaching, elastic, seemingly without effort, smooth and rhythmic, covering the maximum amount of ground with the minimum number of steps. At a walk it covers a great deal of ground, with long stride of both hind legs and forelegs. At a trot the dog covers still more ground with even longer stride, and moves powerfully but easily, with coordination and balance so that the gait appears to be the steady motion of a well-lubricated machine. The feet travel close to the ground on both forward reach and backward push. In order to

Germane to Shepherds

Some GSDs have a "blue" (actually a silver-gray) color in place of the normally black hairs, caused by a recessive allele ("d"). These dogs tend to have a grayish cast to their noses and eye rims. GSDs may also be "liver" in which the normally black hairs are instead shades of brown, caused by another recessive allele ("b"). These dogs have brown noses and eye rims, and often yellowish eyes.

achieve ideal movement of this kind, there must be good muscular development and ligamentation. The hindquarters deliver, through the back, a powerful forward thrust which slightly lifts the whole animal and drives the body forward. Reaching far under, and passing the imprint left by the front foot, the hind foot takes hold of the ground; then hock, stifle and upper thigh come into play and sweep back, the stroke of the hind leg finishing with the foot still close to the ground in a smooth follow-through. The overreach of the hindquarter usually necessitates one hind foot passing outside and the other hind foot passing inside the track of the forefeet, and such action is not faulty unless the locomotion is crabwise with the dog's body sideways out of the normal straight line.

Transmission—The typical smooth, flowing gait is maintained with great strength and firmness of back. The whole effort of the hindquarter is transmitted to the forequarter through the loin, back and withers. At full trot, the back must remain firm and level without sway, roll, whip or roach. Unlevel topline with withers lower than the hip is a *fault.* To compensate for the forward motion imparted by the hindquarters, the shoulder should open to its full extent. The forelegs should reach out close to the ground in a long stride in harmony with that of the hindquarters. The dog does not track on widely separated parallel lines, but brings the feet inward toward the middle line of the body when trotting, in order to maintain balance. The feet track closely but do not strike or cross over. Viewed from the front, the front legs function from the shoulder joint to the pad in a straight line. Viewed from the rear, the hind legs function from the hip joint to the pad in a straight line. Faults of gait, whether from front, rear or side, are to be considered very *serious faults.*

Temperament: The breed has a distinct personality marked by direct and fearless, but not hostile, expression, self-confidence and a certain aloofness that does not lend itself to immediate and indiscriminate friendships. The dog must be approachable, quietly standing its ground and showing confidence and willingness to meet overtures without itself making them. It is poised, but when the occasion demands, eager and alert; both fit and willing to serve in its capacity as companion, watchdog, blind leader, herding dog, or guardian, whichever the circumstances may demand. The dog must not be timid, shrinking behind its master or handler; it should not be nervous, looking about or upward with anxious expression or showing nervous reactions, such as tucking of tail, to strange sounds or sights. Lack of confidence under any surroundings is not typical of good character. Any of the above deficiencies in character which indicate shyness must be penalized as very *serious faults* and any dog exhibiting pronounced indications of these must be excused from the ring. It must be possible for the judge to observe the teeth and to determine that both testicles are descended. Any dog that attempts to bite the judge must be *disqualified*. The ideal dog is a working animal with an incorruptible character combined with body and gait suitable for the arduous work that constitutes its primary purpose.

Disqualifications:

Cropped or hanging ears

Dogs with noses not predominantly black

Undershot jaw

Docked tail

White dogs

Any dog that attempts to bite the judge

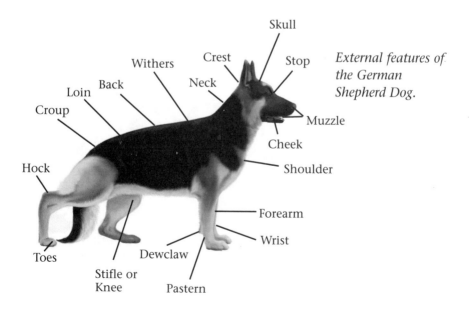

External features of the German Shepherd Dog.

Stepping Out

The standard of perfection is more than just arbitrary beauty marks. In theory, the dog that is built right will move right. This works in theory, but not always in practice. That's why a big part of evaluating a German Shepherd is watching it move from every angle.

The German Shepherd was developed to trot tirelessly for a full day of work, acting as a moving fence while performing its duties as a herding dog. Subsequent jobs also required tireless athleticism, whether it was as a patrol dog, service dog, or just plain companion.

The German Shepherd standard describes the most efficient trot in dogdom. The hallmark of the GSD's trotting gait is its great elasticity, strength, and fluidity, covering the ground in long, ground-eating strides. The GSD is the dog that invented the so-called "flying trot," in which all four feet are off the ground at full extension so that the dog actually floats forward with every stride. No other breed of dog can approach the trotting ability of the German Shepherd Dog.

Good trotters also have to be sound when viewed from the front or rear. In general this means that the legs converge in a straight line toward the center line of gravity without interfering with one another. Any deviation from a straight line of support (such as cowhocks, turned pasterns, or bow legs) weakens the dog's stride and detracts from its strength.

Observing the German Shepherd Dog in action is truly a moving experience.

Real Character

The best-looking, best-moving GSD in the world is nothing without character. This is a breed with work to do, and no matter how well built a dog is, the desire and temperament to do its job is not something you can force on a dog. It is either there or it is not. If it is not, then you might have a lovely pet, but you won't have a real German Shepherd.

The German Shepherd standard emphasizes temperament perhaps more than the standard of any other breed. Look also at what the SV standard says about temperament:

Under General Attributes:

> "With an effervescent temperament, the dog must also be cooperative, adapting to every situation, and take to work willingly and joyfully. He must show courage and hardness as the situation requires to defend his handler and his property. He must readily attack on his owner's command but otherwise be a fully attentive, obedient and pleasant household companion. He should be devoted to his familiar surroundings, above all to other animals and children, and composed in his contact with people. All in all, he gives a harmonious picture of natural nobility and self-confidence."

And under Temperament, Character and Abilities:

> "Sound nerves, alertness, self-confidence, trainability, watchfulness, loyalty and incorruptibility, as well as courage, fighting drive and hardness, are the outstanding characteristics of a purebred German Shepherd Dog. They make him suitable to be a superior working dog in general, and in particular to be a guard, companion, protection and herding dog. His ample scenting abilities, added to his conformation as a trotter, make it possible for him to quietly and surely work out a track without bodily strain and with his nose close to the ground. This makes him highly useful as a multipurpose track and search dog."

The German Shepherd has remained the most popular breed in the world not because of its looks, not because of its movement, but because of its character. It is the dog at its best, a true companion that is what we wish our best human friends could be: noble, courageous, loyal, but in private moments saved for you alone, a bit of a clown and a puppy at heart—a real character!

The perfect German Shepherd would conform to every point of the standard and trot with great, sound strides. Beyond that, it would be of strong and noble temperament and of robust health. There is no perfect German Shepherd, but yours will come close, I hope, and it will surely be your perfect friend.

The Least You Need to Know

➤ The GSD standard of perfection describes a dog that can best do the job for which it was bred.

➤ The AKC GSD standard includes disqualifications for cropped or hanging ears, a nose that isn't predominantly black, an undershot jaw, a docked tail, a white coat, or an attempt to bite the judge.

➤ A disqualification means the fault is considered so severe the dog cannot compete in conformation shows.

➤ The GSD is noted for its "flying trot."

➤ A dog that is built right and moves right is still not all it should be unless it is healthy and has a sound temperament.

Chapter 3

Have You Met Your Match?

"You can choose your friends, but you can't choose your family." Whoever said that obviously never picked out a dog. With a dog, you can choose both your friend and family.

Despite this great opportunity, most people devote about as much time to choosing their new dog as they do to ordering lunch from a drive-thru window—certainly less than they spend choosing the other choosable family member (their spouse). Not surprisingly, more people divorce their dogs than their spouses in this country. The problem is that, unlike divorcees, spurned dogs don't end up in singles bars, but in animal shelters. For most of them, it's a one-way trip. So my first mission in this section is to talk you out of getting a dog, and to try even harder to talk you out of getting a German Shepherd. If you're still not convinced it's the mistake of a lifetime, then you just might be ready to choose the friend of a lifetime.

Obviously, you're supposed to answer "yes" to each "Pup Quiz" question (you're not getting a passing score that easily), so let's get into the essay answer part of the quiz.

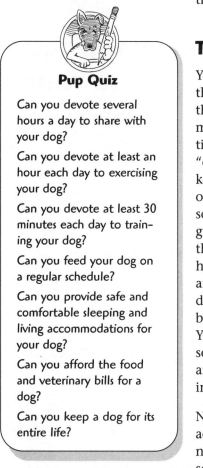

Pup Quiz

Can you devote several hours a day to share with your dog?

Can you devote at least an hour each day to exercising your dog?

Can you devote at least 30 minutes each day to training your dog?

Can you feed your dog on a regular schedule?

Can you provide safe and comfortable sleeping and living accommodations for your dog?

Can you afford the food and veterinary bills for a dog?

Can you keep a dog for its entire life?

Time-Sharing

You're late to work again, you push the dog outside, hustle the kids out the door and spend a grueling day making a buck. You come home dead tired, but determined to spend that "quality time" with the kids. The dog keeps butting in and dancing on top of the Monopoly board on the floor, so back outside he goes. Dinner guests arrive, and the dog is sniffing them in embarrassing places. How'd he get back inside anyway? Guests are gone—oh yeah, time to feed the dog (patting yourself on the back for being such a responsible dog owner). You go in the yard, fall in a hole, and see the day's laundry scattered about and the plants all dug up. That dog is incorrigible!

No, that dog is neglected. Dogs are active, intelligent animals that cannot be subjected to a life sentence in solitary confinement. Nor are they toys that can be put away until the next time you feel like playing with them, or breathing furniture there to provide an all-American backdrop for your perfect family picture. If you plan to get a family dog, make sure it's a real member of the family.

German Shepherds are smarter than the average dog. They need companionship and activity, even more than most other breeds. You don't have to quit your job to get a German Shepherd, but you do have to make time for your dog, just as though it were a second job with no time off and no sick leave.

Active Duty

For some perverse reason, dogs love to exercise. This is incredibly irritating to many dog owners (although a major appeal to the health-crazed minority). German Shepherds really love to exercise. They were bred to cover miles of territory every day and to keep on the move for hours. A stroll around the block is not going to cut it, so you have a few choices. You can buy about 20 acres of land and fence it securely so your Shepherd can patrol the perimeter, you can buy a doggy treadmill and run up your electric bill, or you can get up off the sofa and become healthy yourself! Walk, even jog, your dog a couple of miles every day. You can cheat by shortening the walk, but adding a play session. This way you get to stand relatively still while throwing sticks and balls. If physical exertion is out of the question for you, then strongly reconsider getting a German Shepherd.

Intelligence Testing

Most people think they want a canny canine, but very few people are prepared to deal with and nurture that intelligence. An intelligent child who is given no direction or stimulation is on its way to becoming a problem child; the same is true for an intelligent dog. If you plan to keep your dog in a cage a good part of the day, or even locked in the house alone while you work, then you don't want a dog whose mind is racing with ideas and a need for entertainment. You want a dumb dog (actually, if you plan to ignore your dog, you want a stuffed dog). A dog cannot read a book or watch TV when things are slow; it needs things to do. A smart dog looks for ways to entertain itself, and it finds them. The problem is that the most intelligent dog is still not smart enough to think of helpful things to do for entertainment. True, it may decide to redecorate your house, but chances are the ripped drapes and chewed paneling will not be the new styling you had in mind. The bored dog digs, barks, gets into the garbage, chews, escapes, and comes up with some amazingly mischievous ideas. Then what happens? Their owners try to remove all possible items the dog could entertain itself with, or they lock the dog in a cage or run. The dog can always find a way to do something, even if it's only barking or biting itself—and when it finally gets a chance to do something, it's so crazed with relief and ecstasy that its owners consider it uncontrollable. They conclude that this supposedly intelligent dog is actually stupid and wild, and take it on a one-way trip to

25

the dog pound. An intelligent dog needs intelligent things to do—and an intelligent owner who realizes that.

Making a success of owning a German Shepherd means never forgetting the extent of your dog's intelligence.

German Shepherds are intelligent dogs. This means you need to exercise your German Shepherd's mind as well as its body. Training your dog not only tires out its little brain, but, because it's a German Shepherd, actually results in learning on the dog's part! You have it within your power to create perhaps the one being in the world who will pay attention to what you say and even mind you. For some breeds, training is a nice option; for German Shepherds, it is a necessity. They are too smart, too powerful, and too active to remain without a leader. If you don't plan to lead, then get out of their way, because they will gladly take over. Unfortunately, although they may be smart for dogs, they really aren't leadership material.

Despite (or perhaps because of) them being the near-equivalent of canine Einsteins, you still need plenty of patience with your German Shepherd. Can you calmly say "Now give me my wallet—oh, I see you've eaten a $50 bill? Gee, I sure hope it doesn't upset your delicate tummy!" and then walk away without contemplating home surgery? Can you return to your car to find your dog's face poking up from a sea of upholstery foam and simply get in and sit on the springs as you drive serenely home without detouring to the dog pound? German Shepherds are ingenious geniuses, and, like all gifted children, they are prone to occasional experimentation.

Cost of Loving Index

"All you add is love"—and a lot of work and a mound of money. Dogs are the best love money can buy, but they don't come cheap. Besides the initial cost of your German Shepherd (which could range from $100 to $10,000), you need to feed the dog, house the dog, and fix the dog, not to mention all the fun stuff you can spend money on, such as toys, accessories, classes, and competitions, and all the un-fun stuff, like replacing your carpets, doors, and plants.

Feeding the Dog

Dogs not only like to eat, they have to eat. Despite this novel nugget of biological information, some dog owners think that if they have to stay late at work, spend the night away from home, or use their money for a new outfit, their dog can just go without. It's not right, and it's not healthy. Then there's always the case of the "child who promised to feed the dog." Of course, this is a promise never kept, but too often the parents resolve they will teach the child a lesson by not giving in and feeding the dog. Huh? Feeding the dog does not require the combined efforts of the great chefs of Europe, but it does require consistency and some outlay of money to buy a decent quality food. You can't just throw your leftovers in a vat and slop the dog, or you will spend all the money you think you are saving at the vet's office.

Germane to Shepherds

German Shepherds are good-sized dogs, and they need to eat about 3 to 6 cups of food each day. A typical feed bill for an adult GSD is about $300 to $500 per year.

Housing the Dog

Where will your new family member live? In the basement? The garage? A pen? What a lovely welcome! These places can be modified to serve as temporary quarters, but if you want your German Shepherd to be part of the family, unless you plan for your family to hang out in the basement, garage, or pen, you need to make some compromises so your dog can share your household. This doesn't mean you have to give your dog the run of the house and first rights to all your furniture. Dogs need their own place, so wherever you want your dog to sleep, you need to make it a special spot all its own, complete with soft bedding. A cage fulfills this role and is a suggested purchase.

Keep in mind that like all dogs, German Shepherds shed. In fact, German Shepherds shed a lot. If you cannot tolerate hair in any part of your home, a Shepherd is not the dog for you. Also consider that Shepherds are large dogs. If you live in tight quarters, the addition of a dog to step over every time you need to cross the room may not be a good idea.

Some people who want their dog to function as a guard dog reason that sleeping inside will spoil it for its duties, but your dog is far more likely to guard its family if it actually knows who its family is.

If you plan for your dog to spend a good deal of its time outside, you must provide a warm shelter for winter, shade for summer, and a fence for year-round security. The German Shepherd's intelligence is at once its greatest asset and perhaps its greatest undoing. Owners convinced of their dog's high IQ figure their Rin Tin twin is too smart to need supervision, so they allow it to roam at will. After all, who ever saw Rin Tin Tin in a fenced yard? Actually, Rin Tin Tin lived in another era when the highways weren't crowded with high-speed cars, and you can bet Rin Tin Tin never roamed at will. The smartest dog is nonetheless dumb by (most) human standards, and a loose dog is eventually likely to be a dead dog. If the dumbest thing you can do is to let your dog run loose, the next dumbest is to chain it up. Dog chains are the perfect recipe for strangled or aggressive dogs. They are not acceptable. Nor are little dog pens stuck out in the "back forty." Even if you live in the middle of the country, you need a fenced yard for your German Shepherd, a yard that it shares with the rest of the family.

Expense Calculator

One-time Expenses

      Dog: _____

      Puppy vaccinations: _____

      Fence: _____

      Collar: _____

      Leash: _____

      Neuter/spay: _____

      Toys: _____

      One-time total: _____

Yearly Expenses

      Food: _____

      Checkup/vaccinations: _____

      More toys: _____

      Yearly total: _____

When You Least Expect It

      Replace carpeting: _____

      Replace interior of car: _____

      Emergency trip to vet to remove carpeting
and auto upholstery: _____

      Unexpected total: _____

Optional Expenses

      Classes: _____

      More classes: _____

      New home with bigger yard: _____

      Optional total: _____

Grand Estimated Total Over Next 10 Years: _____

Fixing the Dog

Some people rush to their own doctor at the slightest bump, but then ignore their dog's ailments until it mercifully keels over (at which

Germane to Shepherds

German Shepherds are pre-disposed to several serious health problems, including hip and elbow dysplasia, osteochondrosis dissicans, cauda equina, gastric torsion, and perianal fistulas, all of which can be very expensive to treat. See Chapter 17 for more details.

point their owners are shocked at its sudden demise). On the other hand, just as many dog owners rush to the vet when their dog has a bump, yet never see the inside of a doctor's office themselves. The truth is your German Shepherd will have to go to the veterinarian, and although vets may be nice folks, they don't work for free. Your dog will probably need at least vaccinations, worming, neutering, heartworm checks, and preventives. Add a couple of visits for when your dog is puking on your couch or other assorted pleasantries, and you have a normal year's vet expenses of about $150 to $400. As with people, the threat of catastrophic illness looms. Cancer, trauma, and all sorts of weird ailments can cost thousands of dollars to treat. Chances are they won't happen, and you can't be expected to spend your children's college fund on your dog, but you need to be aware of the possibility of such a problem. Veterinary bills are usually highest in the first and last years of your dog's life.

'Til Death Do Us Part

How will a dog fit into your long-term plans? Do you know where you will be living a year from now? Can you say with assurance you will live somewhere that allows you to have your dog and that you will not allow your circumstances to change to the point you can no longer keep a dog? If you add a baby to the household, does the dog go? Do you dream of taking a cruise around the world? Plan on having your Shepherd for about the next 10 years, and on caring for it every single day of those 10 years. Shepherds make great dogs in part because of their loyalty to their families. Don't get a Shepherd on a trial-run basis. They are sentient beings who will not understand why they have been banished to the back yard or abandoned to the dog shelter. After you have used up your dog's irresistibly cute puppy months, few people will line up to offer it a new home. If the old standby line "We found him a home in the country" were true, then country roads would be impassable with the millions of these former city-slicker dogs. That home in the country was most likely called the city pound, and most dogs don't leave there alive.

The number one pet problem in this country is lack of responsibility and of commitment. Our disposable society thinks nothing of trading in a dog for another model at the slightest whim. It is always the human half who is the unfaithful one; your dog will remain loyal to you no matter how big a jerk you are. Can you be as responsible as your dog? Before you get a dog, can you take a vow to care for it "in sickness and in health, for richer or poorer, 'til death do us part?"

Now is the time to sit down for a serious reality check with your entire family, and if your reality check bounces—fish make great pets!

The Least You Need to Know

➤ German Shepherds are large, intelligent, active, hairy dogs, so consider the pros and cons of owning such a dog.

➤ A German Shepherd needs daily physical exercise, at least an hour a day, and mental exercise, at least a half hour per day of challenging tasks.

➤ Running loose, being tied out, or being kept in a small pen are not acceptable ways to keep your dog outside.

➤ Think long term: Are you sure you can keep a dog for the next 10 to 12 years?

Part 2

A Good (Ger) Man Is Hard to Find

If you have come this far, I assume you passed the acid test and have decided you are German Shepherd Dog material. Now all that's left is to hop in the car, answer that newspaper ad and speed down to get your very own dog that will put Rin Tin Tin to shame, right? How shall I put this delicately—a fool and his money are soon parted? There's a sucker born every minute? You're smart enough to read this book, so be smart enough to seek, choose, and buy your German Shepherd wisely. To do this, you just need to be pointed in the right direction. As a popular breed, a German Shepherd is easy to find. As a popular breed, a good German Shepherd is hard to find. How will you know a good one from a not-as-good one? Where will you look? Those answers, and more, can be found in this section.

Chapter 4

Familiarity Breeds Contentment

In This Chapter

➤ American versus European Shepherds

➤ Understanding American and German registration

➤ The meaning of pet, show, and breeding quality

If you want a cookie-cutter breed in which all the dogs look and act alike, don't start looking at German Shepherds. They come in different colors, different styles, and different coats, and they have been bred with different emphases. Besides the generally accepted colors, you will see white German Shepherds, and you will also see long coated German Shepherds. You will see show GSDs, obedience GSDs, service GSDs, and Schutzhund GSDs. You will see American GSDs and German GSDs and sometimes GSDs from other countries, too. This is a breed with a lot to offer, not only with respect to its incredible abilities, but also its variety. When it comes to German Shepherds, one size usually does not fit all.

What Is a German German Shepherd?

A great way to get an argument started among GSD breeders is to ask them whether an American or a European (usually German) GSD is better. The pages of popular dog magazines are crowded with more

35

ads for European German Shepherds than for those with American lines. Part of this is the implied prestige that comes with owning a dog either directly imported or tracing immediately back to its country of origin. It's obviously more than that, however, since you don't see a similar flood of people importing other breeds from their homelands.

Many people feel that the continued control of the SV, the organization that created such an incredible breed in the first place, continues to ensure that the best GSDs come from Europe. With the SV's system of Breed Wardens and surveys, it is unlikely that some of the poor quality, unhealthy dogs routinely bred in America would ever pass muster there. In fact, though, most of the poor specimens bred in America have not passed muster here either, as they have seldom earned Championship titles or other awards. Unfortunately, the average GSD pet buyer is unaware of the meaning of titles, awards, and health clearances. One advantage of the German system is that the Breed Wardens and surveys have done much of the work for you. German GSDs are not approved for breeding unless they have passed certain conformation, temperament, training, and health requirements. This means that SV registration, unlike AKC registration, does carry with it some seal of approval, no matter how minimal.

Even the very best American and German GSDs do differ, however, and your choice of lines will depend on your personal taste and just what it is you want your GSD to do. Each type has its own admirers, but keep in mind: They are all German Shepherds, members of one of the best breeds around, no matter where they're from.

If you have your heart set on showing in AKC shows, by all means get an American-bred GSD. American GSDs have been selected for generations for exquisite type, showy attitude, and the most fluid, powerful movement known in the world of dogs. Compared to European Shepherds, such a dog tends to have a more refined head, yet be a bit larger overall. Perhaps most noticeable is the more extreme angulation (bend) of the hind legs, accompanied by a greater slope of the torso from front to rear. Detractors of American GSDs claim they are exaggerated, have lost their working ability, and tend to lack courage. Admirers strongly disagree!

European GSDs tend to act and look a bit different. Because of the emphasis on working ability, if you want a GSD for protection or

The individual dog's quality is determined by how closely it conforms to the breed Standard in the opinion of the observer. (William Brown)

obedience, you might have a better chance with a GSD from German lines. They tend to have thicker, stronger heads, less angulation of the hind legs, and less slope from front to rear. Their bodies tend to be slightly shorter and thicker, and their toplines often show a noticeable arch. Detractors of European GSDs claim they are bred with little regard for looks, and may be overactive and exhibit too high a prey drive for the average owner. They agree European GSDs are great for protection work, but are impractical for most people who need a quieter, more easygoing companion.

A disadvantage of buying a dog directly from Europe is that you probably won't be able to visit the kennel or meet the dog beforehand (although it does give you a good excuse for that European vacation!). You should be able to see pictures and a video of the dog, however, and you should also be able to check the importer's references. You should have a signed contract, too, before parting with your money. Many American breeders have GSDs from European lines, so you need not get a dog directly from overseas to acquire a GSD of this type.

Remember that the differences in conformation between the European and American dogs mean that a big winner in SV shows will not necessarily be any kind of a winner in AKC shows (and vice versa).

The Bone-A-Fidos

Like all the best things in life, there are always imposters and fakes. How can you be sure your new dog is a bona-fide German Shepherd Dog? Papers.

Papers are for more than housebreaking; they are proof of your German Shepherd's pure ancestry. They consist of a litter or individual registration certificate issued from a registry. In most cases, this is the American Kennel Club (AKC), but German imports are registered with the SV.

These are not the only registering bodies. The United Kennel Club is also a respected dog registry in the United States, and most developed countries have a national kennel club that registers dogs. Many also have "imposter" registries. Many small registries have popped up offering to register dogs even if the dogs lack proof of pure breeding. You should be wary of dogs registered with one of these unknown organizations (no matter how high-falutin' the registry's name sounds) because they often are no more registered or purebred than you or I.

Some unscrupulous breeders promise to provide registration documents "soon" and never deliver them. By the time you figure this out, you are already too attached to the puppy to ask for a refund.

Al Says

If registration papers are not available at the time you buy the puppy, ask to see both parents' registrations and get a written statement that the proper documents will arrive within a mutually acceptable time frame. In the meantime, get a bill of sale that identifies your puppy.

Don't confuse the registration certificate with a pedigree. A dog with a pedigree is not necessarily registered, although a dog registered with a legitimate registry must have a pedigree. Registration papers are the actual documents that record a dog's registration numbers. The pedigree is more often an unofficial document (although you can purchase official certified pedigrees through the AKC, and the pedigree is part of the SV registration certificate). The pedigree is a listing of your dog's family tree. To the experienced breeder, it is a history of breeding decisions that can be traced through generations. Incidentally, all registered German Shepherds can have a pedigree "as long as your arm"; the length of the pedigree doesn't mean one dog is somehow more "pure" than another. It just means a bigger piece of paper is attached to it.

Finally, remember that neither AKC nor SV registration is a seal of quality. AKC registration means only that the dog's ancestry is pure and registered (and even that can sometimes be subject to faking); many AKC-registered dogs are poor examples of their breed. SV registration implies that the parents have at least met certain minimal standards of health, breeding, and quality; nonetheless, nothing can guarantee how an individual puppy will turn out.

AKC Registration

AKC registration papers consist of a registration certificate or application form, which you complete and send to the AKC to register the dog in your name. If these papers are not available when you buy the puppy, the breeder is required by AKC rules to give you a signed statement or bill of sale that includes the breed, sex, and color of the dog, its date of birth, the breeder's name, and the registered names of the dog's sire and dam (with numbers, if possible). The AKC takes about three weeks to process registrations, so any claims by the breeder that lack of papers are because of delays any longer than that should be met with suspicion.

Often a breeder sells a pet-quality dog with a Limited Registration, which means that if the dog is bred, its offspring will not be registered by the AKC. Breeders do this because they do not think the dog should be bred, and it is extra insurance in case the new owners fail to have the dog neutered or spayed. Such dogs can still compete in AKC Obedience Trials and other performance competitions. Limited Registration may be changed later to regular status only by the breeder.

SV Registration

SV certification is far more extensive than its AKC counterpart. It includes a four-generation pedigree complete with breed survey information, color, hip certification, titles and show ratings, and information about littermates. Unfortunately, because all the information is in German, it is all "Greek" to most Americans.

Learnin' German

The parent German Shepherd Club in Germany is the SV (Verein für Deutsche Schaferhunde). The SV registration papers are called **Rasse-Echtheitszertifikat,** and the pedigree, the **Ahnentafel.**

First, it may be either white (with green borders) or pink; the "pink papers" are more desirable because they are issued only when both sire and dam are recommended for breeding. In either case, the first page contains information on the individual dog, such as its name, color, birth date, breeder, and registration number. The top right-hand corner may also contain the "a" stamp for hip certification and survey remarks, if any. It also contains information about ancestors found more than once on either the sire's or dam's side of the pedigree, listing these dogs' names and the generation of the pedigree in which they can be found, with sire and dam sides separated by a dash. The second and third pages contain the dog's pedigree, complete with the color and survey reports of the parents and grandparents, as well as the names of littermates. Dogs in the pedigree that were recommended for breeding have an asterisk preceding their name. The fourth page is used to record ownership transfers.

Learnin' German for Real, or How to Read SV Papers

Inzucht auf: linebreeding

Geschlecht: sex

Haarart: coat

Farbe und Abzeichen: color and markings

Besondere kennzeichen: special marks

Tatowier-Nr.: tattoo number

Wurftag: day and month of birth

Wurfjahr: year of birth

Züchter: breeder

Anschrift: address

Lebenszeit: surveyed for life

"a" Zuerkannt: hip certification

Eltern: parents

Grosseltern: grandparents

Urgrosseltern: great-grandparents

Geschwister: littermates

Vater: sire

Mutter: dam

KB: breed survey report

Working /Training Titles

BIL: guide dog for the blind

DH: service dog

DPH: police service dog

FH: Tracking Dog

HGH: Herding dog

INT: international Schutzhund title

PFP: police Tracking Dog

PH: police dog

SchH: Schutzhund

ZH: customs service dog

1: beginning level

2 or 3: competition level

ZB: Show Ratings

VA: excellent select

V: excellent

SG: very good

G: good

Ausr: sufficient

M: faulty

U: insufficient

Quality Quandaries

Experienced breeders rate their dogs as pet, competition, and breeding quality. A pet-quality dog is generally the least costly because it has some trait that would prevent it from winning in conformation (or sometimes other) competitions. These traits should not be flaws in temperament or health; such dogs are obviously not ideal pets and should usually not be available for sale. Being a pet is one of the most important roles a dog can fulfill, and pet quality is an essential trait of every good GSD.

Competition (usually Schutzhund or conformation) quality dogs should first of all be pet quality; that is, they should have good temperament and health. Those destined for the show ring should portray the attributes called for in the breed Standard, such that they could reasonably be expected to become conformation champions. Those destined for Schutzhund or Obedience competition or for working should be of sound body and mind. Be somewhat cautious if a breeder contends they never have anything less than competition quality.

Breeding-quality dogs come from impeccable backgrounds and should be of even higher quality than competition-quality dogs. These dogs must pass a battery of health clearances and be of sound temperament and conformation. Breeding quality means more than the ability to reproduce, but far too often these are the only criteria applied to prospective parents by owners unduly impressed by a registration certificate or a pedigree. Be extremely wary if a breeder claims all the pups in a litter are breeding quality. It is difficult to pick a competition-quality puppy at an early age; it is impossible to pick a breeding-quality puppy.

If you want a competition-quality Shepherd, or especially if you want one of breeding quality, it would be worthwhile to pay someone knowledgeable in the breed to go with you and give you an educated opinion. Even then, an educated opinion is still only an opinion.

Decide well ahead of time what your intentions are for your new dog. A lot of hard feelings have arisen because of misunderstandings revolving around quality. Don't get a pet-quality dog with plans of showing or breeding it. A reputable breeder has reasons for labeling a pup as pet quality; it could prove very embarrassing if you show up in the ring with it as other breeders will assume you were sold the pup as show quality. Don't get a pet-quality pup with plans of breeding it; again, the breeder has good reasons for not believing this dog should be bred. Many ethical breeders sell pet-quality dogs with only Limited Registration privileges, which were explained earlier in this chapter. Others give you the full ownership of the dog only upon proof that you have had it spayed or neutered. Some buyers accuse these breeders of making those demands so they can curtail their competition for puppy sales; although this may occasionally be true, most often such non-breeding clauses are signs of a responsible breeder.

By the same token, don't get a show-quality Shepherd and then never show it unless you have cleared this ahead of time with the breeder. Good breeders lose money with every pup they sell. Their compensation comes in part with the pride of seeing the dogs they so carefully produced represent them in the show ring. When you promise to show that dog and then never do, you are cheating the breeder—and maybe the breed.

The better quality you demand, the longer your search—and your wait—will take. A couple of months is a reasonable time to look for a pet puppy; a couple of years for a breeding-quality dog. Begin your search for a high-quality GSD by seeing as many GSDs as possible, by talking to GSD breeders, by attending GSD competitions, by reading every available GSD publication, and by joining GSD discussion groups on the Internet.

The Least You Need to Know

➤ European German Shepherds differ from American ones in looks and temperament.

➤ Registered dogs or dogs eligible for registration should come with the appropriate documents.

➤ True breeding quality is the rarest and most expensive quality, followed by competition (or show) quality, and then pet quality.

Pick of
the Litter

Knowing where to look and what you want is half the battle. Now it's time to narrow the field and get the dog of your dreams. Getting to see the parents and even grandparents of your prospective puppy is the best indicator of how your pup will turn out. Remember the essentials: looks, temperament, and health.

The Essentials

For looks, the essentials of the German Shepherd Standard are your most reliable guide. The GSD has an outline of smooth curves on a body that is longer than tall, somewhat higher at the shoulders than the rear. It is strong, agile, and substantial. It has a strong, chiseled head with medium-sized, almond-shaped eyes and erect, moderately pointed ears. It has a double coat, with the outer coat consisting of dense, straight, or slightly wavy, harsh, close-lying hair of medium length, with a bushy tail. Its trot covers the ground in great strides. Its color is typically either tan or silver with a black saddle, or entirely black or sable.

For temperament, look first to the parents. They should neither try to attack you nor slink away from you. If the pups are quite young, you may have to make allowances for the dam, as she may be somewhat protective of them. Pups raised with minimal (or aversive) human contact during their critical period of development (from about 6 to 10 weeks of age) may have some lifetime personality problems. Notice how the breeder interacts with the adults and pups, and whether the puppies are being raised underfoot (good) or out of sight (bad).

For health, ask the breeder how old the dogs in the first two generations of the pedigree lived to be. Ask to see health clearances, especially certification for hip dysplasia and elbow dysplasia. Ask the breeder about health problems in the line, and look at the parents and puppies to see if they appear healthy. Is the puppy being raised in sanitary conditions? Does it have its puppy vaccinations? Has it been checked or treated for internal parasites? No matter how much research you do into the background of any puppy, there is no guarantee that your dog will live a long and healthy life. But why not go with the odds and choose a dog from the healthiest background possible?

Many breeders supply health guarantees with their puppies. Unfortunately, a guarantee is of little value if, for you to be compensated, it requires you to return or euthanize a dog you have grown to love. At the same time, a breeder never has total control over the future health problems of any puppy and generally cannot afford to offer you your money back for every problem, especially without veterinary certification. A good compromise is a guarantee that

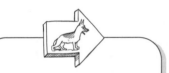

Germane to Shepherds

In America, OFA certification is most usual. OFA rates hips as Normal (with Excellent rated better than Good), Transitional (with Fair rated better than Borderline), and Dysplastic (with Mild rated better than Moderate and both rated better than Severe). Elbow certification is either Normal or Dysplastic. See page 178 for more information about hip and elbow dysplasia.

covers certain problems that can be well documented (most commonly hip and elbow dysplasia) and that compensates you with a replacement pup, while allowing you to keep your original pup as long as you supply documentation of the condition, return the registration of the original pup, and supply proof that it has been neutered or spayed.

Both parents should have certifications for their hips and elbows and optimally also for their blood (screening for von Willebrand's disease). Hip certification can be an Orthopedic Foundation for Animals (OFA), PennHIP, Ontario Veterinary College (OVC), "a" stamp (Germany), or FCI (international) certification.

Like all popular breeds, the German Shepherd has hereditary predispositions to several health problems (see Chapter 17, Hereditary Headaches). Don't be scared off by what may appear to be a long list of problems. The typical German Shepherd is healthy and free of hereditary disease—but don't be oblivious to these problems either.

The Fairer Sex?

Many people have strong ideas about whether a male or female is better. Usually these ideas are wrong, but there are a few differences.

GSD males are larger (about 25 inches at the shoulder and from 75 to 95 pounds) and have heavier bone structure and a larger head than females. Females are about 23 inches tall and from 60 to 70 pounds. Males tend to be somewhat prouder and more territorial, and some people contend they are more courageous; the drawback is they don't always get along well with other males. Males, given the opportunity, are also apt to go off in search of females, and often think nothing of repeatedly lifting their leg on your furniture to mark your house as their territory. On the other hand, females may be a bit more "levelheaded." They fight less with each other, but when they do fight it can be especially ferocious. The main drawback with a female is the period of estrus ("season" or "heat") which normally occurs twice a year; this lasts for 3 weeks, during which time she must be kept away from amorous neighborhood males who will consider your house a singles bar. You must also contend with her bloody discharge and possible attempts to elope with her suitors. It will be the longest 3 weeks of your life. The solution for both sexes is neutering.

Al Says

If you want a GSD male for conformation (or breeding), be sure he has both testicles descended into the scrotum by the time you take him home. They should both be down by 8 weeks of age, although some may be as late as 16 weeks (or in very rare cases, longer).

Age of Consent

Most people only consider a puppy when they set out to get a dog, but that's not always the best idea. No one can deny that a puppy is cute and fun, but a puppy is much like a baby; you can't ever be too busy to walk, feed, supervise, or clean (and clean and clean). If you work away from home, have limited patience or heirloom rugs, or demand a competition- or breeding-quality dog, an older puppy or adult would probably be a better choice.

Buying a puppy, no matter how promising, is always a risk. The buyer with specific needs is always better served to look for an older Shepherd. (Jean Keller)

GSDs are an exception among breeds in the ready availability of high-quality or highly trained adults. It seems more common to find European titled adults available than American ones. A dog shown in the conformation ring in Germany will have a Kör report (breed survey) that supplies a detailed analysis of the dog's conformation and temperament, as well as a recommendation of whether it should be used for breeding. If you intend to eventually breed your GSD, a titled adult from any country gives you a good head start. Buying an adult that is already Schutzhund or obedience trained can save you countless hours of hard work and provide you with a well-trained partner, but as always, be forewarned that not all trainers are created equal. Of course, be prepared to pay top dollar the more training, titles, and accolades the dog has. Several to many thousands of dollars is commonplace. As an aside, if you plan to get such a dog for breeding, you might want to have some assurance that it's fertile.

If you simply want a mature companion, contact an established breeder. Breeders may have adult dogs available that would relish the chance to live as a pampered pet. They might have adults that simply didn't win as much in the ring as anticipated or that have not proved to be good producers. Several rescue groups are devoted to finding homes for GSDs in need of loving homes. Keep in mind that an adult GSD may need a longer adjustment period. No matter what the age, if the dog has been properly socialized (that is, treated gently and exposed to a variety of situations, people, and dogs), your GSD will soon blend into your family life and love you as though it has always owned you.

The Chosen One

Let's get to the puppies! You've chosen the litter, the color, the sex— now all that's left is to pick your special puppy. As you look at this undulating mass of fur balls nipping at your feet, everything you've learned will be lost and you will find yourself with a bad case of "I'll take that one!" as you point to every little wiggle-worm in sight. How will you ever choose? One way is to let the breeder pick. The breeder knows the pups' personalities and traits better than you could in the short time you can evaluate them, so listen carefully to any suggestions the breeder may have. Most people are drawn to extremes, either the most outgoing or most introverted pups in a litter. Your best bet is to go with the middle pup, however, one that is neither shy nor overconfident. An overconfident one could be somewhat better as a working dog; a shy one, unfortunately, is not better suited for any role.

Many people put great stock in puppy temperament testing, although there's little evidence of its predictive value. A common test is to place the pup on its back. Ideally, the pup will struggle for a few seconds and then allow you to hold it there without struggling. Another test is to see if the puppy is inclined to follow you. Many people who can't decide let the puppy pick them. It's hard to say no to a little tyke that comes over to say hello and ends up falling asleep in your lap.

The Least You Need to Know

➤ Never lose sight of the essential qualities your dog must have: looks, temperament, and health.

➤ You should be aware of the health problems German Shepherds are predisposed to.

➤ Both parents of your new dog should have hip and elbow certification.

➤ Do the best you can to pick the healthiest, best-looking pup with the best temperament—and then love whatever pup you get.

Part 3

Puppy Love

Half the excitement of welcoming a new dog is preparing for the big homecoming. Puppy-proofing your home will be a lot easier if you do it before your new puppy is underfoot, undoing everything as fast as you can do it. Much of the fun comes from showering your Shepherd with stuff. The best sources for supplies are large pet stores, concessionaires and vendors at dog shows, and discount mail-order pet catalogs. Of course, your new puppy thinks the best sources are your dresser drawers, closets, and wastebaskets.

Chapter 6

A Shepherd Shopping Spree

> ## In This Chapter
>
> ➤ How to spoil your Shepherd rotten
>
> ➤ What you really need to make life good
>
> ➤ The products you don't want to buy
>
> ➤ Precautions about even the best products

One of the best things about getting a new dog is the excuse it gives you to go on a major buying trip. True, your new pup will just as likely ignore its fancy store-bought toy in favor of an old sock, or choose a pile of rags to sleep on instead of its new velvet pad, but you will have the satisfaction of knowing you have the most spoiled-rotten dog in the neighborhood. Even if you have more spartan ideas, you at least need some fundamentals.

Do Fence Me In

The number one GSD accessory and lifesaver is a securely fenced yard. In today's world of automobiles and suburbs, a loose dog is at best an unwelcome visitor and, more often, a dead dog. GSDs can be gifted jumpers, climbers, diggers, and wrigglers, and are often tempted by the greener grass on the other side of the fence. Running stray dogs, playing children, racing bicycles, or just the call of the wild may prove irresistible to your dog.

Invisible containment systems have become a popular alternative to traditional fences, but do have some shortcomings. Because they work only with a dog wearing a special collar receiver that is activated by the buried boundary wire, they can't keep out stray dogs that aren't wearing such a collar, nor can they keep out unscrupulous dog-nappers. In addition, an excited, determined, or fast-moving GSD can be over the boundary before it has a chance to stop, and then find itself blocked out of its own yard. Nonetheless, most owners report good results with these fences, and they are ideal choices for front yards in neighborhoods where a regular fence would be out of place.

Never tie your dog out. It is cruel and dumb, and it's the perfect recipe for creating an aggressive, neurotic, unhappy dog. Also, your GSD could choke to death, hurt its neck, be the target of teasing by children, or be attacked by strays. Trolley lines do not make tying out acceptable. The foregoing perils apply equally.

A secure kennel run can be a convenient asset. It should be at least 8 feet high and preferably have a top. Dogs can get more exercise in a long, narrow run as opposed to a square run of equal area. If the run is separated from the house, it should be parallel to it. This encourages the dog to run back and forth along its length, whereas in a run set at right angles to the house, a dog tends to just stay at the end closest to the house. The most convenient runs have a doggy door leading to an inside enclosure, often another small run or area in the garage or laundry area. This affords your dog shelter in case of bad weather. If not, your kennel will need both shade and shelter. If you place a doghouse in the run, be sure the dog cannot jump on top of the house and then out of the kennel run. Dirt flooring can become muddy and harbor germs, as well as encourage digging. Cement flooring is easy to clean but holds odors and is expensive. The best compromise flooring is probably pea gravel, which is fairly easy to keep clean. The run can provide a secure area for your GSD when you are away from home, but is not a substitute for a yard or a home.

In the Doghouse

If your dog will be spending a lot of time outside, you may need a doghouse. The best doghouses have a removable top for cleaning and a doorway system that prevents wind and rain from whipping into the sleeping quarters. This means a design with two offset doors and an "entrance hall." One of the doors should have a hanging rubber or fabric "doggy door"–type flap. The floor should be slightly raised, and soft bedding should be in the sleeping quarters. For warm weather, shade must be available.

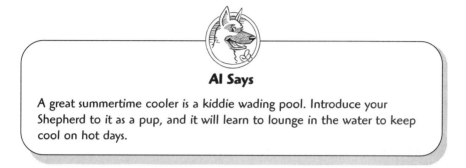

Al Says

A great summertime cooler is a kiddie wading pool. Introduce your Shepherd to it as a pup, and it will learn to lounge in the water to keep cool on hot days.

Get Cagey

Many new dog owners are initially appalled at the idea of putting their pet in a cage as though it were some wild beast. At times, though, your GSD pup can seem like a wild beast, and a cage is one way to save your home from ruination and yourself from insanity.

Learnin' German

Most dog people prefer the term "crate" instead of cage. I don't.

A cage can provide a quiet haven for your youngster. Just as you find peace and security, you hope, as you sink into your own bed at night, your pup needs a place it can call its own, a place it can seek out whenever the need for rest and solitude arises. Used properly, your GSD will come to think of its cage not as a way to keep itself in, but as a way to keep others out!

A cage should be the canine equivalent of a toddler's crib. It is a place for naptime, a place where you can leave your pup without worry of it hurting itself or your home. It is not a place for punishment, nor is it a storage box for your dog when you're through playing with it. Rethink getting a GSD (or any dog) if you plan for it to live in a cage.

Cages are convenient, sometimes so convenient that they are overused. Don't expect your dog to stay in a cage all day, every day, while you are at work. Overuse of the cage is not only unfair, and even cruel, to the dog, but can also lead to behavior problems. A GSD is an intelligent, active dog. To lock it in a cage without stimulation can result in such frustration and anxiety that the dog can begin to resent the cage and act uncontrollably when out of the cage.

Nonetheless, the cage has its place in training. Place the cage in a corner of a quiet room, but not too far from the rest of the family. Place the pup in the cage when it begins to fall asleep, and it will become accustomed to using it as its bed. Be sure to place a soft blanket in the bottom. By taking the pup directly from the cage to the outdoors when it awakens, the cage will be one of the handiest housebreaking aids at your disposal.

The ideal cage is large enough for a puppy to stand up in but not walk around in. Cages that a dog can walk around in tend to be used as bathrooms. If money were no object, then you could keep buying ever-expanding cages as your GSD got bigger. A less expensive option is to buy a large cage and then place a divider in it that you gradually move to accommodate the growing pup. The adult cage can be larger once your dog is housebroken. Certainly, if your dog must spend some long stretches in the cage, it should be large enough to stretch out in. If you plan to travel with your cage, make sure it can fit into your car and that it is easy to transport.

Most cages are either of the wire variety or the plastic variety. Wire cages provide better ventilation and a view for your dog, and most (especially the "suitcase" models) are easily collapsible for storage or transport. They can be drafty, however, and don't provide the coziness of plastic cages. It can also be tempting for a bored dog to pull things through the grates, effectively "straining" the new coat that you happened to place on top. Most wire cages are not approved for airline shipping. Plastic "airline" cages are relatively inexpensive. Their ventilation isn't as good, but they can be cozy, especially in winter. They take up more room when storing because they only break down into halves. They are the most common cage used for flying. Fancy metal cages are also available, for a fancy price. They are the choice of the elite for shipping, but out of the price range of the average owner. Whatever type of cage you choose, pay special attention to the latching mechanism. Make sure a determined dog can't spring the door.

The X-Pen Files

An exercise pen (or "X-pen") fulfills many of the same functions as a cage. X-pens are transportable wire folding "playpens" for dogs, typically about 4 feet × 4 feet. They are a reasonable solution when you must be gone for a long time because the pup can relieve itself on paper in one corner, sleep on a soft bed in the other, and frolic with its toys all over! It's like having a little yard inside. The X-pen provides a safe time-out area when you just need some quiet time for yourself. But before leaving your pup in an X-pen, make sure it cannot jump or climb out. Covers are available for incorrigible escapers. If you use an X-pen, cover the floor beneath it with thick plastic (an old shower curtain works well), and then add towels or washable rugs for traction and absorbency. Again, do not expect to stick your GSD pup in an X-pen all day every day and still have a sane dog.

Al Says

Don't forget baby gates! They are better than shut doors for placing parts of your home off-limits. Do not use the accordion-style gates because a dog can get its head stuck in them and asphyxiate.

Creature Comforts

If you're like most people, you sleep in a bed. If you're like most new dog owners, you are adamant that your dog won't be sharing it. The chances of you sticking to that promise will be much better if your dog has a bed of its own. Yet so many dog owners go off to bed at night and leave their dog wandering aimlessly around the house without a bed to call its own. When they discover the dog sleeping on the sofa, they label the dog as sneaky, but dogs need comfortable beds just as much as you do.

There are many kinds of good dog beds your Shepherd can use. If you give him his choice, though, he might take yours and bring his friends. (Dr. Zoë M. Backman)

A bed can be a folded blanket, a baby crib mattress, a papa-san cushion, a fancy dog bed, or anything moderately soft and preferably washable. It can be placed in a corner, a box, a dog cage, or anywhere out of drafts and excitement. Whatever you use and wherever you put it, the most important thing is that it is a place your dog can call its own. The second most important thing is that you don't use the traditional wicker basket unless you have an insatiable desire to play the world's largest game of pick-up sticks with the remains of the basket or Russian roulette with your puppy's life.

Bowling 'em Over

Your dog will need food and water bowls, and although you could just let it use yours, most people prefer for the dog to have its own. Your choices are plastic, ceramic, or stainless steel. Forget plastic. Dogs can chew it up, and many dogs are allergic to it. It's also harder to keep clean. Ceramic is also not a great choice, simply because it can be awkward to clean and if it cracks will harbor germs. You should strive for stainless steel bowls. They last forever (except for the one used by the occasional dog that chews its bowl) and are easily washed.

Make sure the bottom of the food bowl is flat. If you keep the bowl outside and you have an ant problem, you can buy a special ant-resistant bowl, or you can simply place your bowl in a shallow pan of water so the ants would have to cross a moat to get to the food.

As far as what to put in the bowl, see Chapter 11, "Eating High on the Dog." Meanwhile just start with whatever your puppy has been eating at its breeder's.

Al Says

Don't forget a camera! Telephoto lenses are best for taking outdoor pictures. Be sure to get down at dog level for the best shots.

Collaring Your GSD

Few items of such importance are as incorrectly chosen for dogs as the simple leash and collar. Just like your clothing, one size does not fit all, and one style does not fit all occasions.

For collars, you can choose between buckle, choke, or martingale models. Every dog should have a buckle collar to wear around the house. On it should be your dog's license tags (preferably the flat plate type). You will have to buy several buckle collars as your pup grows, but just get the little nylon puppy collars that don't cost much. When your dog reaches maturity, you can splurge on a handsome leather or web collar (the rhinestone variety isn't too popular with GSDs!). The problem with buckle collars is that long-term constant wearing can wear away the hair. You can avoid this by removing the collar at night when your dog is sleeping. Another problem is that they can sometimes slip over the head if the dog tries to back out of them, or give the handler little control if the dog is strong and strongminded.

For this reason, a choke (or slip) collar may be a better choice for walking the dog on a leash. Choke collars come in nylon or chain, with chain giving you a little bit more control. The main problem with choke collars of any type is their tendency to literally choke dogs to death. Countless dogs have gotten their choke collars caught on sticks, fences, car interior parts, or even a playmate's tooth and died—sometimes in front of their desperate owners who could not dislodge them

Germane to Shepherds

The best choice for GSD choke collars is called a "fur-saving" chain choke, which has very large oval links, each about 1 inch long.

because of the dog's frantic actions. Never, never leave a choke collar on a dog unattended. It's like sending your child out to play with a hangman's noose around his neck.

A compromise between a buckle and choke collar is the martingale collar. It tightens when pulled, but can tighten only so much. Most martingale collars are nylon. A special type of martingale is the prong collar; it has links with prongs that bite into the dog's neck when the collar tightens. Needless to say, their use is controversial. In some cases when the person is physically unable to control the dog, they might be the only safe choice, however. Any person using a prong collar needs to get professional advice on the collar's proper use and on training the dog.

A problem with any kind of collar is that it is somewhat difficult to control a dog by its neck. When the collar slips down low on the neck, the dog can throw its weight into it and pull with reckless abandon, oblivious to all your pulling. Head collars can control your dog better by controlling its head. They work on the same principle as a horse halter; where the nose goes, the body follows. Head collars are a humane and effective alternative for headstrong Shepherds.

Harnesses that fit around the chest are seldom used because they afford the least control of any restraining devices. They were created to distribute weight so that a horse or sled dog could pull the most with the least effort. They are very safe for obedient dogs, but you will be unable to control a Shepherd wearing a harness if it decides it wants to go elsewhere.

A Leash on Life

First of all, the most stupid leash ever designed is the chain leash. You can't grab one because it can cut your hand off, and they are actually more likely to break than a good web leash. So get a sturdy web, nylon, or leather leash—anything but chain! Chain leashes are impractical, heavy and uncomfortable. Do yourself and your Shepherd a favor and stay away from them. All dogs should have a 4- or 6-foot leash. Shorter leashes are better when walking in crowded places. Puppies can use a lighter leash. For early leash training, a light adjustable "show lead" works well.

Retractable leashes are popular and useful, but often carelessly used. They are not for use around other dogs or people, which too often get in the way and get all tied up in the long line. Nor are they for use next to roadways; dogs are too apt to run in the road before you can put the brakes on, and dogs can be just as dead hit by a car when on a lead as off. Finally, be careful! Several people have lost finger parts when the line whipped across their hands. In addition, if you drop one of these leashes, they retract toward the dog, which can cause the dog to think it's coming after it, creating a horrifying chase in which the panicked dog runs faster and farther in a futile attempt to get away. Those retractable leashes are great, but should be used with care.

Brush Up on Grooming Supplies

Your new Shepherd needs a few health and beauty aids to keep it looking and feeling its best. Being a Shepherd, it doesn't need all the foo-foo beauty aids of some other dogs, but it still needs a few essentials.

A natural bristle brush is ideal for brushing the hair, especially for puppy coats. Although a Shepherd's hair doesn't get tangled, a brush helps remove dead hair, stimulate the skin, and distribute oils, and a brushing session is also an act of bonding. For an adult dog, a shedding rake can help get out the loose hair. Don't forget the dog shampoo; although you can use human baby shampoo, dog shampoo is better suited for dogs. Be sure to get some no-rinse shampoo for quick fixes. See pages 124-126 for specialized shampoo choices. A good-smelling dog deodorant is also handy.

Now is also the ideal time to get your dog used to having its teeth brushed. Get a soft doggy toothbrush or a child's toothbrush. Doggy toothpaste is also available.

Nail clippers are absolute essentials. Two types are available: guillotine and scissor. Both are good. Be sure to get heavy-duty clippers for an adult GSD.

Start getting your first-aid kit together (see page 146).

The Scoop on Poop

The least glamorous thing on your shopping list will be the poop scoop. It will also be one of the handiest. If you have a yard, don't try to clean it with makeshift shovels and buckets. Use something designed to make the job easy and less yucky. Get a poop scoop! The two-part model is easier to use than the hinged one. Those with a rake are better for grass, and the flat ones are better for cement. Then where to put it? It depends on your city ordinances. You may just chuck it in the trash or in your own toilet. You can also get a dog poop disposal system that digests the dog wastes in a little bucket you bury in your yard. These work great (as long as you don't have too many dogs).

If you are walking your dog on city streets, a number of poop disposal baggy systems are available. Use them.

The Least You Need to Know

➤ A secure fence is number one on your list of items.

➤ A cage is a great thing to have as long as you don't overuse it.

➤ Your dog should wear a choke collar only when on a lead.

➤ Don't forget bowls, brushes, shampoo, nail clippers, first-aid kit, and poop scoop.

Chapter 7

House Rules

In This Chapter

➤ How to save your rugs, furniture, walls, and sanity

➤ Do Shepherds make strange bedfellows?

➤ The five essential unbreakable housebreaking rules

➤ Dealing with the third type of "stuff"

Do you pride yourself on your beautiful home? Do you cherish your white velvet chairs and oriental rugs? Are you having a nervous breakdown envisioning a puppy in its midst? Oh, come now—why on Earth would you worry about unleashing a mobile set of barracuda teeth set on auto-chew, powered by four mud-tracking pistons and armed with a variety of orifices prone to randomly squirt out assorted yuck when you least expect it?

I know I said you have to treat your new German Shepherd like a real family member, but at least at first, let's think of your new dog as a very sloppy family member.

German Shepherd pups don't wipe their feet, they chew like beavers, they are covered none too securely with fur, and they are not overly particular about where they deposit bodily wastes. Your idea of a better home and garden will seldom mesh with your dog's view of this topic. Unless you are trying to make sure your in-laws and neighbors quit coming over, you have to set up some house rules for your new family member, or your new family member will rule the house—its way!

Off-Limits!

Your puppy is a natural born explorer, and it will follow its nose into every nook and cranny of your house. Part of the pup's exploratory tools are its teeth, and any chewed items left in its wake are your fault, not your pup's—you are the one who should have known better. Harsh corrections are no more effective than a tap on the nose along with a firm "No" and removal of the item. If you come across one of your cherished items chewed to bits and feel compelled to lash out, go ahead—hit yourself in the head a few times for slipping up. It might teach you a lesson!

Like all intelligent creatures, German Shepherds enjoy the creature comforts of your chairs and sofas. Keep in mind that your nice furniture won't be nice for long after your dog sheds all over it, tries to dig a hole in it, dances all over it with muddy paws, and chews on the arms while drifting off to sleep. If you don't want your dog on the furniture, keep it off from the beginning. Don't pick the pup up to sit on your lap; instead, sit on the floor with it. When your pup does get on forbidden furniture, simply say "No" and place it—don't fling it!—on the floor. If you don't seem to be making progress, you can buy a device that emits a loud tone when a dog jumps on furniture (and in really hard cases, you can get a mat that provides an electric buzz when the dog steps on it). Such devices, however, shouldn't be necessary if you train your puppy gently and consistently from the beginning. Make sure every family member knows the rules and they understand that sneaking the puppy onto off-limits furniture, for example, is not doing the puppy any favors at all.

Shep Heard

...that setting mouse traps on the furniture is a good way to teach your dog to stay off. Shep heard wrong! Mouse traps are a good way to spend a lot of money at the vet's office fixing broken toes and noses.

Should your GSD sleep on the bed? Certainly not at first. Your pup needs to learn to sleep by itself, and it needs to have the security of a bed of its own. How would you like to have to wander around at night wondering if you'd have a place to sleep? Consider this before sharing a bed with a German Shepherd: No matter how large your bed, you will end up hanging off the edge while your dog stretches to its full length. In addition, a dog in bed can cause problems between couples when the dog decides to be jealous or overly protective. Finally, unless you change your sheets almost every day, you will be covered with hair and whatever else was on your dog's paws. Just as with the furniture issue, it is easier to later invite your dog up than to suddenly make the bed off-limits.

But how can you treat your dear dog like a less privileged member of the family? You can make compromises. Your dog can learn that it is allowed on only certain pieces of furniture, or only if its special blanket is on the furniture. Your dog can have its own special bed, maybe next to your own. Restricting your dog doesn't mean making it second-class; it just means making sure it has a place it can consider its own.

Puppies, like toddlers, can get into way too much trouble when unsupervised. You can always extend the area of your home where your dog is welcome later, but it's a lot harder to suddenly tell your dog it is no longer allowed in certain areas when it is used to wandering at will. The easiest way to keep your dog out of your pristine living room is to simply shut the door. You can also set up a baby gate or cardboard panel. You can eventually teach your dog to stay out by praising it for stopping at the doorway, but your young pup is not ready to assume such responsibility yet.

Shep Heard

...that the correct way to discipline a puppy is to grab it by the nape of its neck and shake it, just as its dam would do. Shep heard wrong! Mother dogs may grasp a pup by its neck, but they don't shake it as a means of correction while holding the pup. Shaking a puppy (or adult) is no safer than shaking a baby. It's a good way to cause neck injuries or brain damage.

Piddle, Puddle, Soil, and Trouble

You know you've lived with a puppy when the sound of running water awakens you from a deep slumber and you blindly stumble toward the source yelling "Out!" while the hapless person who turned on the spigot watches in amazement. Welcome to the club! Don't think you can raise a puppy and never have to learn Carpet Cleaning 101. All puppies "go" in the house. As dogs go, though, Shepherds go less than most others. Maybe not at first, but they are fairly easy to housebreak. Nonetheless, most people have unrealistic expectations of their dog's ability to become housebroken, based in part on friends' boasting about their little genius that was house-broken at two weeks of age or something similarly ludicrous.

No matter how gifted your GSD is, it will probably still leave occa-sional "gifts" for you until it is around 6 months of age, and may still not be reliably housebroken until a year old. If you want to eliminate household elimination, you need to start by never breaking the housebreaking rules. Even so, as soon as you are hopeful that your precocious puppy is housebroken, it will take a giant step backward and convince you there is no link between its brain and its bowels.

Water, Water, Everywhere

Housebreaking Rule #1: Restrict your pup's unsupervised freedom in the house.

If you plan on letting your dog roam freely about the house, then plan on stepping in a lot of soggy spots (or worse!) on the carpet in remote areas. Your dog is not being sneaky; your dog is being a good little wolf. All canines have a natural desire to avoid soiling their den area, and as soon as wolf pups can teeter out of their den, they walk away from the entrance to eliminate. The wolf den area is consider-ably smaller than your entire house, however, and your pup probably considers only its own bed to be the equivalent of the den. It may walk to another part of the room and eliminate there, not under-standing that it has just soiled the carpet in your den!

The solution is to restrict your puppy to a wolf den–sized area when you cannot supervise it. You can use your dog's cage as its den, but if the cage is too large for it, the puppy may simply step away from the area it sleeps in and relieve itself at the other end of the cage. A large cage that is the right size for an adult GSD can be divided with a secure barrier until the puppy is larger or housebroken. Even so, your puppy may step just outside the door of the cage and eliminate there. If the cage is near the door, you have a better chance of getting from the cage to the door accident free.

Al Says

If you can't place the pup's bed or cage near the door, you can fashion a runway out of portable construction fencing or even cardboard that you set in place when you let the pup out. You can also line the floor with plastic or scatter rugs.

Water over the Bridge

Housebreaking Rule #2: Don't let accidents happen.

When a puppy has to go, it has to go *now*! Not when you finish this last bite or this TV show. "Just a second" is not in your pup's vocabulary. Puppies have very weak control over their bladders and bowels, so if you don't take them to their doggy outhouse often and immediately, they may not be able to avoid soiling. When a pup soils in the house, it brands that area as its bathroom and is likely to go there again. If your pup does have an accident indoors, clean and deodorize the spot thoroughly and block the pup's access to that area.

Shep Heard

...that ammonia products are great for cleaning up pet urine. Shep heard wrong! Ammonia is a component of urine, so using an ammonia cleaner is like posting a sign that says "go here"! Sop up as much urine as possible, and use a pet deodorizer cleaner that neutralizes odor.

Learn to predict when your puppy will have to relieve itself. Immediately after awakening, and soon after heavy drinking or playing, your puppy will urinate. Right after eating, or if nervous, your puppy will have to defecate. Car rides also tend to elicit defecation—even in the car (you'll be the one riding with your head out the window!). Circling, whining, sniffing, and generally acting worried usually signals that the big event is imminent. Even if the puppy starts to relieve itself, quickly but calmly scoop the pup up and carry it outside (the surprise of being picked up usually causes it to stop in midstream, so to speak).

Wait-and-Pee Attitudes

Housebreaking Rule #3: Know your puppy's limits.

Learn how long you can expect your pup to hold it. A rule of thumb is that a puppy can, at most, hold its bowels for as many hours as the pup is months old. This means that a 3-month-old can hold itself for 3 hours (but note there are limits; your 12-month-old can't hold it for 12 hours). If the pup is forced to stay in the house or in a cage longer, you are causing an accident and teaching your pup to go in the wrong place.

You can't just stick a puppy in a cage all day while you're at work and think you won't return home to a messy cage and an equally messy pup. If you cannot be with your puppy for an extended period, you might want to leave it outside (only in good weather and with cover) so that it isn't forced to have an indoor accident. If this is not possible, you may have to paper-train your puppy. Place newspapers on the far side of the room (or X-pen), away from the puppy's bed or water bowl; near a door to the outside is best. Place the puppy on the papers as soon as it starts to relieve itself. Note of caution: Few more nauseating odors exist than that of urine-soaked newsprint.

A better option is to use sod squares instead of newspapers. Place the sod on a plastic sheet, and when soiled, take it outside and hose it off or replace it. By using sod, you are training the pup to relieve itself on the same surface it should eventually use outside. And chances are you won't have any sod squares just accidentally sitting on the floor next to your chair to confuse the dog. Place the soiled squares outside in the area you want your dog to use.

Rub Your Own Nose in It

Housebreaking Rule #4: Punishment doesn't help.

Dog owners have been rubbing their dogs' noses in their mess for years, and it hasn't been working for years. Dog owners, unfortunately, are slow learners. The dogs trained this way appear to learn just as slowly. Punishing a dog for a mess it has made earlier is totally fruitless; it succeeds only in convincing the dog that every once in a while, for no apparent reason, you are apt to go insane and attack it. It is a perfect recipe for ruining a trusting relationship. That "guilty" look you may think your dog is exhibiting is really a look of fear that you have once again lost your mind.

Even if you catch your dog in the act, overly enthusiastic correction only teaches the dog not to relieve itself in your presence, even when outside. This doesn't mean you ignore it as it ruins your carpet. You can clap your hands or make a loud noise to startle the pup so that it stops, or swoop it up and run for the door. You can add a firm "No," but yelling and swatting are actually detrimental.

Shep Heard

...that rubbing a dog's nose in its mess is the best way to teach it a lesson. Shep heard wrong! It doesn't work, and besides—it makes kissing your dog no fun at all!

Spend a Penny!

Housebreaking Rule #5: Reward correct behavior.

If punishment isn't going to teach your pup, what is? Reward. Punishment doesn't make clear what is desired behavior, but reward makes it clear very quickly. When the puppy does relieve itself in its outside toilet, remember to heap on the praise and let your pup know how pleased you are. Adding a food treat really gets the point across. Keep some tidbits in a jar near the door and always accompany your pup outside so that you can reward it.

Get Out of Here!

Housebreaking Rule #6: Go outside (I mean you!).

If you want your dog to go outside for its duties, you also need to go outside and watch it. Most owners think they've done their part by opening the door and pushing the pup outside. After 5 minutes, the pup is let back in and promptly relieves itself on the rug. Bad dog? No, bad owner. Chances are the pup spent its time outside trying to get back inside to its owner. Puppies do not like to be alone, and knowing you are on the other side of the door makes the outdoors unappealing. In bad weather, the pup probably huddled against the door so it didn't miss when it was opened again. The solution? You must go outside with the pup every time. Don't take it for a walk, and don't play with it; simply go with it to its relief area, say "hurry up" (for some curious reason, the most popular choice of command words), and be ready to praise and perhaps give a treat when the pup does its deed. Then you can go to its play area or back inside.

A Day in the Life

As with any baby, prepare to lose some sleep when your pup first comes home. Your typical day will begin early—roughly 1 to 2 hours earlier than you want to get up, whatever time that may be. Puppy will be whining or perhaps mouthing objects or starting to get up. You must stumble out of bed and go immediately to the pup's bed, ushering it quickly to the door. Raining outside? Once the pup is out, you are allowed to reach back inside for your umbrella. Go with the pup to the appointed place, say "hurry up!" in the most enthusiastic voice you can muster under the circumstances, and wait. Wait while the pup sniffs every blade of grass and then, when it seems the big event is about to unfold, forget what it's doing and start biting your feet. Repeat "hurry up!" as the rain increases, and watch the pup again examine every square inch as though the world's fate rested on the placement of its wastes. Success at last—"goooood"—then give the pup a tidbit. Not so fast—there's still that other bodily function. Back inside, it's time for breakfast. Breakfast finished, back outside. If you spend the day at home, your day will be punctuated by rushes to the door. If you will be gone, you have to make plans for letting the puppy relieve itself in your absence. When you come home, dead-tired, your pup (and probably a mess) will greet you, and it's time to take the puppy out. After pup's dinner, out you both go. Of course there will be playtime, but remember the pup will have to go out after all the excitement. Before bed, take the puppy out. And better get some rest, because you'll probably need to take the pup out one or two or three times in the middle of the night. Besides, tomorrow is another day…

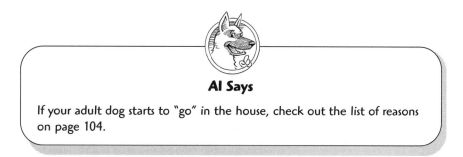

Al Says

If your adult dog starts to "go" in the house, check out the list of reasons on page 104.

What Goes Down, Must Come Up…

…if it doesn't go out. Next to the sound of running water, the other sound that could awaken a dog owner from a coma is the ominous *urp, urp, urp, urp, gaaaaag* signaling that what went down is in fact coming back up and out all over your carpet. At the first urp, rush your dog to a washable floor or, if you're lucky, outside. Don't get complacent just because your dog has now deposited a good-sized mound on the floor; with dogs, one good urp deserves another. They seem to always puke twice (even three times). I have never been able to teach my dogs that puking falls under the housebreaking credo; perhaps it's because they don't do it enough for training to take effect, or because I usually feel sorry for them and really don't try that hard. You can avoid it somewhat by not allowing your puppy

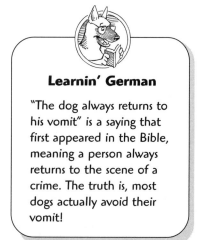

Learnin' German

"The dog always returns to his vomit" is a saying that first appeared in the Bible, meaning a person always returns to the scene of a crime. The truth is, most dogs actually avoid their vomit!

to play hard after it has eaten, or not allowing it too eat too much at one meal, and dissuading it from eating too much grass. If your dog does vomit on your carpet, be forewarned that dogs apparently have battery acid in their stomachs, so you have to clean it up immediately if you don't want abstract yellow splotches all over your rug. In fact, dog vomit can even take the finish off hardwood floors!

The Least You Need to Know

➤ Don't give your puppy the run of the house. Unsupervised puppies become unhousebroken dogs.

➤ Decide now if you want to let your pup on furniture, and be consistent! However, it needs a bed it can call its own.

➤ Rewarding your pup for going in the right place works better than punishing it for going in the wrong place.

➤ No matter what, you will clean up some kind of doggy excrement. Stock up on pet stain and odor removers.

Brave New World

The next few months will be filled with learning, adventure, confusion, and wonder for your new pup, and of learning, adventure, laughter, and frustration for you. "They grow up so fast" is even more true for puppies than for children, and you can't put off introducing your German Shepherd to the real world or you will lose your dog's once-in-a-lifetime opportunity to become wise to the ways of the world. So get out there and explore your world.

German About Town

Too many people, especially those who live in rural areas, forget that there's a whole big world out there. So, if your dog spent its puppyhood down on the farm, it really will be a case of "country comes to town" when you finally take your new friend to the big city. The reason you can't put this off is that puppies are born basically fearless. As they open their eyes and begin to explore the world, they can't afford to be afraid of every new thing they see because everything they see is new. So when they are very young, up to the age of about 12 weeks, they take new experiences right in stride. Of course, a dog without fear is called a dead (or stupid) dog, and starting at around 12 weeks, puppies begin to get a little more suspicious of anything new. This suspicious nature continues to grow. That means pups should be exposed to as many novel experiences as early in puppyhood as possible.

Al Says

Although never scientifically documented, many breeders believe there is a second "fear-imprinting" stage that occurs in adolescence. It seems that dogs that experience somewhat traumatic experiences in late puppyhood or early adulthood seem to suffer especially lasting bad effects.

But what about disease? You're right—you can't trot your puppy all around town without worrying about it catching something nasty. The thing about socialization, though, is that a little bit is enough. Take your dog to a "clean" area (one in which unvaccinated dogs or puppies are unlikely to have been) a few times when it is young. If you expose it to other puppies, make sure they have been vaccinated.

One more important thing about socializing puppies: A bad experience is worse than no experience at all. Puppies do learn from their outings, and they are just as likely to learn that strangers are mean as they are that strangers are kind. Be very careful your pup doesn't get hurt or frightened. Don't think that if a little is good, a lot is better. For example, if you want your pup to enjoy a stroll downtown and meeting new people, don't figure that by taking him to the Macy's Thanksgiving parade you will be socializing even more. You won't. You will be overwhelming your pup and achieving the opposite result you had planned on.

Social Affairs

In many towns, Obedience groups offer puppy kindergarten classes. They are a great opportunity to expose your pup to nice people and other pups its own age. Especially if yours is a single dog, it may not have many opportunities to interact with other dogs. But again, this doesn't mean that running amuck with its new buddies is necessarily good. If your dog gets beat up or is the bully, that might not be the best thing. You need to know when to step in and say enough is enough.

Al Says

Ask your veterinarian's opinion about your pup's immunity status before taking it around other dogs.

In general, though, these are great classes, and you are lucky if you can find one in your area. At the same time, your pup can start practicing its first simple Obedience exercises and learn to control itself in public. You can also get advice about some common puppyhood problems (although it would, of course, be impossible for the advice to be better than what's in the bible you now hold in your hands). As with all classes, there are good ones and rotten ones, so check it out first and don't be shy about complaining or quitting if things don't seem right to you after you're enrolled.

Shepherding in a Second Pet

There are certain advantages, and disadvantages, to having more than one dog. Two dogs are twice the fun of one, without being twice the work. Consider adding another dog or pet if you will be gone for most of the day and your Shepherd would otherwise be home alone. Most dogs enjoy having a canine companion, but don't worry—they will still be loyal to you. Problems can arise with fighting between dogs, especially between dogs of the same sex. Two males are most likely to fight, but two females can be most persistent and vicious in their fighting. A male and female works best, but only if at least one of them is neutered. It also works best if one dog is older than the other, so that it is clearly the undisputed leader of the pack.

Al Says

If two dogs are better than one, what about three? Yes! The problem with two dogs is that one is always jealous or lonely when you train the other separately. With three, it always has a companion. What about four? No way! Four is one more than you can grab hold of and try to control in a pinch.

When introducing dogs, it's best to do so on neutral ground. Have both dogs on a leash and walk them alongside each other, letting them focus on a lot of diversions. When they seem trustworthy around each other, feed them together, again on neutral ground. Ignore the newcomer around the older dog, and always make a fuss over the old dog whenever the new dog comes around. You need to reinforce the older dog's feelings of leadership by always petting it and feeding it first, and letting it know it's still the special one.

The same procedures are applicable for introducing your pup to cats and other pets, except you can't take them to neutral areas. Feed both in the presence of one another, and consider using a muzzle or cage for the protection of both.

Don't leave animals together unsupervised until you are absolutely sure they are getting along well.

And Baby Makes Three

Many a devoted dog owner has been known to get rid of the dog when a new baby comes home, often because of the stories they've heard about what dogs can do to babies. Just as many glibly bring the new baby home and hand it over to the dog to guard. Neither is the correct response. Dogs can hurt babies. They can also save babies.

The way you introduce them could make the difference. Start now if you are expecting to add a baby to the home.

➤ Dogs should know how to come, sit, stay, and lie down on command.

➤ Keep the dog on a leash when first introducing it to the baby. If you are uneasy, you can muzzle the dog, but you don't want the dog to associate muzzling with the baby. This means it should already be familiar with the muzzle before the baby comes home, and sometimes wear it when not around the baby.

➤ When first bringing the baby home from the hospital, keep the dog away. Let it get used to the sound and scent of the new family member. Some dogs may not understand this is a small human, not a prey animal, so be very careful at this time.

➤ Have the dog sit and stay, bring the baby in the room, and reward the dog for remaining in place. Gradually move the baby closer, all the while rewarding the dog for its good behavior.

➤ Only when you feel confident about the dog should you allow it to sniff the baby.

➤ Do not leave the dog and baby alone together.

➤ Always make a fuss over the dog when the baby is present. Never shuttle the dog out of the room because the baby is coming in. You want the dog to associate the baby with good things coming to itself, not become jealous or resentful of it. Remember, your dog probably used to be the baby of the family.

Al Says

In humans, direct eye contact is seen as a sign of sincerity, but staring directly in your dog's eye is interpreted by the dog as a threat. It can cause a fearful or dominant dog to bite. Teach children not to stare at a strange dog.

Some dogs are afraid of children, either because they don't understand what they are or because they have had bad experiences with
them. Introduce dogs and children carefully, encouraging the child
to be gentle and to offer the dog a treat. Do not allow young children
to sit on a dog, fall on it, or pull its hair, ears, or tail. Instruct children that they are never to run from a dog, scream shrilly around it,
stare at it, or hurt it. It's not fair even to the most saintly of dogs to
allow it to be picked on. Never take chances with a child's safety, but
do give your dog a chance—safely.

German Language 101

Living with a German Shepherd is like having a wolf in the house—
sort of. As much as they have shaken off their wild vestiges, GSDs
still speak the ancestral language of their feral relations.

Part of training is communication. Despite being "man's best friend,"
the relationship between human and dog is a one-sided one. Humans
expect their dogs to understand them, seldom bothering to try to
learn the dog's language. With very little effort, you can meet your
GSD halfway and learn to speak German (Shepherd, that is). Here are
some key signals you should understand:

➤ A wagging tail and lowered head upon greeting is a sign of submission.

➤ A lowered body, tucked rear, urination, and perhaps even rolling
over is a sign of extreme submission.

➤ A yawn is often a sign of nervousness.

➤ Drooling and panting can indicate extreme nervousness (as well
as carsickness).

➤ Exposed teeth, raised hackles, very upright posture, stiff-legged
gait, and a direct stare indicate very dominant behavior.

➤ Elbows on the ground and rear in the air, the classic "play-bow"
position, is an invitation for a game.

The Least You Need to Know

➤ Very young puppies are relatively fearless, but become increasingly suspicious with age.

➤ You need to expose your young puppy to all of life's experiences, without overwhelming it.

➤ Don't forget to teach your puppy to be by itself.

➤ Introduce new dogs on neutral territory, and let the older dog know you still consider it the special one.

➤ Your dog and your baby or child can be great friends, but you need to introduce them carefully and never take chances.

➤ Dogs use body language to communicate. Learn it!

Part 4

The Good Shepherd

Dog-training methods have changed little through the years—but they should have. Do both you and your dog a favor, and don't listen to your next-door neighbor's training advice or use the same techniques your grandparents (or even your parents) may have used to train their dogs. New training methods are easy, fun, and, most of all—they work! Combine this with one of the smartest dogs on Earth, and you have the makings of a canine Einstein!

A well-trained dog is more than a trick dog. The most gifted of obedience performers can still be a problem child in some circumstances. Behavioral problems are one of the major causes of dog death in this country, whether that death results directly from the problem or because the owner had to give up on the dog as incorrigible. Many times these problems could have been solved, if only the right advice had been available.

Chapter 9

You Can Teach an Old Dog New Tricks

In This Chapter

➤ The right way to train your dog

➤ What's with choke collars?

➤ Teaching the commands come, sit, down, stay, and heel

➤ Plus a few tricks!

Whether your dog is a bubbly bubble-headed baby or a grumpy growling grown-up, you can guide it toward being a competent canine companion. You may use slightly different rewards and techniques, but your basic training methods will be the same.

There is no such thing as an untrainable dog, but there are many untrained dogs. A surprising number of untrained dogs have been "trained," but ineffectively. Their owners usually give up and decide their dog is dumb or dog training works only for people who devote their lives to training dogs. You can train your dog without devoting your life to it. You just have to know the rules.

The Ten Commandments

1. Think like a dog.

Dogs live in the present; when you punish or reward them, they can only assume it is for their behavior at the moment of punishment or reward. So if you discover a mess, drag your dog to it from its nap in the other room and scold, the dog's impression is that either it is being scolded for napping, or that its owner is mentally unstable. Good lesson!

2. You get what you ask for.

Dogs repeat actions that bring them rewards whether you intend for them to do so or not. Letting your Shepherd out of its cage to make it quit whining might work momentarily, but in the long run, you end up with a dog that whines incessantly every time you put it in a cage. Make sure you reward only those behaviors you want the dog to perform more often.

3. Mean what you say.

Sometimes a puppy can be awfully cute when it misbehaves, or sometimes your hands are full, or sometimes you just aren't sure what you want from your dog. But lapses in consistency are ultimately unfair to the dog. If you feed your dog from the table because it begs "just this one time," you have taught it that while begging might not always result in a handout, you never know—it just might pay off tonight. This intermittent payoff produces behavior that is the most resistant to change, just like a slot machine jackpot. You could hardly have done a better job of training your GSD to beg if you tried.

4. Say what you mean.

Your GSD takes its commands literally. If you have taught that "Down" means to lie down, then what must the dog think when you yell "Down" to tell it to get off the sofa where it was already lying down? Or "Sit down" when you mean "Sit"? If "Stay" means not to move until given a release word, and you say "Stay here" as you leave the house for work, do you really want your dog to sit by the door all day until you get home?

5. Guide, don't force.

Your German Shepherd already wants to please you; your job is to simply show it the way. Training by force can distract or intimidate the dog, actually slowing down learning.

6. Punish yourself, not your dog.

Striking, shaking, choking, and hanging are extremely danger-ous, counterproductive, and cruel; such treatment has no place in the training of a beloved family member. They are the hall-mark of a dumb trainer. Plus, they don't work. Owners some-times try to make this "a correction the dog will remember" by ignoring or chastising the dog for the rest of the day. The dog may indeed realize that its owner is upset, but it doesn't know why. Besides, chances are you're the one doing things the wrong way, not your dog.

7. Give your dog a hunger for learning.

Your GSD works better, and is more responsive to food rewards, if its stomach isn't full. Never try to train a sleepy, tired, or hot dog.

8. You can be the quitter.

You, and your dog, have good days and bad days. On bad days, quit. It makes no sense to continue when one or the other is not in the mood. Do one simple exercise and then go do something else. Never train your dog when you are irritable or impatient.

9. Happy endings make happy dogs.

Begin and end each training session with something the dog can do well. Keep sessions short and fun—no longer than 10 to 15 minutes. Dogs have short attention spans, so after about 15 minutes, you will notice that your dog's performance is begin-ning to suffer unless a lot of play is involved. To continue train-ing a tired or bored dog results in teaching bad habits, causing resentment in the dog, and producing frustration for the trainer. Especially when training a young puppy, or when you have only one or two different exercises to practice, quit while you are ahead! Keep your GSD wanting more, and you will have a happy, willing obedience partner.

10. Once is enough.

Repeating a command over and over, or shouting it louder and louder, never helped anyone, dog or human, understand what is expected of them. Your GSD is not hard of hearing.

11. The best-laid plans don't include dogs.

Finally, nothing ever goes just as perfectly as it seems to in all the training instructions. Although there may be setbacks, you *can* train your dog, as long as you remember to be consistent, firm, gentle, realistic, patient—and have a good sense of humor.

Yeah, I know. So you got an extra commandment, no charge.

Even the best of canine students welcome a little clowning now and then. (Suzy Lucine)

The Right Stuff

You could go out and spend a few hundred dollars on a radio-controlled collar, but your dog won't learn any more than if you used an old rope. The secret is not in the tools; it's in the trainer. Still, having the right tools can make things go a bit easier, and besides, they make you look like you know what you're doing.

Basic training equipment usually includes a short (six-foot) lead, a long (about 20-foot) lightweight lead, and a collar. Traditionally, a choke collar has been used, but most GSDs can be effectively trained with a buckle collar.

A choke collar is not for choking! In fact, it is more correctly termed a "slip collar." The proper way to administer a correction with a choke collar is with a *very* gentle snap, and then an immediate release. The choke collar is placed on the dog so that the ring with the lead attached comes up around the left side of the dog's neck, and through the other ring. If put on backwards, it will not release itself after being tightened (since you will be on the right side of your dog for most training).

Al Says

Never leave a choke collar on a dog! See pages 59-60 for more information about collar choices.

Basic Training

It's never too early or too late to start the education of your GSD. With a very young GSD, train for even shorter periods. By the time your GSD reaches 6 months of age, it should know the commands sit, down, stay, come, and heel.

Al Says

A common problem when training any dog is that the dog's attention is elsewhere. You can teach your dog to pay attention to you by teaching it the "watch me" command. Say "Wolfman, watch me"; when he looks in your direction, give him a treat or other reward. Gradually require the dog to look at you for longer and longer periods before rewarding it. Teach "watch me" before going on to the other commands.

We'll demonstrate how easy it can be by training an imaginary pup named "Wolfman" (it's my book, so I get to name him). You, of course, can name your dog something else and use your dog's name in place of Wolfman's.

The Comely Shepherd

If your dog knows only one command, that command should be to come to you when called. Coming on command is more than a cute trick; it could save your dog's life. Your puppy probably already knows how to come; after all, it comes when it sees you with the food bowl, or perhaps with the leash or a favorite toy. You may have even used the word "Come" to get its attention; if so, you have a head start. You want your puppy to respond to "Wolfman, come" with the same enthusiasm as though you were setting down his supper; in other words, "Come" should always be associated with good things.

Think about what excites your GSD and makes it run to you. For most young GSDs, the opportunity to chase after you is one of the grandest games ever invented. And of course, most young GSDs jump at the chance to gobble up a special treat. Combine these two urges and use them to entice your GSD to come on the run.

The best time to start is when your GSD is a young puppy, but it is never too late. You need a helper and an enclosed area. A hallway is perfect for a very young pup. Have your helper gently restrain the puppy, while you back away and entice the puppy. Do whatever it takes at first: Ask the pup if it wants a cookie, wave a treat or favorite toy, even crawl on your hands and knees. The point is to get the pup's attention and to get it struggling to get away and get to you. Only at this point should you call out "Wolfman, come!" with great enthusiasm, at the same time turning around and running away. Your helper releases the pup at the same time, and you should let it catch up to you. Reward it by playing for a second, and then kneel down and give it the special treat. Repeat this several times a day, gradually increasing the distance, taking care never to practice past the time when your pup begins to tire of the game. Always keep up a jolly attitude and make the pup feel lucky to be part of such a wonderful game.

Once your puppy has learned the meaning of "Come," move your training outdoors. With the pup on lead, command "Wolfman, come!" enthusiastically, and quickly run away. When he reaches you, praise and reward! If he ignores you for more than a second, tug on the lead to get his attention, but do not drag him. Responding to the "Come" command can't be put off until your dog feels like coming. In addition, the longer you separate the tug from the command, the harder it is for your pup to relate the two, and, in the long run, the harder the training will be on the youngster. After the tug, be sure to run backward and make the pup think it was all part of the grand game.

Next, attach a longer line to the pup, allow it to meander about, and in the midst of its investigations, call, run backward, and reward. After a few repetitions, drop the long line, let your GSD mosey around a bit, and then call. If he begins to come, run away and let him chase you as part of the game. If he doesn't come, pick up the line and give a tug, and then run away as usual. If at any time your GSD runs the other way, never give chase. Chase the line, not the dog. The only game a GSD likes more than chasing you is being chased by you. It will always win. Chase the line, grab it, give it a tug, and then run the other way.

As your dog becomes more reliable, you should begin to practice (still on the long line) in the presence of distractions, such as other leashed dogs, unfamiliar people, cats, and cars. In most of these situations, you should not let the dog drag the line, but hold on just in case the distractions prove too enticing.

Al Says

Never have your dog come to you and then scold it for something it has done. In the dog's mind, it is being scolded for coming, not for any earlier misdeed. Nor should you call your dog to you only at the end of an off-lead walk. You don't want the dog to associate coming to you with relinquishing its freedom. Call it to you several times during the walk, reward it and praise it, and then send it back out to play.

Some dogs develop a habit of dancing around just out of your reach, considering your futile grabs to be another part of this wonderful game. You can prevent this by requiring your dog to allow you to hold it by the collar before you reward it. Eventually, you can add sitting in front of you as part of the game.

This might seem like a lot of work to teach a simple command that your dog can almost teach itself, but it will save you a lot of wasted time in the long run, and perhaps a lot of grief. Besides, it should be fun, not work!

Sitting Pretty

"Sit" is the prototypical basic dog command, and with good reason. It is a simple way of controlling your dog, and it's easy to teach.

The easiest way to teach the sit command is to stand in front of your pup and hold a tidbit just above its eye level. Say "Wolfman, sit," and then move the tidbit toward your pup until it is slightly behind and above his eyes. You might have to keep a hand on his rump to prevent him from jumping up. If your dog backs up instead of sitting down, place his rear against a wall while training. When the puppy begins to look up and bend his hind legs, say "Good!" and then offer the tidbit. Repeat this, requiring him to bend his legs more and more until he must be sitting before receiving the "Good!" and reward.

Al Says

Teach stationary exercises, like "sit," "down," and "stay," on a raised surface. This allows you to have eye contact with your dog and gives you a better vantage from which to help your dog learn. It also helps keep your little one from being distracted and taking off to play.

Good Things Come to Those Who Wait

You might have noticed that you can get your dog to sit, but he may have a habit of bouncing back up once you've rewarded him. Require him to remain sitting for increasingly longer intervals before giving the reward. You can also teach the stay command, which is another handy thing for your dog to know.

A dangerous habit of many dogs is to bolt through open doors, whether from the house or car. Teach your dog to sit and stay until given the release signal before walking through the front door or exiting your car.

Have your dog sit, and then say "Stay" in a soothing voice (for commands in which the dog is not supposed to move, don't precede the command with the dog's name). If your dog attempts to get up or lie down, gently but instantly place him back into position. Work up to a few seconds, give a release word ("Okay!"), and then praise and give a tidbit. Next, step out (starting with your right foot), and turn to stand directly in front of your dog while it stays. By stepping off on your right foot when you want your dog to stay, and your left foot when you want your dog to heel, you can give your dog an extra cue about what to expect.

Work up to longer intervals, but don't ask a young puppy to stay longer than 30 seconds. The object is not to push your dog to the limit, but to let it succeed. To do this you must be patient, and you must increase your times and distances in very small increments. Finally, practice with the dog on lead by the front door or in the car. For a reward, take your dog for a walk!

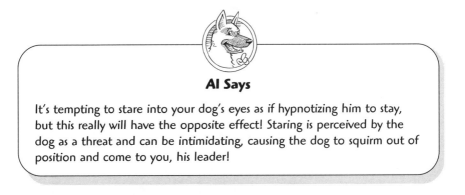

Al Says

It's tempting to stare into your dog's eyes as if hypnotizing him to stay, but this really will have the opposite effect! Staring is perceived by the dog as a threat and can be intimidating, causing the dog to squirm out of position and come to you, his leader!

You Can Keep a Good Dog Down

When you need your GSD to stay in one place for a long time, you can't expect it to sit or stand. This is when the down command really comes in handy.

Begin teaching the down command with the dog in the sitting position. Say "Wolfman, down," and then show him a tidbit and move it below his nose toward the ground. If he reaches down to get it, give it to him. Repeat, requiring him to reach farther down (without lifting his rear from the ground) until he has to lower his elbows to the ground. Never try to cram your dog into the down position, which can scare a submissive dog and cause a dominant dog to resist. Practice the down/stay command just as you did the sit/stay command.

Well-Heeled

One of the many nice things about having a dog is taking it out in public. You know you look good when you stroll down the sidewalk with your eye-catching German Shepherd stepping along smartly at your side. You should also know you don't look good if your dog is dragging you along behind it as it visits every fire hydrant, bush, and other dog in sight. Not only that, but your dog will be out of control and perceived as a menace, and you will be exhausted by the end of what should have been a pleasurable walk. Walking alongside you on lead doesn't come naturally, but it *can* come easily to your Shepherd.

Walking on a leash may be a new experience for a youngster, and he might freeze in his tracks once he discovers his freedom is being violated. In this case, do not simply drag the pup along, but coax it along a few steps at a time with food or a favorite toy. When the puppy follows you, praise and reward. In this way, the pup comes to realize that following you while walking on lead pays off.

Once your pup is prancing alongside, it's time to ask a little more of him. Even if you have no intention of teaching a perfect competition "heel," you need to teach the heel command as a way of letting your GSD know it's your turn to be the leader.

Have your GSD sit in heel position—that is, on your left side with its neck next to and parallel with your leg. If you line up your feet and your dog's front feet, that's close enough. Say "Wolfman, heel," and step off with your left foot first (remember that you stepped off on your right foot when you left your dog on a stay; if you are consistent, the leg that moves first provides an eye-level cue for your dog). During your first few practice sessions keep him on a short lead, holding him in the heel position and, of course, praising him. The traditional method of letting the dog lunge to the end of the lead and then snapping it back is unfair if you haven't first shown the dog what is expected. Instead, after a few sessions of showing the dog the heel position, give him a little more loose lead and use a tidbit to guide him into correct position.

If your GSD still forges ahead after you have shown it what is expected, pull it back to position with a quick gentle tug and then release the lead. If, after a few days' practice, your dog still seems oblivious to your efforts, then turn unexpectedly several times; teach your dog that it must keep an eye on you and be alert to all your movements. Keep in mind that every time you do this, you cause your GSD to heel a little bit farther back in relation to your position. It's easier for your dog to keep an eye on you from behind you than from any other position. In the long run, more dogs have a problem

Learnin' German

Many Shepherd owners train their dogs with German commands. Here's a few you might want to consider trying:
Sit: Setz
Down: Platz
Come: Komm
Stay: Bleib
Heel: Bei Fuss
Fetch: Bringen
No: Nein
Watch: Achtung
Let go: Aus

with lagging behind than with forging ahead. In other words, don't go overboard when trying to correct forging. It tends to self-correct with just a little guidance.

As you progress, add some right, left, and about-turns, and walk at several speeds. Then practice in different areas (still always with the dog on lead) and around different distractions. You can teach your GSD to sit every time you stop. Vary your routine to combat boredom, and keep training sessions short. Be sure to give the "Okay"

Al Says

Keep up a pace that requires your GSD to walk fairly briskly; too slow a pace gives your dog time to sniff, look all around, and in general become distracted; a brisk pace focuses the dog's attention on you and generally aids training.

command before allowing your dog to sniff, forge, and meander on lead.

Tricks and Treats

The only problem with basic obedience skills is that they don't exactly astound your friends. For that you need something flashy, some incredible feat of intelligence and dexterity: a dog trick. Try the standards: roll over, play dead, catch, shake, speak. All are easy to teach with the help of the same obedience concepts outlined in the training section.

➤ Teach "Play dead" by teaching your dog to lie down from a standing position. You can do this by guiding it with a treat. Require it to drop quickly to get the reward. Then lure it over on its side, requiring it to stay down for longer periods before getting the reward. Getting the dog to put its head down is the hard part. You can try placing the reward on the floor and not giving it unless the dog places its head down, but you may have to use your hand for a little extra guidance.

➤ Teach the roll over trick by telling your dog to lie down, and then saying "Roll over" and luring the dog over on its side with a treat. Once the dog is reliably rolling on its side, use the treat to guide it on its back. Then guide it the rest of the way, eventually giving the treat only when the dog has rolled all the way over.

➤ Teach your dog to catch by throwing a tidbit (or ball) in an arc coming down toward its muzzle. When the dog fails to catch the treat or ball, grab the item off the ground before the dog can snatch it. Repeat this until your dog gets the idea that the only way to beat you to the prize is to catch it in the air. Only then do you let your dog eat the treat or play with the ball.

➤ Teach the shake trick by having your dog sit. Say "Shake" and hold a treat in your closed hand in front of your dog. Many dogs pick up a foot to paw at your hand. These are the naturals! With others, you have to give a little nudge on the leg to get it up, or lure the dog's head far to one side so it has to lift the leg up on the opposite side. As soon as the paw leaves the ground, reward! Then require the dog to lift it higher and longer.

➤ Teach the speak trick by saying "Speak" when it appears your GSD is about to bark. Then reward. Don't reward barking unless you've first said "Speak."

If your dog can physically do anything, you can teach your dog when to do it. Just use your imagination. Rin Tin Tin, look out!

The Least You Need to Know

➤ The cornerstones of good training are consistency, timing, rewards, and patience—plus a good sense of humor.

➤ Guiding your dog with food helps it learn faster than forcing it into position.

➤ Never call your dog to you to reprimand it.

➤ Basic obedience can save your dog's life!

Chapter 10

Rin Tin Tin Never Did That!

In This Chapter

➤ What to do when you're at the end of your rope

➤ Why your dog destroys your home

➤ Dealing with aggression

➤ Barking, digging, messing in the house, jumping, and escaping—it's gotta stop!

German Shepherds are the best dogs in the world. Since you've read this far, you are no doubt among the best dog owners in the world. Then why are you having problems? Why is your dog going against the rules?

Even the best dogs with the best owners can sometimes do the worst things. The situation is often made worse by well-meaning but misguided training advice from the next door neighbor or even dog trainers who don't have a scientific background in dog behavior analysis. Great strides have been made in recent years in canine behavioral therapy. Despite the popular perception of doggy shrinks asking the neurotic dog about its childhood, real dog behaviorists are educated in canine behavior and therapy, and consider both behavioral and medical therapies. They hold either a Ph.D. in behavioral science or a veterinary degree, and are certified as companion animal behaviorists. Veterinarians can sometimes offer advice, but few are extensively trained in behavior patterns. As a first step in any serious behavior problem, a thorough veterinary exam should be performed.

The most common improper advice is to punish the dog, and if that doesn't work, punish it some more. If punishment doesn't work the first time, why do owners think it will work the second, third, or fourth time? As the misbehavior continues in the face of punishment, the owners lay the blame on the dog. Finally the dog is labeled as stupid or incorrigible, and banned to the far reaches of the yard, offered "to a good home," or taken to the pound.

The Wrecking Crew

One of the great joys of German Shepherd ownership is the knowledge that after a hard day at work, you can come home and be greeted by your loyal dog. Then you can spend some quality time relaxing and playing. Dream on! That might happen, but just as likely you will fling open your door and stop dead in your tracks, finally gasping out "Vandals! We've been ransacked!" Your vandal is your loving dog, telling you how much it loves you as only a dog can do.

Before we get to how your dog destroying your home is a token of its love for you, let's talk about the ones in which it isn't. Puppies are natural demolition experts, and they do it for the sheer ecstasy that only a search-and-destroy mission can provide. The best cure (besides adulthood) is supervision and prevention. Remove everything your pup can get into; no need for a costly paper shredder or garbage disposal when you have a puppy loose in the house! Adult German Shepherds still may destroy items through frustration or boredom. The best way to deal with these dogs is to supply both physical interaction (such as chasing a ball) and mental interaction (such as practicing a few simple obedience commands) an hour or so before leaving

Shep Heard

...that dogs spite their owners for leaving them alone by redecorating the house. Shep heard wrong! Dogs never destroy out of spite. Owners who continue to believe this erroneous idea never cure their dogs' destructive behavior.

your dog. Several toys are available that can provide hours of entertainment; for example, some can be filled with peanut butter or treats in such a way that it takes the dog a long time to extract the food.

Often adult dogs continue their search-and-destroy mission, but the cause is seldom boredom, and they won't just outgrow it. The German Shepherd is an extremely devoted dog, and its owners tend to be equally devoted. They chose a GSD in part because of the breed's desire to be close to its family. The problem for many Shepherds arises when its people leave it all alone. Being left alone is an extremely stressful situation for these highly social animals. They react by becoming agitated and trying to escape from confinement. Perhaps they reason that if they can just get out of the house they will be reunited with their people. The telltale signature of a dog suffering from this *separation anxiety* is that most of its destructive behavior is focused around doors and windows. Most owners believe the dog is "spiting" them for leaving it, so they punish the dog. Unfortunately, punishment is ineffective because it actually increases the dog's anxiety level, as it comes to both look forward to and dread its owner's return.

The proper therapy for separation anxiety is treating the dog's fear of being left alone. This is done by leaving the dog alone for short periods and gradually working up to longer periods,

Learnin' German

Separation anxiety is the fear of being left alone or separated from particular people or even dogs.

taking care to never allow the dog to become anxious during any session. When you *must* leave your dog for long periods during the conditioning program, leave it in a different part of the house than the one in which the conditioning sessions take place. This way you won't undo all your conditioning if the dog becomes overstressed by your long absence.

When you return home, no matter what the condition of the house or how much you missed your dog, refrain from a joyous reunion scene. Greet the dog calmly or even ignore it for a few minutes, to emphasize the point that being separated was really no big deal. Then have the dog perform a simple trick or obedience exercise so that you have an excuse to praise it. It takes a lot of patience, and often a whole lot of self-control, but it's not fair to you or your dog to let this situation continue. It will only get worse.

Shep Heard

...that the best way to deal with a scared dog is to inundate it with the very thing it's afraid of, until it gets used to it. Shep heard wrong! This concept (called "flooding") doesn't work because the dog is usually so terrified it never gets over its fear enough to realize the situation is safe. The cardinal rule of working with a fearful dog is to never push it into situations that might overwhelm it.

'Fraidy Dogs

Known for its bravery, even the bravest of German Shepherds can sometimes develop illogical fears or phobias. The most common are fears of strange people or dogs, gunshots, and thunder. Every once in a while, a particularly imaginative Shepherd comes up with a bizarre fear all its own, but it can usually be treated using the same general concepts.

Never coddle your GSD when it acts afraid because it reinforces the behavior. It is always useful if your GSD knows a few simple commands; performing these exercises correctly gives you a reason to praise the dog and also increases the dog's sense of security because it knows what is expected of it. Whether it is a fear of strangers, dogs, car rides, thunder, or being left alone, the concept is the same: Never hurry, and never push the dog to the point that it's afraid.

Al Says

In the worst-case scenario, the dog is petrified at even the lowest level of exposure to whatever it is scared of. You may have to use anti-anxiety drugs along with training to calm your dog enough to make progress. This is when you need the advice of a behaviorist.

Friend or Foe?

German Shepherds are characteristically cautious with strangers. Some take this caution to an extreme and are downright shy. Shy dogs are like shy people in some ways: They are not so much afraid of people as they are of being the center of attention. Unfortunately, the most common advice given to cure shyness in dogs is to have a lot of strange people pay attention to the dog. This usually does little except petrify the dog and further convince it to be afraid of strangers. From the dog's viewpoint, it is learning that for some reason, strangers seem alarmingly interested in it. Never force a dog that is afraid of people to be petted by somebody it doesn't know; it in no way helps the dog overcome its fear and is a good way for the stranger to get bitten. Strangers should be asked to ignore shy dogs, even when approached by the dog. When the dog gets braver, have the stranger offer it a tidbit, at first while not even looking at the dog.

Big Bang Therapy

Fear of thunder or gunshots are common problems in older dogs. To see a normally courageous German Shepherd quivering and panting in the closet at the slight rumblings of a distant thunderstorm is a sad sight, and it only gets worse with time. The time to do something about it is at the first sign of trouble. Try to avoid fostering these fears. Act cheerful when a thunderstorm strikes, and play with your dog or give it a tidbit. Once a dog develops a noise phobia, try to find a recording of that noise. Play it at a very low level and reward your dog for remaining calm. Gradually increase the intensity and duration of the recording. A program of gradual desensitization, with the dog exposed to the frightening person or thing and then rewarded for calm behavior, is time-consuming but the best way to alleviate any fear.

Digging Up Some Dirt

Perhaps you remember the days when your lawn was lush and green. You should have taken a picture because those days are long gone. Don't get a German Shepherd if you can't appreciate the stark beauty of a moonscape. Just think of the extra physical exercise your thoughtful dog has arranged for you as you leap over holes and

Shep Heard

...that you can teach a dog to quit digging by filling the hole with water and half-drowning the dog in it. Shep heard wrong, wrong, wrong! It doesn't work, it's cruel, and it's dangerous.

shovel the dirt back into them, and the mental exercise as you ponder why there's never enough dirt to fill them back up. If, however, you remain unappreciative, the best you can do is to try to confine the digging to certain parts of the yard. Most digging goes on when you're not around, so fence off those parts of the yard you want to remain presentable and let your dog in them only when you're there to supervise. Give your dog its own sandbox or area for digging; when it digs in the nice parts, redirect it to the digging area. And take heart—it's one problem that time will cure.

Tales from the Bark Side

Having a doggy doorbell can be handy, but there's a difference between a dog that warns you of a suspicious stranger and one that warns you of the presence of oxygen in the air. The surest way to make your neighbors hate your dog is to let it bark unchecked day and night. Allow your Shepherd to bark momentarily at strangers, and then call it to you and praise it for remaining quiet, distracting it with an obedience exercise if necessary. If your dog won't stop barking when you tell it to, distract it with a loud noise of your own. Begin to anticipate when your dog will start barking, distract it, and reward it for quiet behavior. You may worry that you will ruin your dog's watchdog ability by discouraging barking, but the opposite is true. A watchdog that cries wolf is useless. By discouraging your dog from barking at nonthreatening objects and encouraging it to bark at people acting suspiciously, you will create the ideal watchdog.

Isolated dogs often bark through frustration or as a means of getting attention and alleviating loneliness. Even if the attention gained includes punishment, the dog continues to bark to get the owner's temporary presence. A dog stuck in a pen or tied to a chain in the backyard will bark. What else is there for it to do?

Rin Tin Tin's Tsali at 9 months traces back 10 generations to Rin Tin Tin IV. (Daphne Hereford)

The simplest solution is to move the dog's quarters to a less isolated location. Let the dog in your house or fence in your entire yard. Take the dog for long walks where it can interact with you and other dogs. If barking occurs when you put your dog to bed, move its bed into your bedroom. If this is not possible, the dog's quiet behavior must be rewarded by your presence, working up to gradually longer and longer periods. The distraction of a special chew toy, given only at bedtime, may help alleviate barking. Remember, a sleeping dog can't bark, so exercise can be a big help. The dog that must spend the day at home alone is a bigger challenge. Again, the simplest solution is to change the situation, perhaps by adding another animal—a good excuse to own two dogs!

Al Says

For stubborn barkers, a citronella collar is sometimes effective. These collars spray a squirt of citronella (which dogs don't like) whenever the dog barks. They are more effective and safe than bark-activated shock collars.

For Adults Only

What happens when your housebroken dog appears to be broken? If your adult GSD soils the house, it could be caused by a physical or emotional problem. A physical examination is warranted any time a formerly housebroken dog begins to soil the house. You and your veterinarian need to consider the following possibilities:

➤ Older dogs simply might not have the bladder control they had as youngsters; a doggy door is the best solution.

➤ Older spayed females may "dribble"; ask your veterinarian about drug therapies.

➤ Several small urine spots (especially if bloody or dark) may indicate a bladder infection, which can cause a dog to urinate frequently.

➤ Sometimes a housebroken dog is forced to soil the house because of a bout of diarrhea, and afterward continues to soil in the same area. If this happens, restrict that area from the dog, deodorize the area with an enzymatic cleaner, and revert to basic housebreaking lessons.

➤ Male dogs may "lift their leg" inside the house as a means of marking the area as theirs. Castration often solves this problem as long as it is performed before the habit has become established; otherwise, diligent deodorizing and the use of some dog-deterring odorants (available at pet stores) may help.

➤ Submissive dogs, especially young females, may urinate upon greeting you; punishment only makes this "submissive urination" worse. For these dogs, be careful not to bend over or otherwise dominate the dog and to keep greetings calm. Submissive urination is usually outgrown as the dog gains more confidence.

➤ Some dogs defecate or urinate because of the stress of separation anxiety; you must treat the anxiety to cure the symptom. A dog that messes its cage when left in it is usually suffering from separation anxiety or anxiety about being closed in a cage (claustrophobia). Other telltale signs of anxiety-produced elimination are drooling, scratching, and escape-oriented behavior. You need to treat separation anxiety and start cage training over, placing the dog in the cage for a short period and working up gradually to longer times. Dogs that suffer from cage anxiety but not separation anxiety do better if left loose in a dog-proofed room or yard.

The Escape Artist

German Shepherds are smart dogs—sometimes too smart for their own good. Some Shepherds are geniuses when it comes to applying their intelligence to finding escape routes from their own yard. In most cases, their owners have helped to make them that way. They have helped their dog learn how to escape by making it easy at first, and then gradually trying to see if the minimal fix will work. Take the example of the new Shepherd owner and the old fence. The new owner surveys the fence and decides it might be tall enough and strong enough. When the dog demonstrates it's not tall enough, the owner tries to fix it by adding an extension to make it a bit taller. The problem is the dog has just graduated from crime school and learned a bad lesson: Fences can be beaten, so it will likely test the new fence. If that one, too, can be jumped over or dug under, the owner is in for a problem. Adding to the fence bit by bit is just the way you would teach a dog to jump Olympic heights; in fact it is how Shepherds are trained to scale military obstacle courses. So why would you use the same technique to teach your dog not to jump? If you want your dog to stay in the yard, make your yard escape-proof from the very beginning.

Al Says

For diggers, try burying a wire mesh fence under the ground for a foot or two inside the fence perimeter. As a last-ditch effort for an incorrigible fence jumper or digger, you might have to string electric wire just inside your fence.

When the Bite Is Worse than the Bark

Let's face it—many people are afraid of German Shepherds. Some Shepherd owners derive immense (if perverse) enjoyment from this, but most would protest that their puppy dogs are just big pussycats. Nonetheless, some German Shepherds can be aggressive, and their large size and powerful jaws makes this sort of behavior dangerous. Understanding aggression could save you a lot of grief and save your dog its life. The first step is admitting you have a problem.

It's Just a Game

Puppies and dogs play by growling and biting. Usually they play with their littermates this way, but if yours is an only puppy, you will just have to do. So many people have seen horror stories about dogs that when their pup growls and bites, they immediately label it as mean. You need to know the difference between true aggression and playful aggression. Look for these clues that tell you it's all in good fun:

➤ Wagging tail

➤ Down on elbows in front, with the rump in the air (the play-bow)

➤ Barks intermingled with growls

➤ Lying down or rolling over

➤ Bounding leaps or running in circles

➤ Mouthing or chewing on you or objects within reach

On the other hand, look for these clues to know you had better watch out:

➤ Low growl combined with a direct stare

➤ Tail held stiffly

➤ Sudden, unpredictable bites

➤ Growling or biting in defense of food, toys, or bed

➤ Growling or biting in response to punishment

Simply because your dog is playing doesn't mean you should let it use you as a chew stick. When your pup bites you, simply say "Ouch! No!" and remove your bloodied stump from its mouth. Replace it with a toy not made of flesh and bone. Hitting your dog is uncalled for; your dog was just trying to play and meant no harm. Hitting is also a form of aggression that could give your dog the idea it had better try (bite) harder next time because you're playing the game a lot rougher. You don't want to encourage playful aggression, but you don't want to punish it. You want to redirect it.

Biting the Hand that Feeds

Aggression toward humans is one of the most severe behavioral problems a dog can have. The potential for human endangerment often leads to the dog's demise. Many times the dog is dearly loved but the owners can no longer cope with the threat to the safety of humans. Dog aggression toward humans can be roughly divided into aggression toward family members and aggression toward strangers. Aggression toward family members or other people known to the dog tends to be the most troubling. Because of the gravity of this problem, the best advice is to seek the counsel of a certified companion animal behaviorist.

Much has been made of dominance problems in dogs; they probably occur less often than is thought, but when they do occur, the result can be aggression toward family members. This aggression most often occurs because of competition over a resource (such as trying to remove food or a toy, encroaching on the dog's sleeping quarters, or trying to step past it in a narrow space) or during a perceived display of dominance by the owner (such as petting, grooming, scolding, leading, or bending over it). Dogs may act more aggressively toward family members than strangers and treat the family members in a dominant way, such as walking stiffly, staring, standing over them, and ignoring commands. Punishment usually elicits only further aggression.

Owners of such dogs inevitably feel guilty and wonder "Where did I go wrong?" The fault is not entirely theirs. Although some actions of the owner might have helped create the problem, these same actions would not have produced dominance aggression in dogs that were not already predisposed to the problem. In predisposed dogs, owners who act to foster the dog's opinion of himself as king can lead to problems. What would convince a dog that he ranked over a person? The most likely causes include:

➤ petting the dog on demand

➤ feeding the dog before eating your own meal

➤ allowing the dog to go first through doorways

➤ allowing the dog to win at games

107

➤ allowing the dog to have its way when it acts aggressively

➤ fearing the dog

➤ not punishing the dog for initial instances of aggression

Al Says

Dominance aggression is more common in males than females, and occasionally (but not always) castration can help. Your veterinarian can give your intact (un-neutered) male dog a drug that temporarily causes its hormonal state to be that of a neutered dog as a test to see whether castration might help. Spaying a female does not help correct (and may even hinder) dominance aggression.

Treatment consists of putting the dog in its place, without direct confrontation. Your Shepherd has the ability to win in a serious direct confrontation with you. If you try to beat it into submission, you will just as likely end up the loser. At least at first, it's best to avoid situations that might lead to a showdown. If, however, your dog only growls, and *never* bites, you may be able to nip the behavior in the bud before you get nipped yourself by scolding or physically correcting the dog. If your dog is likely to bite, but you still want to try, talk to your veterinarian about temporary drug therapy to calm it sufficiently during initial training, and consider having your dog wear a muzzle.

Shep Heard

...that you should roll a dominant dog over on its back into a submissive position. Shep heard wrong! Attempting this with a dominant dog is a good way to get bitten.

You must cease and desist any of your behaviors that tell the dog it is the boss. As much pleasure as you may get from petting your dog absentmindedly as you watch TV or read, you can't. There will be no more free lunches, and no more free pets, for your dog. From now on, your dog must work for its petting, its praise, and even its food. The work will be simple—just obeying simple commands from you. It must sit when you tell it to sit and wait until you have gone through doorways first. When your dog thrusts its head into your lap to be petted, you must ignore it. When you want to pet your dog, you must first have it obey some simple commands, and then pet it sparingly as a reward. Yes, it's tough love, but it may be your dog's only chance.

Al Says

Another cause of aggression toward people can arise from fear. The owner may be bitten if the dog has come to fear overzealous physical punishment, or a stranger may be bitten if she approaches and tries to touch the dog when it's fearful. In both cases, the dog is biting out of perceived self-defense. Obviously punishment will only make matters worse. The cure is to refrain from placing the dog in fearful situations or to try to alleviate the dog's fears.

Beware of Dog

Aggression toward unfamiliar humans is not only dangerous, but a lawsuit waiting to happen. Some dogs may be afraid of strangers and bite when approached by them. Others actively go after strangers, treating them as they would intruding dogs. Still others bite visitors to their home. Each case must be treated differently. The fear biter must have its fear treated, and never be put in a situation in which a stranger is forced upon it. The dog that goes after strangers is very likely being territorial. It must be corrected and scolded. When a stranger appears, the dog should be required to perform a few obedience commands and be rewarded with a tidbit for good behavior. The dog that attacks visitors should also be corrected and required to do some simple obedience when visitors come. Shuttling the dog into another room only increases its aggressive tendencies. You want your dog to associate visitors with good times. Eventually, you might even have your visitors give your dog treats. Regardless, don't take chances. Keep your dog on lead at all times around strangers, and keep it muzzled if you must.

The German Jumping Bean

German Shepherds are big heavy dogs, and big heavy dogs can wreak havoc when they jump on people, especially little frail people in nice clothes. Puppies naturally greet their mother and other adult dogs by licking them around the corners of their mouth. This behavior translates to humans, but to reach your face, they need to jump up on you. Sometimes owners love this display of affection, but not when they are all dressed up or when company comes over. Since you can't expect your GSD to know the difference, teach it to sit and stay so that you can kneel down to its level for greetings. When your dog does jump up, simply say "no" and step backward, so that its paws meet only air. Teaching your dog a special command that lets it know it's okay to jump up (when you're in your grungy clothes) can actually help it discriminate the difference.

Shutting your dog in another room when guests arrive just makes it more crazed to greet people and ultimately worsens the problem. The more people it gets a chance to greet politely, the less excited it will be about meeting new people, and the less inclined it will be to jump up. Have your guests kneel to greet your calmly seated Shepherd.

The Least You Need to Know

➤ If punishment doesn't work at first, escalating the punishment never works.

➤ The most common cause of home destruction is separation anxiety, a type of fear. Therapy for any fear involves gradual desensitization in which the dog is never overwhelmed.

➤ Loss of housebreaking in an adult dog may be caused by a medical problem.

➤ Aggression can be directed at familiar people, strange people, or small animals, and may be based on dominance, territoriality, fear, or prey drive behavior.

➤ Dogs with behavioral problems, especially dominance-related ones, should never get "something for nothing." They must be made to earn all petting, praise, and food.

Part 5

A Dog's Life!

It's the little things in life that are the big things in the long run, the everyday things you do to take care of your dog. The good part is they're usually pretty easy and pretty enjoyable for both of you. Here you'll find information on what foods are best for your dog (and what foods your dog likes best besides whatever happens to be on your plate), what kind of exercise is best for your dog, and all the health and beauty tips of the professionals. So let's see: Your dog has you giving it a tasty nutritious meal like clockwork, taking it all over the countryside for recess and playtime, brushing its coat and teeth and manicuring its nails—this is a dog's life?

Chapter 11

Eating High on the Dog

In This Chapter

➤ Dry versus semi-moist versus canned food

➤ What the dog food labels are telling you

➤ What about natural diets?

➤ What not to feed

➤ Coping with weight problems

Your German Shepherd's athletic build, as well as its energy, condition, health, and ultimately, longevity depend in part on what you choose to set in front of it. Unlike humans, dogs have a limited diet because they are usually fed one type of food. This makes choosing that food even more important and intimidating. All it takes is one dizzying trip through the dog food section of a supermarket, pet supply store, or dog show vendor aisle to leave you utterly baffled and feeling like the worst dog owner who ever lived. Before you become paralyzed with indecision, keep in mind that dog nutritionists have done most of the work for you; as long as the food you choose passes some basic guidelines, it will be adequate to sustain your dog's life. It may not make it bloom with health, however. For that, you do need to do a little investigating.

Shepherd's Pie

Although dogs are members of the order *Carnivora* ("meat-eaters"), they are actually omnivorous, meaning their nutritional needs can best be met by a diet derived from both animal and plant sources. Most dogs do have a decided preference for meat over non-meat foods, but a balanced meal combines both meat and plant-based nutrients. These nutrients are commercially available in several forms. Most Shepherd owners feed a combination of dry and canned food, supplemented with dog biscuits as treats.

Dry food (containing about 10 percent moisture) is the most popular, economical, and healthy—but least enticing—form of dog food.

Semi-moist foods (with about 30 percent moisture) contain high levels of sugar used as preservatives. They are tasty, convenient, and handy for traveling, but are not an optimal nutritional choice as a regular diet. Pay no attention to their meat-like shapes; they all start out as a powder and are formed to look like meat chunks or ground beef.

Canned food has a high moisture content (about 75 percent), which helps make it tasty, but it also makes the food comparatively expensive, since you are in essence buying water. A steady diet of canned food would not provide the chewing necessary to maintain the dog's dental health. In addition, a high meat content tends to increase levels of dental plaque.

Dog biscuits can help supply the chewing action necessary to rid teeth of some (but far from all) dental plaque. The better varieties of dog biscuits offer complete nutrition. They are most commonly used as snacks or treats.

The Association of American Feed Control Officials (AAFCO) has recommended minimal nutrient levels for dogs based on controlled feeding studies. Unless you are a nutritionist, the chance of you cooking up a homemade diet that meets these exacting standards is remote. So the first rule is to select a food that states on the label that it not only meets the requirements set by the AAFCO, but also has been tested in feeding trials. You should also realize that when you add table scraps and other enticements, you are disrupting the balance of the diet. A few table scraps don't hurt, but a diet with a high percentage of scraps will almost certainly not be balanced.

Feed a high-quality food from a name-brand company. Avoid food that has been sitting on the shelf for long periods, or that has holes in the bag or grease that has seeped through. Always strive to buy and use only the freshest food available. Dry food loses nutrients as it sits, and the fat content can become rancid.

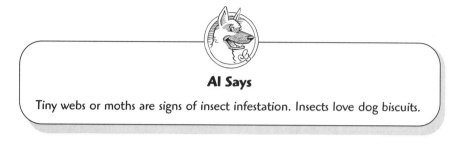

Al Says

Tiny webs or moths are signs of insect infestation. Insects love dog biscuits.

Shop around for a food that your Shepherd enjoys. Mealtime is a highlight of a dog's day; although a dog eventually eats even the most unsavory of dog foods if given no choice, it hardly seems fair to deprive your family member of one of life's simple and, for a dog, most important pleasures. But beware: Dogs often seem to prefer a new food when first offered, but this may simply be due to its novelty. Only after you buy a cupboard full of this alleged Shepherd ambrosia will you discover it was just a passing fancy.

Shep Heard

...that dogs don't like variety in what they eat. Shep heard wrong! Most dogs, unless they've been raised on only one food, prefer a varied menu.

Although you shouldn't devise your own home-cooked diets, you can prepare nutritious meals at home for your dog. Many balanced diets are available as guidelines; just be sure to examine the credentials of the diet's creator.

Avoid feeding:

➤ Chicken, pork, lamb, or fish bones. They can be swallowed and their sharp ends can pierce the stomach or intestinal walls.

➤ Any bone that could be swallowed whole. It could cause choking or intestinal blockage.

➤ Any cooked bone. Cooked bones tend to break and splinter.

➤ Mineral supplements (unless advised to do so by your veterinarian).

➤ Chocolate. It contains theobromine, which is poisonous to dogs.

➤ Onions. Onions can cause red blood cells to break down, sometimes causing serious illness in dogs that eat them.

➤ Alcohol.

What about B.A.R.F.?

Bones And Raw Food (BARF) diets have gained a lot of attention and supporters. These diets advocate more natural feeding by feeding dogs whole raw animal carcasses, particularly chicken. Feeding consists of throwing a chicken carcass to the dog, which is then eaten bones and all. Proponents point out that such diets are more like the natural diet of ancestral dogs, and claim good health, clean teeth, and economical food bills. Detractors point out that these diets may have safety problems because of the possibility of salmonella and E. coli associated with meat processing. Dogs can get salmonella and E. coli poisoning, but they are more resistant to them than humans are. Detractors also point to the lack of scientific data to support the assertion of improved health. Little incentive exists for dog food companies to publish data that would support the benefits of homemade diets. As the popularity of these diets increases, funding will, it is hoped, become available for such studies. Meanwhile, the worth of these diets is still under question. If you decide to go this route, avoid feeding raw meat to dogs with compromised immune systems, and try to find meat that is fresh and locally processed.

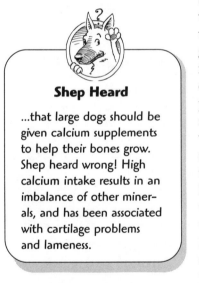

Shep Heard

...that large dogs should be given calcium supplements to help their bones grow. Shep heard wrong! High calcium intake results in an imbalance of other minerals, and has been associated with cartilage problems and lameness.

Boning Up on Nutrition

When comparing food labels, keep in mind that differences in moisture content make it difficult to make direct comparisons between the guaranteed analyses in different forms of food unless you first do some calculations to equate the percentage of dry matter in the food. The components that vary most from one brand to another are protein and fat percentages.

Protein provides the necessary building blocks for growth and maintenance of bones, muscle, and coat, and for the production of infection-fighting antibodies. The quality of protein is as important as the quantity. Meat-derived protein is more highly digestible than plant-derived protein and is of higher quality. Most Shepherds do fine on regular adult foods having protein levels of about 20 percent (dry food percentage).

Fat is the calorie-rich component of foods, and most dogs prefer the taste of foods with higher fat content. Fat is necessary to good health, aiding in the transport of important vitamins and supplying energy. Dogs whose diets are deficient in fat often have sparse, dry coats.

Choose a food that has a protein and fat content best suited for your dog's life stage, adjusting for any weight or health problems (prescription diets formulated for specific health problems are available). Puppies and adolescents need particularly high protein and somewhat higher fat levels in their diets, such as the levels found in puppy foods. Stressed, highly active, or underweight dogs should be fed higher protein levels or even puppy food. Obese dogs or dogs with heart problems should be fed a lower fat formulation. Older dogs, especially those with kidney problems, should be fed moderate levels of very high quality protein. Studies have shown that high-protein diets do not cause kidney failure in older dogs, but given a dog in which

Shep Heard

...that the food with the most protein is the best. Protein is an important component of dog foods, but most dogs don't need super-high-protein foods unless they are under a great amount of physical stress.

Germane to Shepherds

German Shepherds are among the breeds predisposed to hip dysplasia, and studies have shown that extremely rapid growth can increase the probability of developing it. Current recommendations for these breeds is to discontinue feeding puppy food at about 4 or 5 months of age. Switch to a lower protein formulation (about 21 percent to 24 percent). The puppy will grow more slowly, but still reach the same adult size.

kidney stress or decompensation exists, a high-protein diet can do a lot of harm.

As important as the guaranteed analysis is the list of ingredients: A good rule of thumb is that three or four of the first six ingredients should be animal derived. They tend to be tastier and more highly digestible than plant-based ingredients; more highly digestible foods generally mean less stool volume and less gas problems.

You might have to do a little experimenting to find just the right food, but a word of warning: One of the great mysteries of life is why a species, such as the dog, that is renowned for its cast-iron stomach and preference to eat out of garbage cans, can at the same time develop a violently upset stomach simply from changing from one high-quality dog food to another—but it happens. So when changing foods, you should do so gradually, mixing in progressively more and more of the new food each day for several days.

Feeding a quality diet will be clearly evident in your Shepherd's overall condition. (Christine Alderson)

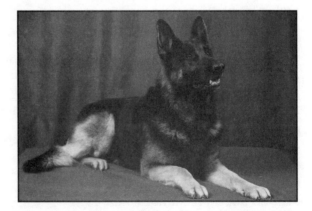

Eschewing the Fat

The dog's wild ancestor, the wolf, evolved to survive feast and famine, gorging after a kill, but then perhaps waiting several days before another feast. In today's world, dogs can feast daily, and without the period of famine, can easily become obese.

A Shepherd of the proper weight should have a slightly hourglass-shaped figure when viewed from above or the side. There should be no roll of fat over the withers or rump. The stomach should be slightly tucked-up. The ribs should be easily felt through a layer of muscle. The GSD is an athlete, and should have an athlete's body: lean and muscular.

Overweight German Shepherds should be fed a high-fiber, low-fat, and medium-protein diet dog food. Such commercially available diet foods, which supply about 15 percent fewer calories per pound, are preferable to the alternative of just feeding less of a fattening food. Home-prepared diets are available that are tasty and less fattening.

Many people find that one of the many pleasures of dog ownership is sharing a special treat with their pet. Instead of giving up this bonding activity, substitute a low-calorie alternative such as rice cakes or carrots. Make sure family members aren't sneaking the dog forbidden tidbits. Keep the dog out of the kitchen or dining area during food preparation or at meal times. Schedule a walk immediately following your dinner to get your dog's mind off your leftovers; it will be good for both of you.

Al Says

Dogs have most of the same taste receptors that we do, including similar sugar receptors (which explains why many have a sweet tooth). But their perception of artificial sweeteners is not like ours, so they seem to taste bitter to dogs. Research has shown that dogs in general prefer meat (not exactly earthshaking news), and while there are many individual differences, the average dog prefers beef, pork, lamb, chicken, and horsemeat, in that order.

If your dog remains overweight, seek your veterinarian's opinion. Heart disease and some endocrine disorders, such as hypothyroidism or Cushing's disease, or the early stages of diabetes, can cause the appearance of obesity and should be ruled out or treated. A dog in which only the stomach is enlarged, without fat around the shoulders or rump, is especially suspect and should be examined by a veterinarian. However, most cases of obesity are simply from eating more calories than are expended. Obesity predisposes dogs to joint injuries and heart problems and aggravates many pre-existing problems. An obese GSD cannot enjoy one of its greatest pleasures in life—the ability to run, jump, and frisk with boundless energy.

Skin and Bones

Many picky eaters are created when their owners begin to spice up their food with especially tasty treats. The dog then refuses to eat unless the preferred treat is offered, and finally learns that if it refuses even that proffered treat, another even tastier enticement will be offered. Try a couple of dog food brands, but if your Shepherd still won't eat, then you may have to try some tough love. Give your dog a good, tasty meal, but don't succumb to Shepherd blackmail or you could be a slave to your dog's gastronomical whims for years to come.

A sick or recuperating dog might have to be coaxed into eating. Cat food or meat baby food are both relished by dogs and may entice a dog without an appetite to eat.

Underweight GSDs may gain weight with puppy food; add water, milk, bouillon, or canned food and heat slightly to increase aroma and palatability. Milk causes many dogs to have diarrhea, so try only a little bit at first.

Your veterinarian should examine your dog if its appetite fails to pick up or if it simply can't gain weight. Some GSDs have enzymatic deficiencies that can be treated by adding digestive enzymes to their food (see page 185). Even more worrisome is a dog that suddenly loses its appetite or weight. Such problems can be warning signs of a physical disorder.

Feeding Time

Very young puppies should be fed three or four times a day, on a regular schedule. Feed them as much as they care to eat in about 15 minutes. From the age of 3 to 6 months, pups should be fed three times daily, and after that, twice daily. Adult dogs can be fed once a day, but it is actually preferable to feed smaller meals twice a day.

Some people let their dog decide when to eat by leaving food available at all times. If you choose to let the dog "self-feed," monitor its weight to be sure it is not overindulging. Leave only dry food down. Canned food spoils rapidly and becomes both unsavory and unhealthy. If your dog overindulges, you have to intervene before you have a roly-poly Shepherd on your hands.

Overfeeding your Shepherd puppy is one of the worst things you can do. Studies have shown that overfed GSD pups are more likely to develop hip dysplasia. It's not that overfeeding causes hip dysplasia; rather, if a dog has a genetic predisposition to be dysplastic, overfeeding makes it much more likely for that genetic predisposition to express itself in the future.

Puppies that are fed less grow more slowly, but eventually they attain the same stature as puppies that are fed more. The rapid growth in the latter seems to be a causative factor in making these dogs more prone to hip dysplasia.

Driven to Drink

Water is essential for your Shepherd's health and comfort. Don't just keep your dog's water bowl full by topping it up every day; that allows algae to form along the sides of the bowl and gives bacteria a chance to multiply. Empty, scrub, and refill the water bowl daily. If the water bowl runs dry, your dog may turn to the toilet bowl as an alternative source. In fact, you should make it a practice to keep the lid down because many dogs that can drink from it view the toilet bowl as an especially deluxe watering hole! It should go without saying that drinking from the toilet is not a healthy practice—and definitely not conducive to sweet doggy kisses!

The Least You Need to Know

➤ Feed your dog a brand-name food.

➤ If you prefer homemade diets, follow an established recipe; don't try to make one up yourself.

➤ Avoid feeding cooked bones, spoiled food, chocolate, onions, alcohol, or unprescribed mineral supplements.

➤ Obesity is the most prevalent canine health problem in America; feed your dog low-calorie food for meals and feed vegetables for snacks.

➤ Always have fresh water available.

Rub Your Dog's Fur the Right Way

In This Chapter

➤ The easy way to bathe your Shepherd

➤ The right way to keep your dog's nails trimmed

➤ Keeping your dog's eyes and ears healthy

➤ Why dirty teeth can kill your dog

Before you protest that if you had wanted a sissy dog to brush and coif you wouldn't have chosen a German Shepherd, take heed: Grooming is not only important for the sake of beauty; it can also prevent serious health problems. Just as with people, good grooming involves more than occasionally brushing the hair. Keeping the nails, teeth, eyes, and ears well groomed is just as, if not more, important. The good news is that you don't have to visit the "Shampoodle Hut" to keep your dog groomed to perfection. All you need is a little direction, and you can be your Shepherd's personal beautician.

Making the Fur Fly

You won't need a chest full of fancy brushes to keep your Shepherd's coat just so—luckily Shepherds never have bad hair days. Shepherd hair doesn't tangle and mat, and dirt falls right out of it. You will do just fine with only a few tools.

A pin brush is used to brush the thicker coat and to get down to the skin, but you need to be careful not to irritate the skin with it. You can brush the hair backward to loosen any dead hairs. A bristle brush is better for extended brushing periods; it distributes the natural oils and is easy on the skin. A slicker brush can help remove shedding hair, but it can cut the outer coat. An undercoat shedding rake (the best are Teflon™ coated) is the best grooming tool during peak shedding periods, when it can help you create a pile of shed undercoat roughly equivalent in size to your dog.

Start with the shedding rake and remove as much of the loose undercoat as possible. Then use the pin brush, and finish up with the bristle brush. For an extra sheen, go over the coat with a fine-toothed comb and finish with a couple of swipes with a chamois cloth.

Some dogs have naturally fuller coats than others, and even dogs with thick coats may shed their undercoats and look extra lean and sleek periodically. You can try to increase the appearance of fullness by brushing the hair backward when it is still wet, but don't expect to create miracles with a hair brush!

Utter Dogwash!

You can lead a dog to water, but you can't make it get in—especially if that dog is an 85-pound German Shepherd that's never been taught there is a difference between a tub of water and a tub of battery acid.

You need to start bath training when your Shepherd is still a young puppy. Done right, bath time can even be fun. Done wrong, you will have a lifelong battle on your hands. Start your bath training with semibaths. Use a tub of warm water filled only to your dog's ankles. During this first bath, you wash just the dog's feet. For the next bath, you might wash the rear legs. Bring some treats with you to give your GSD while it's in the tub. Unless your dog has been sprayed by a skunk or has a skin disease, there's little to be gained by deep cleaning. The trick is to make baths, especially the first ones, short and sweet.

On hot summer days, using an outdoor hose is fine, but not on chilly days. Remember to use water that you would be comfortable using in a shower for yourself. Make sure a fractious pup can't accidentally hit a knob and turn the hot water up. It's always a good idea to keep one hand under the spray so you can monitor the water temperature. If you use your own tub, place a nonskid mat in the bottom of it and help your dog in and out so it doesn't slip. Also, place a strainer over the drain so the rest of your day isn't spent trying to unclog it. A hand-held sprayer is essential for indoor bathing.

Start by wetting down the dog to the skin, leaving the head for last. You can try plugging the ears with cotton, but even then you should avoid spraying water into the ears because the cotton gets soggy easily. Beware: Your dog will want to make sure you, too, enjoy the benefits of the bath by shaking water all over you. Once wet (the dog, not you), apply the shampoo, again leaving the head for last. The shampoo goes a lot further and is easier to work with if you mix it with water first. After you've worked up a lather (and got a lather on your dog, too), start rinsing, working from the head, back and down. Rinsing is a crucial step; shampoo remaining in the coat can cause dryness and itchiness. Most GSDs don't require a cream rinse, but you can add a small amount if you like. A cream rinse tends to make the hair lie flatter.

Al Says

To keep your dog from shaking, keep one hand clenched around the base of one ear. When you let go, stand back!

The choice of shampoo is as personal as the choice of dog food. A dog's skin has a pH of 7.5, while human skin has a pH of 5.5; bathing in a shampoo formulated for the pH of human skin can lead to scaling and irritation. Therefore, you generally get better results with a shampoo made for dogs. If you're on a budget and your dog has healthy skin and coat, a mild liquid dishwashing detergent can actually give good results and will kill fleas. No dog owner should be without a no-water, no-rinse dog shampoo. These are wonderful for puppies, spot-baths, emergencies, and bathing when time does not permit a full bath.

After the bath, your dog will shake and splatter the entire area. Cover it with a towel as quickly as possible and rub it vigorously. Some dogs enjoy being dried with a blow dryer, but as with all things, getting the dog used to the feeling a little at a time is the secret. In fact, once the GSD's thick undercoat gets soaked, it takes a long time to dry, so a blow dryer is a big help. Don't let your dog outside on a chilly day while it's still wet from a bath. You have removed the oils from the coat and saturated your dog down to the skin, so it is far wetter than it would ever get by going swimming and, thus, more likely to become chilled.

Shep Heard

...that flea shampoos are the answer for killing fleas. Shep heard wrong! Most shampoos (even people shampoos) kill fleas, but none (including flea shampoos) has any residual killing action on fleas.

Bathing dislodges loose hairs; a good time to get them out is when the coat is almost, but not entirely, dry. Use a comb or brush to get the dead hairs out.

Al Says

Several therapeutic shampoos are available for skin problems:

- Itchy skin: oatmeal-based antipruritics
- Dry scaly skin: moisturizing shampoos
- Excessive scale and dandruff: antiseborrheic shampoos
- Damaged skin: antimicrobials

Finally, step back and admire your canine Adonis. You might even want to take its photo right now because as soon as your dog gets a chance, it's going to dig a hole and give itself a mud bath to get rid of that horrible shampoo stench!

Erasing a Stink

Dogs smell like dogs, but when they smell like dead dogs, you have a problem. Doggy odor is not only offensive; it is unnatural. Don't exile the dog or hold your breath. If a bath doesn't produce results, it's time to use your nose to sniff out the source of the problem. Infection is a common cause of bad odor; check the mouth, ears, feet, anus, and genitals. Impacted anal sacs or perianal fistulas can contribute to bad odor. Generalized bad odor can indicate a skin problem, such as seborrhea. Don't ignore bad odor, and don't make your dog take the blame for something you need to fix.

Al Says

To get rid of skunk odor: Mix one pint of 3 percent hydrogen peroxide, $2/3$ cup baking soda, and 1 teaspoon of liquid soap or citrus-based dog shampoo with 1 gallon of water. Use immediately. Wear gloves and sponge it on the dog. Leave it on the dog about 5 minutes, and then rinse and repeat if needed. Caution: This solution may slightly bleach dark coats. Vinegar douche is reported to work well, too. Tomato-juice rinses don't work that well and will leave your bathroom looking like the scene of a mass murder if your dog shakes.

Hard as Nails

German Shepherds are not in the bear family, nor are they in the cat family. They do not catch fish or climb trees with their long claws. Despite this amazing bit of animal information, many pet owners seem determined to get their dog in the record book for having the world's longest toenails. An old saying goes that a horse is no better than its feet. The same is true of a German Shepherd. And a GSD's feet are no better than its nails. When you can hear your dog's nails clicking as it moves, that means the nails are hitting the floor with every step. When this happens, the bones of the foot are spread, causing discomfort and eventually splayed feet and lameness. If dew-claws (the rudimentary "thumbs" on the wrists) are left untrimmed, they can get caught on projecting objects more easily and be ripped

Shep Heard

...that dogs wear their nails down naturally by running around. Shep heard wrong! Canine nails evolved to withstand traveling 20 miles or so a day. Unless your dog is a marathon runner, you're going to need to help out a little.

out or the dewclaw nails can actually loop around and grow into the dog's leg. You must prevent this by trimming your dog's nails every week or two.

Begin by handling the dog's feet and nails daily, and then cutting the very tips of your puppy's nails every week, taking special care not to cut the "quick" (the central core of blood vessels and nerve endings). After every cut, give your dog a tiny treat. You may find it easiest to cut the nails by holding the foot backward, much as a horse's hoof is held when being shod. This way your GSD can't see what's going on, and you can see the bottom of the nail. Here you will see a solid core culminating in a hollowed nail. Cut the tip up to the core but not beyond. On occasion you will slip up and cause the nail to bleed. Most Shepherds are stoics and will just give you a grievous look that says, "I told you this would happen," but a few take the opportunity to make sure the whole neighborhood knows you are amputating their toes. Give your "victim" another treat, and apply styptic powder to the nail to stop the bleeding. If this is not available, dip the nail in flour or press it to a wet tea bag—and be more careful next time!

In One Ear and Out the Other

My, what big ears you have! The German Shepherd relies on its wonderful large ears to detect and localize sounds that you cannot perceive and to look stunningly handsome and alert. The Shepherd's ears are normally very healthy, but even the healthiest are likely to need occasional cleaning.

The dog's ear canal is made up of an initial long vertical segment that then abruptly angles to run horizontally toward the skull. This configuration provides a moist environment where ear infections can flourish, although the erect carriage of the Shepherd ear does aid in ventilation and health. It's fairly simple to keep your Shepherd's ears healthy by checking them regularly and not allowing moisture or debris to build up in them.

Like the well-fed Shepherd, the well-groomed Shepherd is a positive reflection of the care it gets.

Signs of ear problems include inflammation, discharge, debris, foul odor, pain, scratching, shaking, tilting of the head, or circling to one side. Extreme pain may indicate a ruptured eardrum. Ear problems can be difficult to cure once they have become established, so early veterinary attention is crucial. Bacterial and yeast infections, ear mites or ticks, foreign bodies, inhalant allergies, seborrhea, or hypothyroidism are possible underlying problems.

Al Says

Foxtail awns (barbed seeds) are one of the most common causes of ear problems in dogs that spend time outdoors. If your Shepherd picks up any of these, keep the ear lubricated with mineral oil, and seek veterinary treatment as soon as possible. The problems they cause only get worse and can result in serious damage.

Don't stick cotton swabs down in the ear canal because they can irritate the skin and pack debris into the horizontal canal. Never use powders in the ear, which can cake, or hydrogen peroxide, which leaves the ear moist. The best recipe for disaster is to stick some ear powder in, follow with a little liquid, pack it all down with a cotton swab, allow it all to dry into a solid plug, and then just wait for a full-fledged problem to explode.

So if you look in your dog's ear and see a bunch of gunk, what do you do? It depends. If your dog has no signs of discomfort or itching, you can try cleaning the ear yourself. Your veterinarian and many dog supply mail-order catalogs sell products that dissolve wax and debris. You can also make a mixture of one part alcohol to two parts white vinegar. Armed with this potion, take your dog outside. Hold the ear near its base and quickly squeeze in the ear cleaner (the more slowly you let it drip in, the more it will tickle). Now gently massage the ear to move the liquid downward and coat the area. When your dog can't stand it anymore (usually after about 15 seconds), jump back and let your dog shake it all out. That's why you do this outside, because dissolved ear wax is not a great thing to have on your walls. You might have to repeat this step a few times. If the inside of the ear is so black with gunk that repeated rinses don't clean it right up, your dog has a problem that needs veterinary attention. If the ear is red, swollen, or painful to the touch, do not attempt to clean it yourself. Your dog may need to be sedated for deeper cleaning and could have a serious problem. Cleaning solutions flush debris but do not kill mites or cure infections. Putting medications in the ear of a dog with a ruptured ear drum can do more harm than good. When in doubt, stay out!

Many people automatically assume any ear problem is caused by ear mites, but unless you actually see mites, don't treat the dog for them. You could make another problem worse.

Ear mites, often found in puppies, are highly contagious and intensely irritating. An affected dog shakes its head, scratches its ears, and perhaps carries its head sideways. The ear mite's signature is a dark, dry, waxy buildup resembling coffee grounds in the ear canal, usually in both ears. This material is actually dried blood mixed with ear wax. If you place some of this wax on a piece of dark paper, and have very good eyes or use a magnifying glass, you may be able to see the tiny culprits moving. Over-the-counter ear mite preparations can cause even more irritation, so ear mites are best treated by your veterinarian.

If you must treat your dog yourself, get a pyrethrin and mineral oil ear product. Pyrethrins are a common and safe class of flea-, tick-, and mite-killing chemicals, available through most pet supply catalogs or at many pet supply stores. First, flush the ear with an ear-cleaning solution. Then apply the ear mite drops daily for at least a week, and possibly a month. Because these mites are also found in the dog's coat all over its body, you should also bathe the pet weekly with a pyrethrin-based shampoo, or apply a pyrethrin flea dip, powder, or spray. Separate a dog with ear mites from other pets, and wash your hands after handling its ears. Ideally, every pet in a household should be treated.

An Eye-Full

My, what big eyes you have! The windows to your German Shepherd's soul are no doubt the part of your dog you look at the most. Perhaps because of this, eye problems are usually detected fairly early. German Shepherds don't have a lot of hereditary eye problems, but are more subject to a condition called *pannus* (in which the normally clear cornea gradually becomes opaque—see page 188) than are most dogs. Nonetheless, you need to be watchful for any eye problems.

Squinting or tearing can be caused by an irritated cornea or a foreign body. Examine under the dog's eyelids and flood the eye with saline solution or use a moist cotton swab to remove any debris. If you see no improvement after a day, have your veterinarian take a look. A watery discharge without squinting can be a symptom of allergies or a tear drainage problem. A clogged tear drainage duct can cause the tears to drain onto the face instead of the normal drainage through the nose. Your veterinarian can diagnose a drainage problem with a simple test.

For contact with eye irritants, flush the eye for 5 minutes with water or saline solution. For injuries, cover the eye with clean gauze soaked in water or saline solution. In both cases, get immediate veterinary advice.

As your Shepherd ages, it is natural that the lens of the eye becomes a little hazy. You will notice this as a slightly grayish appearance behind the pupils. But if this occurs at a young age, or if the lens looks white or opaque, ask your veterinarian to check your dog for cataracts. With cataracts, the lens becomes so opaque that light can no longer reach the retina; as in humans, the lens can be surgically replaced with an artificial lens.

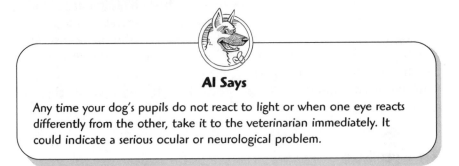

Al Says

Any time your dog's pupils do not react to light or when one eye reacts differently from the other, take it to the veterinarian immediately. It could indicate a serious ocular or neurological problem.

The eyes are such complex and sensitive organs that you should always err on the side of caution. Consult your veterinarian at the slightest sign of a problem.

Armed to the Teeth

My, what big teeth you have! Just how intimidating do you think your German Shepherd will be if all he has to show are gums when he snarls? With a lifetime of neglected tooth care, your dog may develop gum disease and need some of its teeth removed. Dental plaque and tartar are not only unsightly, but also contribute to bad breath and potentially serious health problems. If not removed, plaque attracts bacteria and minerals, which harden into tartar. Neglected plaque and tartar can cause infections to form along the gum line. The infection can gradually work its way down the sides of the tooth until the entire root is undermined. The tissues and bone around the tooth erode, and the tooth finally falls out. Meanwhile, the bacteria may have entered the bloodstream and traveled through-out the body, causing infection in the kidneys and heart valves. Neglecting your dog's teeth can do more harm than causing bad breath; it could possibly kill your dog.

Dry food and hard dog biscuits, carrots, rawhide, and safe, synthetic chewies are helpful, but not totally effective, at removing plaque. Brushing your GSD's teeth once or twice weekly (optimally daily) with a child's toothbrush and doggy toothpaste is the best plaque remover. If you cannot brush, your veterinarian can supply cleansing solution that helps kill plaque-forming bacteria. You might have to have your veterinarian clean your dog's teeth as often as once a year.

Get your dog used to having its teeth examined and brushed while it's still a puppy. Even though we shouldn't eat after brushing, you may have to reward your pup with a tidbit at first for letting you brush one or two of its teeth. While brushing, get to know your dog's mouth so you can spot any developing problems.

Between 4 and 7 months of age, GSD puppies begin to shed their baby teeth and show off new permanent teeth. Often deciduous (baby) teeth, especially the canines (fangs), are not shed, so that the permanent tooth grows in beside the baby tooth. If this condition persists for over a week, consult your veterinarian. Retained baby teeth can cause misalignment of adult teeth. Correct occlusion is important for good dental health. In a correct GSD bite, the top incisors should fit snugly in front of the bottom incisors. Too large a gap between the upper and lower incisors could cause eating difficulties or result in the tongue unnaturally lolling out of the mouth.

Learnin' German

Bite is the canine term for occlusion, the way the teeth and jaws mesh when the mouth is closed. The correct GSD bite is a **scissors bite,** in which the incisors (the six small front teeth between the canines) of the upper jaw just slightly overlap those of the lower jaw. In an **overshot bite,** the top incisors are so far in front of the lower that there's a gap between them. In an **undershot bite,** the upper incisors are behind the lower incisors, Bulldog-fashion.

The Least You Need to Know

➤ A brush and a shedding rake make grooming easy.

➤ Teach your dog to enjoy bath time by giving it mini-baths as a youngster.

➤ Cut your dog's toenails regularly! The easiest way to avoid cutting into the quick is by looking at the underside of the nails.

➤ Look deep into your dog's ears, but don't probe deeply into them.

➤ Eye problems need veterinary attention.

➤ Brushing your dog's teeth can save your dog's life.

Part 6

In Sickness and in Health

Trotting your dog to the veterinarian a couple of times a year does not mean you have done your duty. Your dog's doctor, no matter how good, doesn't have psychic powers. You will not get a phone call saying, "I just had this premonition that your dog has a fever—better bring him in." Nor will your dog say to you, "Gee, I think I have a fever." At least, not in so many words. Unless you marry your veterinarian (an excellent option if you plan on several dogs, by the way), or go to vet school yourself (also possibly a cheaper option in the long run), you need to learn the fundamentals of keeping your dog healthy and recognizing when it is not. You need to understand what your dog's body is telling you.

When something's wrong—how wrong? Is it time for a trip to the vet? The emergency vet? Is there any way you can tell, or do something in the meantime? It's better to be safe than sorry, but it's also better to be rich than poor, so knowing when you really need to go to the veterinarian is an important part of owning a healthy dog and staying solvent. But there's more to it than that. You don't want to be pushy, but hey, this is your beloved dog, and sometimes your veterinarian might not know as much about German Shepherd problems as you do. So here you'll find a special chapter on special German Shepherd problems. You might want to ever so subtly bring them to your veterinarian's attention if your GSD's symptoms match. Finally, I hope you never have to use any information from the emergency care chapter, but don't wait until an emergency to try to learn it.

The Good Doctor

In This Chapter

➤ Recognizing signs of illness

➤ Choosing a veterinarian

➤ Interpreting blood tests

➤ Giving medicine

➤ What you need in your medicine cabinet

In a dog owner's life, there are only three certainties: death, taxes, and vet bills. Owning a dog won't accelerate your own demise, you hope, and unfortunately, you can't declare your dog as a dependent on your tax returns, but you have some control over your vet bills. Although it's impossible to do away with them completely, you can be a savvy veterinary client by protecting your dog from sickness or injury, recognizing when something's not right, and acknowledging when you need professional (veterinary!) help.

Your Shepherd's health care is a team effort directed by your veterinarian but undertaken by you. Preventive medicine encompasses accident prevention, vaccinations, and parasite control, as well as good hygiene and grooming. An ounce of prevention really is worth a pound of cure to the wise dog owner.

Checkpoints

The only way you will know if your GSD may be sick is to become intimately in tune with it when it's well. Take 5 minutes weekly to perform a simple health check, examining:

➤ the mouth for red, bleeding, swollen, or pale gums, loose teeth, ulcers of the tongue or gums, or bad breath

➤ the eyes for discharge, cloudiness, or discolored "whites"

➤ the ears for foul odor, redness, discharge, or crusted tips

➤ the nose for thickened or colored discharge

➤ the skin for parasites, hair loss, crusts, red spots, or lumps

➤ the feet for cuts, abrasions, split nails, bumps, or misaligned toes

➤ the anal region for redness, swelling, discharge, or sores

Watch your dog for signs of lameness or incoordination, sore neck, circling, loss of muscling, and any behavioral change. Run your hands over the muscles and bones and check that they are symmetrical from one side to the other. Weigh your dog and observe whether it is putting on fat or wasting away. Check for any growths or swellings, which could indicate cancer or a number of less serious problems. A sore that does not heal, or any pigmented lump that begins to grow or bleed should be checked by a veterinarian immediately. Look out for mammary masses, changes in testicle size, discharge from the vulva or penis, increased or decreased urination, foul-smelling or strangely colored urine, incontinence, swollen abdomen, black or bloody stool, change in appetite or water consumption, difficulty breathing, lethargy, coughing, gagging, or loss of balance.

Shepherds are sometime so concerned with their tough-guy image that they become amazingly stoic, even when they must be in pain. Because a dog may not be able to express that it is in pain, you must be alert to changes in your GSD's demeanor. A stiff gait, low head carriage, reluctance to get up, irritability, dilated pupils, whining, or limping are all indications that your pet is in pain.

Everything about the German Shepherd proclaims its combination of nobility, intelligence, and courage. (Barbara McGuire)

A German Shepherd may act regal in public, but home is for the puppy in him. (Craig and Cynthia Miller)

Up and over!—clearing the broad jump in style. (Suzy Lucine)

"I believe you dropped this…" (Craig and Cynthia Miller)

Lots of people love the white ones. (Carlo DeVito)

Heroics are all in a day's work for a German Shepherd. (Christine Alderson)

Never too young to commune with nature. (Steven and Nancy Whitworth)

Possession is nine-tenths of the law! (Tom Przewoznik)

A German Shepherd Therapy Dog makes a wonderful ambassador of good cheer. (Dr. Zoë Backman)

"Scarlette" learns about her heritage up close and personal.
(Dr. Zoë Backman)

German Shepherds
and Agility—a natural
combination. (Suzy
Lucine)

Nothing gets past a determined Tracking Shepherd. (Suzy Lucine)

How did this most German of breeds become this most American of dogs? (Craig and Cynthia Miller)

This precocious pup's ears are already standing well, and she's using them to get every sound. (Jean Keller)

"You want to fish in our pond? Sure, no problem..." A group of stalwart dogs owned by members of the German Shepherd Dog Club of Central Massachusetts, Inc. (Craig and Cynthia Miller)

In the Pink

The simplest yet most overlooked checkpoint is your dog's gum color. The gums are the one place you can actually see your dog's blood without taking it out. The fascinating thing about blood is that its color (and the resulting gum color) can say a lot. Normal gum color is a good deep pink. Pale gum color can indicate anemia or poor circulation, and warrants an appointment with the veterinarian.

White or tan gum color can indicate shock, severe anemia, or very poor circulation. Bluish gum or tongue color indicates imminent life-threatening lack of oxygen. Bright-red gum color can indicate carbon monoxide poisoning. Yellowish color can indicate jaundice. Little tiny red splotches (called *petechia*) can indicate a blood-clotting problem. Each of these conditions warrants a call to the emergency vet.

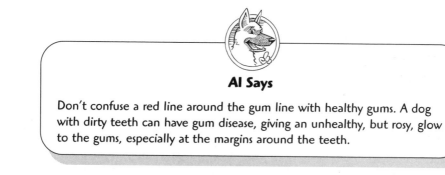

Al Says

Don't confuse a red line around the gum line with healthy gums. A dog with dirty teeth can have gum disease, giving an unhealthy, but rosy, glow to the gums, especially at the margins around the teeth.

Besides color, capillary refill time, which is an index of blood circulation, can be estimated simply by pressing on the gum with your finger and lifting your finger off. The gum where you pressed will be momentarily white, but should quickly re-pink as the blood moves back into the area. If it takes longer than a couple of seconds to re-pink, circulation is poor.

Looking at the gums is so simple, yet almost no one does it—except your vet, who will look at the gums before anything else when your dog comes into the exam room. Get used to looking at your dog's gums, a window to its blood.

Hot-Blooded?

Your dog's body temperature is another clue about what's going on inside. You can't put your hand on your Shepherd's forehead and get

Shep Heard

...that an easy way to take a dog's temperature is with one of those thermometers you just put in the ear. Shep heard wrong! Because the dog's ear canal has a curve that the human ear canal doesn't have, those thermometers don't give an accurate reading for a dog.

an idea, and you can't have your dog hold a thermometer under its tongue. You can get a rough idea by feeling your dog's ears, but for an accurate reading, you need to get a rectal thermometer. The digital ones are a lot easier to use. Your dog will appreciate it if you lubricate it with a bit of Vaseline™ or K-Y Jelly™ first. As in humans, a dog's temperature is slightly lower in the morning and higher in the evening.

Normal temperature for a GSD is about 100° to 102°F. If the temperature is 103° or above, call the vet and ask for advice. If it is 105° or above, go to the emergency vet. A temperature of 106° and above is dangerous. If the temperature is 98° or below, call the vet. If it is 96° or below, go to the emergency vet.

Finger on the Pulse

To easiest way to check your dog's pulse is to feel it through the femoral artery. If your dog is standing, cup your hand around the top of its leg and feel around the inside of it, almost where it joins with the torso. If your dog is on its back, you can sometimes see the pulse in this area. The normal pulse rate for a GSD at rest is about 60 to 120 beats per minute.

Al Says

You can feel your dog's heartbeat by placing your hand on its lower ribcage just behind its elbow. Don't be alarmed if it seems irregular; the heartbeat of many dogs is irregular compared with humans. Have your vet check it out, and then get used to how it feels when it's normal.

While you're at it, you can check your dog's breathing rate. The normal respiration rate for a GSD at rest is about 10 to 30 breaths per minute.

Finally, check your dog's hydration. Pick up the skin on the back just above the shoulders, so that it makes a slight "tent" above the body. It should pop back into place almost immediately. If it remains tented and separated from the body, your dog is dehydrated.

Shep Heard

...that you can tell if a dog is well by whether it has a wet nose. Shep heard wrong! Sick dogs can have wet noses, and well dogs can have dry noses.

The Hospitable Hospital

Your home care maintenance can go only so far in ensuring your GSD's healthy status. No matter how diligent you are, eventually your GSD will need professional medical attention. A good veterinarian is also needed to monitor your dog's internal signs by way of blood tests and other procedures.

When choosing your veterinarian, consider availability, emergency arrangements, costs, facilities, and ability to communicate. Some veterinarians include more sophisticated tests as part of their regular check-ups. Such tests, while desirable, add to the cost of a visit. Unless money is no object, reach an understanding about procedures and fees before having them performed. You and your veterinarian form a team who will work together to protect your dog's health, so your rapport with your veterinarian is important. Your veterinarian should listen to your observations, and explain to you exactly what is happening with your GSD. A veterinarian who is familiar with GSDs and their special health needs is a real asset.

The clinic should be clean and have safe, sanitary overnight accommodations. Trained veterinary technicians are another valuable asset to any clinic, but not all clinics have them. A clinic staffed by several veterinarians is usually better because the staff can confer about tough cases and are more likely to be available for emergencies. Many veterinary clinics refer all clients to a central emergency clinic after-hours, but you should still be able to reach your veterinarian in cases of extreme emergency. A veterinarian with an unlisted phone number should be avoided, and a veterinarian with a listed phone number should not be harassed!

Most veterinarians are general practitioners, and most of their days are filled with routine cases, such as check-ups, vaccinations, skin allergies, spaying and neutering, and some of the more common illnesses. A good veterinarian does not hesitate to utter the phrases "I don't know" and "Perhaps you would like to be referred to a specialist." For any serious disease, you should always ask if a specialist's opinion would be helpful. Most specialists are at university veterinary teaching hospitals, although some can be found in private practice in larger cities. As with humans, expect to pay more for a specialist's opinion. Sometimes even a specialist can do nothing for your dog, but many owners find peace in knowing they did everything they could do and left no stone unturned.

Al Says

Veterinarians are not always right. Do not hesitate to question your veterinarian's diagnosis or treatment, seek a second opinion, and most of all, become informed about German Shepherd health issues.

Blood Will Tell

Why do veterinarians always want blood? Are they aspiring vampires? Are they selling blood on the black market? Or are they trying to run up the bill? Maybe, but usually they have a good reason for wanting your dog's blood. Nothing can tell your vet more about what's going on inside your dog than something that has actually been there, all through your dog's insides, in fact—its blood.

Your GSD's blood can provide valuable clues about its state of health. In fact, it's a good idea to take blood values for your GSD when it is well as a source for later comparison if it ever becomes ill. Also, you should insist on such blood tests before your pet undergoes surgery to make sure it's healthy enough for the procedure. The time to find out your dog has a clotting problem is not when it's on the operating table bleeding.

The most common tests are the Complete Blood Count (CBC) and the Blood Chemistry Test ("chem panel"). Many other specialized tests are fairly common.

A CBC reports on counts of the following:

➤ **Red blood cells:** the cells responsible for carrying oxygen throughout the body

➤ **White blood cells:** the infection-fighting cells

➤ **Platelets:** the components responsible for clotting blood to stop bleeding

A Blood Chemistry Test reports on levels of the following:

➤ **Albumin (ALB):** reduced levels suggest liver or kidney disease, or parasites

➤ **Alanine aminotransferase (ALT):** elevated levels suggest liver disease

➤ **Alkaline phosphatase (ALKP):** elevated levels can indicate liver disease or Cushing's syndrome

➤ **Amylase (AMYL):** elevated levels suggest pancreatic or kidney disease

➤ **Blood urea nitrogen (BUN):** elevated levels suggest kidney disease

➤ **Calcium (CA):** elevated levels suggest kidney or parathyroid disease or some types of tumors

➤ **Cholesterol (CHOL):** elevated levels suggest liver or kidney disease or several other disorders

➤ **Creatinine (CREA):** elevated levels suggest kidney disease or urinary obstruction

➤ **Blood Glucose (GLU):** low levels can suggest liver disease

Germane to Shepherds

German Shepherds can have some hereditary blood clotting problems, including hemophilia and von Willebrand's disease.

➤ **Phosphorous (PHOS):** elevated levels can suggest kidney disease

➤ **Total bilirubin (TBIL):** elevated levels can indicate bile duct dysfunction, liver disease, or red blood cell destruction

➤ **Total protein (TP):** An abnormal level can indicate problems of the liver, kidneys, or gastrointestinal tract

Take Your Medicine

Your dog will often have to take medicine at home. For most dogs, this is no problem. When giving pills, open your dog's mouth and place the pill well to the back of the throat and in the middle of the tongue. Close the mouth and gently stroke the throat until your dog swallows. Pre-wetting capsules or covering them with cream cheese or some other food helps prevent them from sticking to the tongue or roof of the mouth. For liquid medicine, tilt the head back, keep the dog's mouth almost (but not quite tightly) closed and place the liquid in the pouch of the cheek. Liquids are easier to give in a syringe (without the needle!). Then hold the mouth almost closed until the dog swallows.

Then there's the dog that thinks you are trying to feed it thumbtacks and battery acid. Try hiding pills in cream cheese, hamburger, or peanut butter. Give a few decoy treats first so the dog isn't suspicious and is more likely to gulp down the treat. Liquid medications can be almost impossible if your Shepherd says "No way!" You can try injecting the liquid in a bit of meat, cream cheese, or peanut butter, being very careful the medicine doesn't leak out. You can try a sneak attack when your dog is sleeping, but only if you are absolutely sure your dog won't become startled and bite. Besides, this seldom works more than once. If your dog will take capsules but not liquids, you can use a needle and syringe to remove the contents of a vitamin E gel capsule and replace it with medication. You can simply put the medicine on your dog's food if you are sure the bowl will be licked clean. Of course, if you have to go through all this, you really need to ask your vet if the medicine is available in some other form!

For eye medications, first clean any matter out of your dog's eye so it doesn't prevent the medication from reaching the eye. Then do your best to gently pry the eye partially open and place the drops or ointment in the inner corner. Because dogs have an extra eyelid and an extra muscle that pulls the eye back into the eye socket, neither of which are present in humans, they can do a good job of appearing to be eyeless and making your job as difficult as possible.

For ear medication, clean any heavy debris from the ear, if possible. Then place the medicine as deep into the canal as you can. Remember the ear canal first goes down vertically and then turns abruptly toward the center of the dog's head. This means that you should hold the head vertically at first so the medicine can drop down to the curve, and then try to turn the dog's head so the ear you're medicating is turned upward. Since most dogs are rarely this cooperative, your next choice is to massage the base of the ear hoping to spread the medicine inward. It's best to medicate ears outside because as soon as you let go, the dog shakes its head and medicine goes everywhere!

Always give the full course of medications prescribed by your veterinarian. If a medicine is worth giving, it's worth giving in a full course. Don't give your dog human medications unless you have been directed to do so by your veterinarian. Some medications for humans have no effect on dogs, and some can have a very detrimental effect.

Al Says

Aspirin or prescription medications may alleviate some of the discomfort of injuries, but never give them if your dog is on its way to surgery. If you administer pain medication, you must confine your dog; lack of pain could encourage it to use an injured limb, for example, ultimately resulting in further injury.

The Well-Stocked Medicine Chest

For your Shepherd's well-being and your peace of mind, it's always smart to have the medications and related materials you may need for the dog's home health care. Check the following list and make sure you have these items available.

anti-diarrhea medication

antiseptic skin ointment

clean sponge

first-aid instructions

hydrogen peroxide

instant cold compress

ophthalmic ointment

pen light

rectal thermometer

scissors

self-adhesive bandage (such as Vet-Wrap™)

soap

sterile gauze dressings

stethoscope (optional)

syringe

towel

tweezers

veterinarian emergency clinic and poison control center phone numbers

The Least You Need to Know

➤ Normal gum color is a rich pink, not pale pink, whitish, yellowish, bright red, or showing little red spots.

➤ Normal temperature is about 101.5°F.

➤ Normal pulse rate is about 60 to 120 beats per minute.

➤ Normal respiration rate is about 10 to 30 breaths per minute.

➤ Normal hydration is indicated by skin that pops right back into place after being lifted from the body.

➤ A weekly 5-minute once-over lets you become familiar with what's normal for your dog, and recognize what's not.

Chapter 14

Calling the Shots

In This Chapter

➤ Current ideas about vaccinations

➤ Why repeated vaccinations are needed in puppies

➤ The vaccinations your dog must have

➤ Sample vaccination schedules

Many a German Shepherd has succumbed to contagious diseases, diseases that could have been avoided with a simple vaccination. Don't let your precious dog be one of them.

Your pup's breeder should have furnished the first vaccinations before your pup was old enough to go home with you. Bring all information about your pup's vaccination history to your veterinarian on your first visit so that the pup's vaccination schedule can be maintained. Meanwhile, it is best not to let your pup mingle with strange dogs.

Puppy vaccinations are some of the most vital, but most confusing, of all the vaccinations your dog receives. Puppies get their dam's immunity through nursing in the first days of life. That's why it is important your pup's mother be properly immunized long before breeding and your pup be able to nurse from its dam. The immunity

149

gained from the mother wears off after several weeks, and then the pup is susceptible to disease unless immunity is provided through vaccinations. The problem is that there's no way to know exactly when this passive immunity wears off, and vaccinations given before that time are ineffective. You must revaccinate over a period of weeks so that your pup isn't unprotected and gets effective immunity. That's why puppies get a series of shots instead of just one or two.

Vacillating About Vaccinating?

German Shepherds are one of a handful of breeds recognized to have immune system problems. For some reason, they sometimes fail to gain immunity from some vaccinations. One solution is to revaccinate them often, more so than with other breeds. The problem with this solution is that GSDs also tend to be predisposed to autoimmune diseases (in which the immune system turns on parts of the dog's own body in a sort of case of mistaken identity). Autoimmune diseases can be precipitated by vaccinating.

Germane to Shepherds

German Shepherd immunity problems are thought to be caused by a deficiency in IgA, a component of the immune system important in guarding mucous surfaces against bacterial invasion, as well as in other immune functions.

For some autoimmune problems, recent studies have implicated repeated vaccinations that use combinations of vaccines. Some veterinarians, therefore, recommend staggering different types of vaccines and discourage over-vaccination. They also discourage vaccination in any dog that is under stress or not feeling well. Many dogs seem to feel under the weather for a day or so after getting their vaccinations, so don't schedule your appointment the day before boarding, surgery, a trip, or any kind of doggy event.

Most of the time vaccinating doesn't adversely affect your dog, but if you are a worrywart, you can ask your veterinarian about getting titers run every year instead of boosters. A titer tells you if your dog has enough immunity to a disease. The main problem with getting titers is they are more expensive than vaccines.

Vaccinations are available for several diseases. Some vaccinations are mandatory from a legal standpoint, some are mandatory from a good-sense standpoint, and some are optional.

Al Says

Proof of current vaccination is often needed to transport a dog by air, cross international boundaries, attend obedience classes, board at a kennel, or work as a Therapy Dog.

Rabies

Rabies is inevitably fatal once symptoms appear, and unvaccinated dogs remain the principal host for the disease in undeveloped countries. It is passed most often through the saliva of infected carnivores and bats. Because of its deadly consequences, by law all dogs must be vaccinated. The initial rabies vaccination should be given at around 3 to 4 months of age, again 1 year from the first vaccination, and then every 3 years (although to comply with local law, you may have to give a booster every year).

Distemper

The history of purebred dogs is riddled with stories of entire kennels being decimated by outbreaks of distemper. The production of a vaccine was one of the greatest developments in the progress of canine health. Today distemper is primarily seen in unvaccinated puppies. Initial symptoms are upper respiratory problems and fever, followed by vomiting, diarrhea, and neurologic signs. It's not always fatal, but curing distemper is definitely a lot more expensive than getting a simple vaccination would have been! Very young puppies (about 6 weeks old) usually get a distemper/measles vaccination because the measles fraction can give temporary immunity even in the presence of maternal antibodies. Subsequent distemper inoculations are given every 3 to 4 weeks until the pup is about 16 weeks old. Annual boosters are traditionally recommended.

Hepatitis

Infectious canine hepatitis type 1 is caused by an adenovirus (called CAV-1) found mostly in foxes and dogs, but also in coyotes, wolves, skunks, and bears. It is highly contagious and there is no cure. Although it can occur in adults, it is seen most often in young puppies. Some puppies survive; some do not. Vaccination with CAV-2 (which works just as well, but does not result in the "blue-eye" reaction that CAV-1 caused when it was used years ago) is usually given along with distemper vaccinations.

Leptospirosis

Leptospirosis is a bacterial disease that causes serious liver, kidney, and blood abnormalities. It is thought to be more prevalent in rural areas. Vaccination for "lepto" is not particularly satisfying, because it protects for only about 3 to 6 months. The vaccine works more to prevent severe disease, but does not protect against infection or all strains of leptospirosis. A small percentage of puppies have a transient adverse reaction to the vaccination. Therefore, some people prefer not to include lepto in their vaccination regime, although most veterinarians include it as part of a combination vaccine.

Parvovirus

In the late 1970s a worldwide virus broke out that caused often fatal intestinal bleeding. This was an entirely new virus thought to have arisen through mutation. The advent of a vaccination was a major triumph, although breeders still fear parvovirus because it is extremely contagious and can remain in the environment for years. Maternal antibodies often interfere with the vaccination for parvo; for this reason three vaccinations by the age of 16 weeks are recommended, with an optional fourth at around 18 to 20 weeks. Annual boosters are traditionally recommended.

Coronavirus

Coronavirus causes extreme diarrhea that in rare cases results in death. Younger dogs are the most adversely affected. A vaccination is available, but is currently considered optional.

Tracheobronchitis (Kennel Cough)

Kennel cough is highly contagious and tends to spread when dogs share closed spaces. The name comes from its tendency to occur about a week after dogs have been in a boarding kennel, but it is often passed on at dog shows or even veterinary waiting rooms. It's characterized by a dry, honking cough that can last for weeks. Vaccinations are available, but the problem is that kennel cough can be caused by many different infectious agents. The vaccines protect against the most common ones (CPIV, CAV-2, and bordatella), but not all. Their effects also do not last very long. For these reasons, and because kennel cough is not fatal, some people prefer not to vaccinate for it specifically. CPIV and CAV-2 are usually incorporated in combination vaccines, however. Bordatella is usually administered separately (or with CPIV) intranasally and can sometimes cause a transient cough. Nonetheless, kennel cough vaccination can be a good idea for dogs that are boarded or shown. They should be given a week before exposure, or with annual boosters.

Al Says

Bordatella vaccine is usually given by putting drops in the nose.

Lyme Disease

Lyme disease is known to cause severe problems in humans, but its effects in dogs are less noticeable. A vaccination is available, but not universally accepted as necessary. Only dogs living in endemic areas should be considered candidates for Lyme disease vaccination. Consult with your veterinarian about the prevalence of Lyme disease in your local area.

Give It Your Best Shot

Several respected veterinary teaching hospitals have recently revised their vaccination protocols to include fewer booster shots. One such protocol suggests giving a three-shot series for puppies, each shot containing parvovirus, adenovirus 2 (CAV-2), parainfluenza (CPIV), and distemper, with one rabies vaccination at 16 weeks. Following this, a booster is given 1 year later, and then subsequent boosters are given every 3 years. Other respected epidemiologists disagree and prefer the traditional vaccination schedule. The great vaccination debate is far from over, so confer with your veterinarian about current thinking on the matter. One thing is certain: No matter what their possible side effects, vaccinations are a good thing, and all dogs must be vaccinated for their health as well as the health of others.

The Least You Need to Know

➤ All dogs need to be vaccinated with a series of shots as puppies, and at least some boosters as adults.

➤ German Shepherds have a greater tendency to not form sufficient disease immunity, suggesting they may need to be vaccinated *more* often than other dogs...

➤ ...and to complicate matters, German Shepherds also tend to develop autoimmune diseases more, suggesting they may need to be vaccinated *less* often than what is considered normal.

➤ Common vaccinations include rabies, distemper, hepatitis, leptospirosis, parvovirus, coronavirus, tracheobronchitis, and Lyme disease, but not all of them may be necessary.

➤ Ideas about ideal vaccination protocols are continuously changing and always controversial.

Little Bloodsuckers

In This Chapter

➤ How you can save your dog from deadly heartworms

➤ The not-so-wonderful world of worms

➤ Making fleas flee

➤ Ticks and the bad things they cause

➤ Fixing a mangy dog

Parasites can rob your dog of vital nutrients, good health, quality of life, and sometimes, even a long life. The most common internal parasites set up housekeeping in the intestines and heart. The most common external parasites can be found on the skin and in the ears. Every one is either treatable or preventable.

Heartworming Relationships

Heartworms are deadly nematode parasites carried by mosquitoes. Wherever mosquitoes are present, dogs should be on a heartworm preventive. Several effective types of heartworm preventive are available, with some also preventing many other types of worms. Some require daily administration, and others require only monthly administration. The latter type is more popular and actually offers a wider margin of safety and protection. They don't stay in the dog's system for a month, but instead act on a particular stage in the heart-worm's development. Giving the drug each month prevents any heartworms from ever maturing. In warm areas, your dog may need to be on a preventive year-round, but in cooler climates, your dog may need to get preventive drugs only during the warmer months. Your veterinarian can advise you about when your puppy should be started and if year-round protection is necessary in your area.

If you forget to give the preventive as prescribed, your dog may get heartworms. A dog suspected of having heartworms should not be given the daily preventive because a fatal reaction could occur. The most common way of checking for heartworms is to test the blood for circulating microfilariae (the immature form of heartworms), but this method may fail to detect the presence of adult heartworms in as many as 20 percent of all tested dogs. An "occult" heartworm test, although slightly more expensive, tests for the presence of antigens to heartworms in the blood and is more accurate. With either test, the presence of heartworms can't be detected until nearly 7 months after infection. Heartworms are treatable in the early stages, but the treatment is expensive and not without risks (although a less risky treatment has recently become available). If untreated, heartworms can kill your pet.

Some heartworm preventives can also protect your dog from other nematode parasites. Discuss your options with your veterinarian.

Global Worming

Don't assume that only puppies coming from a bad environment have worms. Most puppies do have worms at some point, even pups from the most fastidious breeders. This is because some types of lar-val worms become encysted in the dam's body long before she becomes pregnant, perhaps when she herself was a pup. Here they lie dormant and immune from worming, until hormonal changes caused by her pregnancy activate them, and then they infect her fetuses or her newborns through her milk.

The classic wormy puppy has a dull coat, skinny body, and potbelly, but many pups infested with worms have few of these symptoms. Because you can buy worming medication over the counter, many people figure this is their chance to save a little money. Others have been taught that to be good dog owners, they should "worm" their dog once a month. Over-the-counter wormers are largely ineffective and often more dangerous than those available through your veterinarian. No dog should be wormed unless it actually has worms. When you take your dog to be vaccinated, bring along a stool specimen so that your veterinarian can also check for these parasites.

Hookworms, whipworms, ascarids, threadworms, and lungworms are all types of nematode parasites that can infect dogs of all ages, but have their most devastating effect on puppies. Left untreated, worms can cause vom-

Shep Heard

...that feeding a dog sweets can give it worms. Shep heard wrong! There are good reasons not to feed a dog sweets, but worms have nothing to do with them.

iting, diarrhea, dull coat, listlessness, anemia, and death. Have your puppy tested for internal parasites regularly. Some heartworm preventives also prevent most types of intestinal worms (but not tapeworms).

Ascarids

Ascarids are one of the most common internal parasites in dogs; among the group of ascarids, the most common is *Toxocara canis*, which is found in virtually every puppy. Most puppies get the larva before birth, and eggs can be found in the pups' feces by the time they are three weeks old. *T. canis* can also be spread by dogs ingesting the eggs, and it can be spread to people as well as dogs. Children playing in sandboxes or playgrounds contaminated with *T. canis*–infested feces can contract the parasite and become dangerously ill as a result. Control programs for *T. canis* in puppies come from the Center for Disease Control, and were developed for the purpose of controlling it in humans. Puppies should be wormed at least twice for *T. canis*, and many protocols advocate more frequent worming, with dosages administered at 2, 4, 6, and 8 weeks of age. Feces should be picked up regularly, and dogs should not be allowed to defecate where children play. Infected puppies can also become quite ill, with heavy infestations leading to convulsions or death. Most mortalities occur at around 2 to 3 weeks of age. Symptoms include a rough coat, potbelly, and wasting muscles. Sometimes adult worms can be seen in vomit or feces.

Hookworms

Hookworms are actually a family of species, the most common in dogs being *Ancylostoma caninum*. They are especially prevalent in warm, humid climates. Hookworms can be acquired before birth, or by the larvae penetrating through the skin, or by the dog eating the larvae. Puppies with heavy infestations can become anemic and have bloody, black, or tarry diarrhea. Without prompt treatment, these puppies usually die. Treatment consists of deworming, blood transfusions, and follow-up prevention. Once the intestinal tract has been cleared of worms, larva in the muscle tissue migrate to the intestines and repopulate them, so another deworming treatment is needed 2 weeks after the first. Adult dogs usually build up an immunity to hookworms, although some dogs have chronic hookworm disease. This is seen more often in dogs with compromised immune systems or dogs that live in the midst of feces. Removing feces at least twice a week is the most cost-effective means of hookworm control.

Shep Heard

...that dogs should be regularly wormed every month or so. Shep heard wrong! Dogs should be wormed when, and only when, they have been diagnosed with worms. No worm medication is completely without risk, and it is foolish to use it carelessly.

Whipworms

Whipworms inhabit the large intestine, where they puncture blood vessels and have a blood feast at your dog's expense. A heavy infestation can cause diarrhea, anemia, and weight loss. Dogs get whipworms by ingesting their eggs. Eggs can live in the environment for up to 5 years, especially in cold climates. Unlike some other types of internal parasites, dogs do not develop an immunity to whipworms. Treatment consists of repeated deworming, often every other month for a year. Picking up feces is an essential part of controlling whipworms.

More Worms

Two more types of nematodes that occasionally infect dogs are threadworms and lungworms. Neither is particularly common. Threadworms live in the small intestine and can cause bloody diarrhea and coughing. They are more common in warm weather, and are treated with high doses of Thiabendazole (mintezol).

Lungworms are found in the respiratory tract, lung tissue, and blood vessels. They can cause large, wartlike nodules on the lungs' bronchii, leading to bronchitis, coughing, and lack of appetite. The condition is difficult to treat and has a high mortality rate in puppies.

Another "forgotten" worm is actually carried by earthworms. Capillaria is a type of lungworm that lives in the nasal passages, trachea, and bronchii. Heavy infestations can cause sneezing and coughing. The worms themselves resemble whipworms and are often misdiagnosed as such. The worms are susceptible to regular deworming medication. Dogs get capillaria from eating earthworms—yet another reason not to eat worms!

Even more rare and exotic worms can be found on the insides of dogs. The giant kidney worm must be removed surgically. Dogs can get them from eating earthworms or fish and frogs that have ingested infected worms. In southern climates, *Spirocerca lupi* causes thickened nodules in the esophagus or stomach and narrowing of the aorta or trachea. Dogs can get them from eating dung beetles or from something that ate an infected dung beetle. Treatment is with deworming medication. Physaloptera are found in the stomach or small intestine and can cause anemia, gastritis, and vomiting. Dogs get this parasite by eating infected beetles, crickets, cockroaches, or animals that ate infected beetles, crickets, or cockroaches. Seems like nothing's safe to eat anymore!

Tapeworms

Tapeworms tend to plague some dogs throughout their lives. Several species exist, by far the most common being *Dipylidium caninum*. There is no preventive, except to diligently rid your GSD of fleas because fleas transmit this kind of tapeworm to dogs. Your dog can get some other types of tapeworms by eating raw rabbit or fish.

159

Shep Heard

...that a dog that scoots its rear on the ground must have worms. Shep sort of heard wrong! Although scooting may be a sign of tapeworms, a dog that repeatedly scoots more likely has impacted anal sacs.

On fresh stools, tapeworms look like moving, white, flat worms, or they may dry up and look like rice grains around the dog's anus. Tapeworms are one of the least debilitating of all the worms, but their segments can be irritating to the dog's anal region and are certainly unsightly.

Tapeworms, which are in the cestode family, do not respond to the same dewormers as those in the nematode family. That means the heartworm preventives that also prevent several nematodes do not affect tapeworms.

Germs and Shepherds

Puppies and adult dogs can also suffer from protozoan parasites, such as coccidia and especially giardia. Less common protozoan infections include toxoplasma, *Neospora caninum*, leishmania, and *Trypanosoma cruzi*. Babesia is growing in frequency. Because they are not worms, worm medications are usually ineffective. Your veterinarian can prescribe appropriate medication.

Coccidia

Coccidia are often associated with diarrhea, but many infected dogs show no apparent symptoms, so the importance of coccidia infection in dogs is not well understood at present. A stool sample is needed for diagnosis. Affected dogs respond well to supportive treatment and drugs to do away with the coccidia. The most important preventive measure is frequent removal of feces from the dog's quarters.

Giardia

Giardia is found fairly commonly in puppies and dogs. It can cause chronic or intermittent diarrhea, but might have no symptoms. It can be diagnosed with a stool sample, and is more likely to be found in loose or light-colored stools. Many dogs carry giardia and have no symptoms, so the presence of giardia in the stool may not necessarily account for any illness a dog may be showing. Giardia can be treated with drug therapy.

Keeping your German Shepherd free of parasites is one of your most important responsibilities as a dog owner. (Craig and Cynthia Miller)

Babesia

Potentially fatal parasites, protozoa of the genus *Babesia* are transmitted by ticks and parasitize the red blood cells. This causes the dog to become anemic, and may also precipitate an autoimmune response that destroys the dog's red blood cells. Platelets may also be destroyed. Symptoms include a fever, lethargy, loss of appetite, and in severe cases, darkened urine. Affected dogs can die within a week of the first appearance of these symptoms. Diagnosis is with blood tests.

Babesia is not common in North America, but does occur, mostly in the southern regions. Many of the first cases are thought to have been brought back from Asia with returning military dogs, mostly GSDs.

Al Says

The symptoms of babesiosis are similar to those of autoimmune hemolytic anemia. If your dog is diagnosed with either of these conditions, make sure your veterinarian also tests for the other possibility.

Stuck on You

Your GSD's skin is its largest single organ and the one most accessible to you. It is a major interface between your dog and the environment, and as such is vulnerable to a plethora of problems, many caused by fleas and ticks.

No Flea Zone

Recent advances in flea and tick control have finally put dog owners on the winning side. In any but the mildest of infestations, these new products are well worth their initial higher price. It's a lot cheaper to put an expensive product on your dog once every 3 months than to reapply a cheap one every day.

Fleas can make your dog's life miserable. No dog should be expected to live a life with insects crawling in its coat and biting its body. Remember that fleas can cause secondary problems, such as tapeworms and severe skin irritation. Many GSDs develop flea allergies, and it is essential that these dogs be kept absolutely flea free. For such dogs, products that require a flea to bite the dog before the medication can kill or sterilize the flea may not be optimal, since even one flea bite can elicit severe allergic reaction. Here are some of the newer flea and tick preventives you should know about:

➤ Imidacloprid (for example, Advantage™) is a liquid applied once a month on the animal's back. It gradually distributes itself over the entire skin surface and kills at least 98 percent of the fleas on the animal within 24 hours and continues to kill fleas for a month. It can withstand water, but not repeated swimming or bathing.

➤ Fipronil (for example, Frontline™) comes as either a spray applied all over the dog's body or as a self-distributing liquid applied only on the dog's back. Once applied, fipronil collects in the hair follicles and then wicks out over time. Therefore, it is resistant to being washed off and can kill fleas for up to 3 months on dogs. It's also effective on ticks for a shorter period.

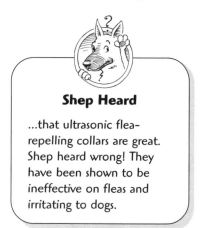

Shep Heard

...that ultrasonic flea-repelling collars are great. Shep heard wrong! They have been shown to be ineffective on fleas and irritating to dogs.

➤ Lufenuron (for example, Program™) is given as a pill once a month. Fleas that bite the dog and ingest the lufenuron in the dog's system are rendered sterile. It is extremely safe. All animals in the environment must be treated for the regimen to be effective, however.

➤ Pyriproxyfen (for example, Nylar™, Sumilar™, and others) is an insect growth regulator marketed in different strengths and formulations that's available as an animal or premise spray. It can protect in the home or yard for 6 to 12 months, and on the animal for 100 days, depending on the particular product.

Shep Heard

...that feeding dogs brewer's yeast or garlic gets rid of fleas. Shep heard wrong! Scientific studies have shown that both are ineffective against fleas. However, many owners swear they work, and they don't seem to do any harm.

Traditional flea control products are either less effective or less safe than these newer products. The permethrins and pyrethrins are safe, but have practically no residual action. The large family of cholinesterase inhibitors (Dursban, Diazinon, Malathion, Sevin, Carbaryl, Pro-Spot, Spotton) last a little longer, but have been known to kill dogs when overused, used in combination with cholinesterase-inhibiting yard products or with cholinesterase-inhibiting dewormers.

Ticked Off

Certain tick species can carry Rocky Mountain spotted fever, tick paralysis, Lyme disease, babesiosis, and most commonly, "tick fever" (erlichiosis)—all very serious diseases. Erlichiosis is being recognized as an increasing threat to dogs (see page 191).

Shep Heard

...that you can burn a tick out. Shep heard wrong! Trying to burn a tick out not only doesn't work, but is also a good way to set your dog on fire.

Ticks can be found anywhere on the dog, but most often burrow around the ears, neck, and chest and between the toes. To remove a tick, use a tissue or tweezers, since some diseases can be transmitted to humans. Grasp the tick as close to the skin as possible, and pull slowly and steadily, trying not to leave the head in the dog. Don't squeeze the tick, as this can inject its contents into the dog. Clean the site with alcohol. Often a bump remains after the tick is removed, even if you got the head, but it goes away with time.

"Mitey Dog"

Mites are tiny organisms in the tick and spider family, so chemicals that are effective on fleas have no effect on mites. Of the many types of mites, only a few cause problems in dogs.

Sarcoptic mange, also called canine scabies, causes intense itching, often characterized by scaling of the ear tips. It is highly contagious and spread by direct contact, even having a transient effect on people. Most of the lesions are found on the ear tips, underside of the body, elbows, and forelegs. Treatment requires repeated shampoos or dips of not only the affected dog, but also other household pets in contact with the infected dog.

Demodectic mange, also called red mange or demodicosis, is not contagious and not usually itchy. The condition tends to run in families and is more common in certain breeds. It is characterized by a moth-eaten appearance, most often around the eyes and lips. Demodectic mange affecting the feet is also common, and can be extremely resistant to treatment. Most cases of demodectic mange appear in puppies, and most consist of only a few patches that often go away by themselves. But in those cases that continue to spread, or in adult-onset demodectic mange, aggressive treatment using an amitraz insecticidal dip is needed. Your veterinarian needs to perform a skin-scraping to confirm the diagnosis before prescribing treatment. In particularly resistant cases, heavy administration of some monthly heartworm preventives can provide an effective cure.

Cheyletiella mites live on the skin surface and cause mild itchiness. Unlike other mites, they are large enough to be seen with the naked eye (but a magnifying glass works better). They look like small white specks in the dog's hair near the skin. Sometimes they are confused with dandruff because they also cause dandruff, especially along the back. They are transmitted by direct contact. Many flea insecticides also kill these mites, but they are better treated by using special shampoos or dips, which must be repeated at least four times on a regular schedule.

Al Says

Another mite that can make your dog miserable is the ear mite. See page 130 for more information.

Lousy with Lice

Lice are not terribly common on dogs, but they can be present and cause problems. They cause itching and poor coat; some types of lice can suck so much blood that the dog can become anemic and even die. You can see lice with a magnifying glass under bright light. Treatment is with an insecticidal shampoo, repeated after a few weeks.

The Least You Need to Know

➤ If your dog can get bitten by a mosquito, it can develop heartworms—and die—unless you have your dog on a heartworm preventive.

➤ Even puppies from the healthiest litters and in the cleanest environments usually must be treated for intestinal parasites, and the best preventive against transmitting intestinal parasites is cleaning up feces.

➤ New flea products are available that really do get rid of fleas! But you have to read the labels.

➤ Ticks can transmit several potentially fatal diseases.

➤ Demodectic mange can be localized or generalized. The former is easily cured; the latter can be very difficult to cure.

Chapter 16

Sick as a Dog

In This Chapter

➤ Common symptoms and what they tell you

➤ Behaviors that could indicate physical disease

➤ How to stop vomiting and diarrhea

➤ Eye, ear, and skin problems

➤ How to deal with a lame dog

People get sick. Dogs get sick. The difference is that people can tell you where it hurts. They can also tell you how bad they feel and what may have caused it. With a dog, it's like trying to ask an introverted mime what the problem is. Add to this the German Shepherd's stoic persona, and you have the ingredients for a full-blown undetected problem. On the other hand, it's expensive to run to the vet every time your dog clears its throat.

Instead of running down all the diseases your dog might have, it's more useful to look at what your dog is telling you, narrow it down to the most common problems it might be indicating, and then decide if it's time for a real doctor's opinion.

Know the signs of good health in your German Shepherd as insurance for recognizing the symptoms of illness. (Susan Heit)

Changes in Behavior

When is a change in behavior more than a mood swing? Sometimes it's difficult to know. Some changes are natural consequences of aging or hormonal states. Sexually intact males may become excited and possibly even unmanageable around females in estrous (heat). Females in estrous can be aggressive toward males making unwanted advances, and males may be inclined to fight with one another. Aside from such changes, though, most normal and fairly long-lasting behavioral changes are not so abrupt.

Germane to Shepherds

Sudden pacing and restlessness, combined with unsuccessful attempts to vomit, could indicate bloat. This is a "rush to the emergency vet right now" situation. Do not "wait and see." Bloat is a fast and merciless killer, and it targets German Shepherds. See page 184 for more information.

A dog that is uncharacteristically lethargic could be sick, and the possible causes are endless without narrowing down the list. Does the dog also have a fever? If yes, then consider an infection. If no, then your dog may have pain somewhere. Sudden loss of vision can also cause lethargy. Cancer, poisoning, or metabolic diseases can cause lethargy without fever. In general, extreme lethargy that lasts for more than 1 day or is accompanied by a fever should be checked by your veterinarian.

Aggressive behavior is usually not a sign of disease unless it is totally unprecedented. It can be a sign of pain, an endocrine problem, or a brain problem. Usually such cases are better examined by a neurologist or a veterinarian specializing in behavior.

Sudden loss of balance could be due to an inner ear problem or to unknown causes. Either way, your veterinarian can prescribe drugs to make your dog feel better.

In general, unprecedented persistent circling or pacing, disorientation, head-pressing, hiding, tremors, seizures, lack of bowel or urine control, or dramatic changes in appetite are usually signs of a physical problem and need to be checked by your veterinarian—and sooner is better than later.

Vomiting

When people vomit, it usually means they feel sick. When dogs vomit, it's hard to tell how they feel. Some dogs almost seem to enjoy vomiting, and eat grass to ensure they will do so. Vomiting after eating grass is common and usually of no great concern. A typical vomiting episode begins with retching, followed by upchucking on your best rug, and then within a minute another bout of retching and vomiting (hopefully by now not on your best rug). Following this, the dog usually appears to be just fine. If the vomiting continues, it's not typical "recreational" vomiting but is cause for concern.

Overeating is a common cause of occasional vomiting in puppies, especially if they follow eating with playing. Feed smaller meals more frequently if this becomes a problem. Vomiting immediately after meals could indicate an obstruction of the esophagus. Repeated vomiting could mean that the dog has eaten spoiled food or indigestible objects, or may have some form of stomach illness. Seek veterinary advice. Meanwhile, withhold food (or feed as directed for diarrhea) and restrict water. Repeated vomiting can result in dehydration, so if your dog can't hold anything down for a prolonged period, it may have to be given intravenous fluids.

Consult your veterinarian immediately if your dog vomits a foul substance resembling fecal matter (indicating a blockage in the intestinal tract) or blood (partially digested blood resembles coffee grounds), or if there is projectile or continued vomiting. Sporadic vomiting with

169

poor appetite and generally poor condition could indicate internal parasites or a more serious internal disease that should also be checked by your veterinarian.

Diarrhea

Dogs, especially puppies, get diarrhea. It can result from overexcitement, nervousness, a change in diet or water, sensitivity to certain foods, overeating, intestinal parasites, viral or bacterial infections, or ingestion of toxic substances. Bloody diarrhea; diarrhea with vomiting, fever, or other signs of toxicity; or a diarrhea that lasts for more than a day should not be allowed to continue without veterinary advice. Some of them could be symptomatic of potentially fatal disorders.

The appearance of the diarrhea can provide important information for the veterinarian, so even though your neighbors may think you're a pervert, take a good look at your dog's diarrhea. What is the consistency? Does it contain blood or mucus? If so, how much? Can you identify foreign objects or parasites? What color is it? These are all clues to the severity and possible causes of your dog's problem.

Less severe diarrhea can be treated at home by withholding or severely restricting food and water for 24 hours. Give your dog ice cubes to satisfy its thirst. Administer human diarrhea medication in the same weight dosage as recommended for humans. A bland diet consisting of rice, tapioca, or cooked macaroni, along with cottage cheese or tofu for protein, should be given for several days. Feed nothing else. The intestinal tract needs time off to heal. Note that dogs with some other illnesses may not be candidates for food or water restriction.

Coughing

Allergies, foreign bodies, pneumonia, parasites, tracheal collapse, tumors, and especially kennel cough and heart disease can all cause coughing. Any persistent cough should be checked by your veterinarian. It may indicate a serious problem. Coughing irritates the throat and can lead to secondary infections if allowed to continue unchecked. It can also be miserable for the dog.

Heart disease can result in coughing, most often following exercise or in the evening. Affected dogs often lie down with their front legs spread and point their nose in the air to breathe easier. A low-sodium diet and drug therapy can help alleviate the symptoms for a while.

Kennel cough (canine infectious tracheobronchitis) is a highly communicable airborne disease caused by several different infectious agents. It's characterized by a gagging cough arising about a week after exposure. After a few days, the cough takes on a "honking" sound. Inoculations are available and are an especially good idea if you plan to have your dog around other dogs at training classes or while being boarded. Treatment consists of resting the dog and avoiding situations that may lead to coughing. Cough suppressants may break the coughing/irritation cycle. Left untreated, the cough can irritate the dog's throat and eventually cause more serious problems. Antibiotics may be needed if secondary infections arise from prolonged irritation.

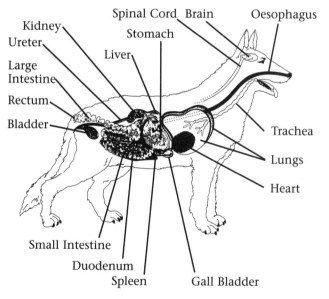

"Outside of a dog, a book is man's best friend. Inside of a dog, it's dark." —Groucho Marx, famed dog anatomist. Seriously, this is the "inside" story.

Urinary Problems

If your dog has difficulty or pain when urinating, urinates suddenly and often but in small amounts, or passes cloudy or bloody urine, it may be suffering from a problem of the bladder, urethra, or prostate. Dribbling urine during sleep can indicate a hormonal problem. Urinalysis and a rectal exam by your veterinarian are necessary to

171

diagnose the exact nature of the problem. Bladder infections must be treated promptly to prevent the infection from reaching the kidneys. Blockage of urine can result in death. An inability to urinate requires immediate emergency veterinary attention.

In males, infections of the prostate gland can lead to repeated urinary tract infections, and sometimes painful defecation or blood and pus in the urine. Castration and long-term antibiotic therapy are required for improvement.

Kidney disease, ultimately leading to kidney failure, is one of the most common ailments of older dogs. The earliest symptom is usually increased urination. Although the excessive urination may cause problems in keeping your house clean or your night's sleep intact, never try to restrict water from a dog with kidney disease. Increased urination can also be a sign of diabetes or a urinary tract infection. Your veterinarian can discover the cause with some simple tests, and each of these conditions can be treated. For kidney disease, a low-phosphorous, low-protein and low-sodium diet can slow the progression.

Under the Skin

Skin problems make up most of the "non-well" cases a veterinarian sees every day, and German Shepherds are prone to several skin problems. They can result from parasites, allergies, bacteria, fungus, endocrine disorders, and a long list of other possible causes.

Allergies

Flea allergy dermatitis (FAD) is the most common of all skin problems. Itchy, crusted bumps with hair loss in the region around the rump, especially at the base of the tail, results from a flea bite (actually, the flea's saliva) anywhere on the dog's body.

Besides FAD, dogs can have allergic reactions to pollens or other inhaled allergens. Allergies to weeds can manifest themselves between the dog's toes. Suspect them when you see the dog constantly licking its feet, or when the feet are stained pink from saliva. Food allergies can also occur. New blood tests for antibodies are much easier and less expensive (although not as comprehensive) than the traditional intradermal skin testing.

Pyoderma

Pyoderma, with pus-filled bumps and crusting, is another common skin disease. Impetigo is characterized by such bumps and crusting most often in the groin area of puppies. Both are treated with antibiotics and antibacterial shampoos. German Shepherd Dog Pyoderma is a type of pyoderma so commonly seen in GSDs that it bears the breed's name. In it, severe, deep draining sores are found over the lower back and hind legs. It often isn't responsive to antibiotics, and lifelong corticosteroid therapy may be necessary for the dog's comfort. Limited evidence suggests it may have a hereditary basis, and be aggravated by hypothyroidism, fleas, and allergies.

Hot Spots

A reddened, moist, itchy spot that suddenly appears is most likely a "hot spot" (pyotraumatic dermatitis), which arises from an itch-scratch-chew cycle resulting most commonly from fleas or flea allergy. German Shepherds tend to get hot spots, especially in hot, humid weather. Wash the area with an oatmeal-based shampoo, and prevent the dog from further chewing. Use an Elizabethan collar (available from your veterinarian or you can fashion one from a plastic pail), or an anti-chew preparation, such as Grannick's Bitter Apple™ (available from most pet stores). Your veterinarian can also prescribe anti-inflammatory medication. As a temporary measure, you can give an allergy pill (Benadryl™—ask your veterinarian about dosage), which alleviates some itching and causes drowsiness, both of which should decrease chewing.

Al Says

Hair loss can also be caused by mange (see pages 164–165), auto-immune problems (see pages 187–189), or endocrine problems (see page 174).

Seborrhea

Seborrhea occurs in an oily form and a dry form. German Shepherds usually get the dry form. In the dry form, the skin feels waxy and greasy, and may also be crusty and dry. Dandruff is often present. It is often associated with excessive earwax and a rancid odor. Sometimes the hair falls out when its roots become coated with grease. Most hair loss occurs on the trunk.

Al Says

Hair may be lost in a bilaterally symmetric pattern, without itching, because of hypothyroidism, Cushing's syndrome, or testicular tumors.

Endocrine Disorders

The most widespread hormone-related disorders in the dog are diabetes, hypothyroidism, and Cushing's syndrome. The most common is hypothyroidism.

Hypothyroidism

Hypothyroidism is one of the most commonly diagnosed conditions in purebred dogs; however, this is one disorder that GSDs seem to get less often than most breeds! Still, no breed is exempt. Symptoms can include weight gain, lethargy, and coat problems such as oiliness, dullness, symmetrical hair loss, and hair that is easily pulled out. It has been implicated in everything from behavioral problems to infertility to lack of energy. Diagnosis is with a blood test; ask your veterinarian about the more sophisticated and accurate tests now available. Treatment is with daily thyroid replacement drugs.

Cushing's Syndrome

Cushing's syndrome (hyperadrenocorticism), seen mostly in older dogs, is characterized by increased drinking and urination, a pot-bellied appearance, symmetrical hair loss on the body, darkened skin, and susceptibility to infections. Diagnosis is with a blood test. Treatment is with drug therapy.

The Least You Need to Know

➤ Sudden changes in behavior could indicate your dog is in pain.

➤ Prolonged vomiting and diarrhea can lead to severe dehydration and should be checked by your veterinarian.

➤ Coughing can arise from several problems, including kennel cough and heart disease.

➤ Inability to urinate is a life-threatening emergency.

➤ When in doubt, get it checked out!

Chapter 17

Hereditary Headaches

Every pure breed of dog is predisposed to its own set of health problems, because every pure breed has its own subset of genes. In some breeds, the selection for particular traits may also inadvertently bring some health problems with it. In other cases, a small number of dogs were used to found a breed, and if one of those dogs happened to carry a gene for a health problem, it could have become widespread throughout the breed because of the restricted gene pool. Finally, in very popular breeds, careless breeding by owners not aware of health problems can cause genetic disorders to become more prevalent. The GSD has several health problems to which it is especially susceptible, although their inclusion in this listing does not mean they are necessarily widespread.

Skeletal Disorders

The skeletal system is the framework for your dog's body. Many large dogs are predisposed to skeletal problems that can lead to lameness.

177

Panosteitis

Panosteitis is an inflammation of the long bones resulting in lameness, which often shifts from leg to leg. It is most common in growing dogs of large breeds, including GSDs. Symptoms may come on suddenly, usually between five and ten months of age, although some GSDs (unlike other breeds) may develop the condition at up to two years of age. The exact cause is not known, but the prognosis for a full recovery is usually excellent. Meanwhile, treatment consists of limiting exercise somewhat and giving the dog analgesics to help control pain.

Elbow Dysplasia

Elbow dysplasia occurs in many breeds, including the GSD. It can be caused by several different types of developmental problems; in the GSD the cause is most often ununited aconeal process (UAP). The anconeal process is a small finger of bone that normally attaches to the head of the ulna (one of the forearm's long bones), and works to stabilize the elbow by fitting snugly into a notch in the humerus (upper arm) where it hinges with the ulna. In some dogs, the anconeal process never attaches properly to the ulna, so the dog's elbow can shift from side to side when the dog places weight on it. The anconeal process breaks loose, floats around, and causes irritation to the elbow.

The dog has varying degrees of lameness in the front legs that originate in the elbow joint, and the joint may be swollen and painful. Radiographs can diagnose the condition. Treatment is with surgical removal of the loose piece.

The Orthopedic Foundation for Animals maintains a registry for elbows, and all GSD breeding stock should have an OFA elbow clearance. Dogs over 2 years of age with normal elbows are assigned a breed registry number. Abnormal elbows are assigned either Grade I, II, or III, with Grade III being the most severely affected. About 20 percent of the German Shepherds that have had their elbow x-rays submitted to OFA have been rated as dysplastic.

Hip Dysplasia

Hip dysplasia is the most well-known hereditary problem of dogs, and the German Shepherd has been the popular poster child for this disorder. The GSD is far from being the most affected breed, however.

Hip dysplasia occurs when the ball of the femur (thigh bone) does not fit properly into the socket (acetabulum) of the pelvic bone. The fit is affected by the depth and shape of the socket and the laxity of the joint. With pressure on the joint, such as what occurs when the dog walks or runs, the combination of laxity and a shallow socket allows the ball of the femur to pop in and out of the socket. This movement further deteriorates the rim of the socket, worsening the condition. This is why early diagnosis and treatment is important.

Hip radiographs can diagnose dysplasia before outward signs of the disorder can be perceived. In the United States, radiographs are most often rated by either the Orthopedic Foundation for Animals (OFA) or the Pennsylvania Hip Improvement Program (PennHIP).

The OFA is the most widely used hip certification organization. Radiographs are subjectively rated by a panel of specialists, based on a number of specific joint characteristics. A dog with "normal" hips (which includes ratings of excellent, good, and fair) receives an OFA number. Borderline ratings indicate that a dog should be rechecked in another 6 to 8 months. Dysplastic hips have ratings of mild, moderate, and severe. Ratings are not given until dogs are 2 years old, but preliminary ratings can be obtained before then.

Shep Heard

...that German Shepherds are plagued with hip dysplasia because of the way breeders have selected for the extremely angulated hips. Shep heard wrong! First of all, many breeds with much less angulated hips have far more hip dysplasia than GSDs. Second, within the breed, no correlation exists between hip angulation and hip dysplasia.

Germane to Shepherds

The "a" stamp given to German dogs includes those with normal, near-normal, and "still-permissible" hips, with the latter category including some mildly to moderately dysplastic dogs. Therefore, the "a" stamp is less informative and more inclusive than OFA or PennHIP certification.

PennHIP evaluation is based on objectively measured degrees of joint laxity, reported as a Distraction Index (DI), with lower numbers reflecting tighter (better) hips. The x-rays must be taken using special procedures by veterinarians approved to do them by PennHIP.

Breeders disagree about which method is better, so many breeders elect to have two radiographs taken at the same time, submitting one to each registry. The only bad choice is no certification at all.

Hip dysplasia becomes progressively more crippling and painful. Mild cases may not need specific treatment, whereas more severe cases can live full lives if given timely surgery. If the condition is detected in a young dog before secondary changes (osteoarthritis) have occurred, a procedure called a triple pelvic osteotomy (TPO) can be performed. In a TPO, the orientation of the dog's hip socket is surgically changed, allowing the femur head to better fit into the socket. Older dogs or dogs with more advanced dysplasia are better candidates for a total hip replacement, similar to the same procedure in humans. The ball of the femur is replaced with a metallic ball, and the socket is replaced with a Teflon™ cup. A third procedure, which is less effective in large dogs, is to simply remove the head of the femur. It might be a reasonable choice for financial reasons in an older dog that needed only to be comfortable walking around the house.

Swimming is an excellent low-impact exercise for a German Shepherd in need of conditioning, but someone should be in constant attention when a Shepherd is in the pool. (Jean Keller)

Osteochondrosis Dissecans

Osteochondrosis dissecans (OCD) is lameness occurring when a flap of cartilage becomes detached from the bone. Lameness starts gradually at around 7 to 10 months of age, and gradually gets worse. The most common site is in one or both shoulders, but almost any joint can be affected. Sometimes absolute rest for several weeks can help, although lameness may actually worsen with rest. It gets better with mild exercise, and is worse with heavy exercise. Surgical repair is usually preferable, and has especially satisfying results with OCD of the shoulder.

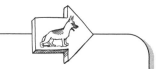

Germane to Shepherds

Some preliminary and controversial evidence exists that giving German Shepherds high doses of vitamin C can improve the mobility of dogs with hip dysplasia. Other studies go further, contending that feeding the pregnant dam and her pups high doses of vitamin C can prevent hip dysplasia. These allegations await more rigorous scientific testing.

Pituitary Dwarfism

Although technically an endocrine disorder rather than a skeletal disorder, pituitary dwarfism has profound effects on the skeleton. Pituitary dwarfism is a failure to grow, normally caused by a lack of growth hormone. It occurs more often in GSDs than in any other breed, and is caused by a simple recessive gene. An affected dog can first be noticed at about 2 months of age, when it is smaller than its littermates. The coat is woolly, lacking guard hairs (the'longer, coarser, outer hairs), and often the hair is missing from the body but remains on the head and legs. The affected dog's bark can be shrill, and it might be more difficult to housebreak because of retarded mental development. Specialized testing can lead to a positive diagnosis. Treatment is with growth hormone replacement, but it must be started early. It will not totally cure the dog, may have some side effects, and can be expensive.

Neural Disorders

The neural system is the computer and wiring of the body. Neural problems can cause incoordination, paralysis, pain, and lack of feeling.

Cauda Equina Syndrome

Cauda equina syndrome is more common in large breeds, particularly German Shepherds. No screening tests are available, and the hereditary component, if any, is not known. Technically, cauda equina syndrome can result from several disorders, but stenosis (narrowing) of the lumbosacral vertebral canal is the most common. When this canal narrows, it presses on the spinal nerve roots within the canal, resulting in pain and perhaps paralysis of the hind legs and incontinence. The pain is localized in the pelvic area, and may worsen when the tail is lifted or the hind legs extended backward. Pain during defecation is a common symptom. The muscles of the hind limbs may be wasted and the dog might drag its toes. These signs can come on slowly, over a period of months, and are often confused with signs of hip dysplasia and degenerative myelopathy.

Specialized x-rays or other imaging techniques are needed for a diagnosis. Mild cases may be treated with rest and medicine, but most cases tend to progress. Better results are usually seen with surgical correction, which requires a good deal of postoperative commitment from the owner. Because of the pain involved in this condition, prompt attention is essential.

Degenerative Myelopathy

Degenerative myelopathy (DM) is a progressive disease of middle-aged to older dogs in which the dog gradually loses control of its hind limbs. The condition is painless but progressive. The earliest signs may include dragging a foot slightly or occasionally placing the top of the foot on the ground. Dogs may have difficulty rising or lying down. More obvious signs follow, including increasing clumsiness, weakness, and partial paralysis. Eventually the hind limbs become completely nonfunctioning. The feet must be monitored for sores that can form from being dragged. Ultimately, the front legs also become affected and paralyzed. Finally, the brainstem is affected, resulting in death. Most affected dogs are euthanized before this point is reached.

There are no health guarantees for all the congenital diseases that can affect a German Shepherd, but buying from relatively sound breeding lines helps. (Barbara McGuire)

Although the cause of DM is unknown, some speculation exists that it may be an autoimmune condition that attacks part of the nerve fibers in the spinal cord of the middle back (thoracolumbar) region. Specifically, the part that is destroyed is the myelin sheath, the fatty insulating covering of the nerve fiber that is important in conducting nerve impulses. This is the same part of the nerve fiber that is destroyed in multiple sclerosis in humans. For diagnosis, spinal fluid proteins may help differentiate DM from other spinal problems. Stress and inactivity seem to worsen the condition. No cure is available, but a special diet, supplements, physical therapy, and exercise

183

may be helpful in slowing or perhaps even halting its progression. The earlier DM is detected and treated, the better the prognosis. Unfortunately, the early signs often go unnoticed or are confused with those of hip dysplasia, delaying the start of treatment.

Al Says

More information about DM can be found at **http://www.vetmed.ufl. edu/sacs/index.htm.**

Digestive Disorders

The GSD is predisposed to several digestive problems, the most life-threatening of which is bloat.

Bloat (Gastric Torsion, Gastric Dilatation-Volvulus)

Bloat is a life-threatening emergency in which gas and fluid become trapped in the stomach. It is most common in large, deep-chested breeds, including GSDs. No screening tests are available, and the hereditary component, if any, is not known.

Symptoms include distention of the abdomen, unproductive attempts to vomit, excessive salivation, and restlessness. A dog with these symptoms needs to go to the emergency clinic right away—not tomorrow, not even in an hour. The veterinarian will try to pass a tube into the stomach so gases can escape. Often the stomach has twisted and rotated on its axis, though, so the tube can't get into the stomach. These dogs need emergency surgery to save their lives. The rotation of the stomach cuts off the blood supply to the stomach wall, which will die and subsequently kill the dog if surgery isn't performed quickly. Other organs may also be compromised. During surgery, the veterinarian should tack the stomach in place to prevent future rotation. Dogs that bloat once often do so again.

In the largest study of bloat to date, several contributing factors emerged. Dogs that are fearful, eat fast, and eat only one meal a day are more likely to bloat. Stress seems to precipitate a bloating episode. Dogs with stable temperaments, and dogs that eat some canned food and table scraps, are less likely to bloat.

To be on the safe side, it is prudent to avoid other suspected risk factors, which means you should:

➤ feed several small meals instead of one large meal

➤ include some canned food or table scraps

➤ not allow the dog to gulp its food

➤ not allow your dog to become stressed near its mealtime

➤ restrict water for an hour after eating

➤ restrict running or jumping for an hour after the dog has eaten

➤ premoisten food, especially foods that expand when moistened

Maldigestion (Pancreatic Exocrine Insufficiency)

Some German Shepherds eat voraciously yet fail to gain weight. In GSDs, this is often caused by lack of a pancreatic enzyme. Affected dogs produce a large volume of feces because the food is not digested efficiently. Your veterinarian can examine the feces for excess fat and get a preliminary diagnosis, but a blood test (measuring trypsinogen-like-immunoreactivity) is needed for a definite diagnosis. These dogs can be treated by adding enzyme powder to an easily digested food, but they must be treated for the rest of their lives.

Inflammatory Bowel Disease

Dogs that have chronic diarrhea may be suffering from inflammatory bowel disease, a syndrome that can be caused by a number of problems. Although the exact causes are as yet unknown, in general the condition involves a hypersensitivity to substances in the bowel. Other symptoms may include vomiting, weight loss, unproductive attempts to defecate, and mucus in the stool. The exact symptoms vary according to what part of the bowel is involved. Blood tests are usually run to rule out other possible causes, and fecal tests are performed to rule out parasites. Diagnosis is with a biopsy of the bowel

185

mucosa. In extreme cases, anemia could result. Feeding a controlled diet sometimes helps, and in some cases suppressing the immune system with drugs is helpful. Other drugs may also be useful in treating this problem.

The dog's diet should be free of additives and preservatives and contain an adequate, but not excessive, amount of protein. The protein should come from a single source that the dog has no previous experience eating. Added dietary fiber can also be helpful. Because there's no such thing as an inherently hypoallergenic food, you might have to search for a novel source of protein. Lamb and rice foods used to be vigorously promoted as hypoallergenic, but because a dog is now likely to have eaten lamb previously, that is no longer true. Your veterinarian can suggest sources of protein (such as venison, duck, or rabbit) that your dog will not, it's hoped, have previously eaten.

Circulatory Disorders

Disorders of the heart and blood are among the most common serious problems in dogs. Compared with many other breeds, German Shepherds have healthy circulatory systems. They, too, have their predispositions, however.

Subvalvular Aortic Stenosis

Subvalvular aortic stenosis is a congenital heart defect in which the opening between the left ventricle and the aorta is abnormally narrow, obstructing the blood flow, with severe cases causing death by 3 years of age. Less severe cases may not exhibit noticeable signs, although some dogs may be weak and collapse during exercise. Diagnosis is with ultrasonography. Open-heart surgery is the treatment of choice, but is expensive and risky. The condition occurs most often in large breeds.

Patent Ductus Arteriosis

One of the most common of all congenital heart defects in dogs, patent ductus arteriosis is seen more frequently in GSDs than in most other breeds. During fetal life, the lungs are not functional, so a vessel (the ductus arteriosis) allows blood to bypass the lungs. This vessel normally closes shortly after birth, but in some dogs it remains open, allowing blood to leak through it and placing a strain on the heart. Affected dogs have a heart murmur and can be diagnosed definitely with an ultrasound. Surgical correction is necessary to cure the condition. Left untreated, heart failure can result.

Hemophilia and Von Willebrand's Disease

Hemophilia and von Willebrand's disease are two different hereditary blood-clotting disorders found in GSDs. Affected dogs lack a factor needed to properly clot blood. Symptoms include pockets of blood beneath the skin, bleeding into the joints (causing lameness), and internal bleeding. Excessive bleeding during surgery or after a toenail is cut too short may be the first signs noticed. Blood tests can provide a definite diagnosis.

Immunological Disorders

The immune system is your dog's defense against microscopic intruders. Sometimes it isn't strong enough, and sometimes it is misdirected. In either case, problems can arise.

Immunoglobulin A Deficiency

The immune system of normal German Shepherds has lower amounts of immunoglobulin A (IgA), which is important for mucosal immunity, especially of the respiratory, gastrointestinal, and genital tracts. This lowered IgA may be related to some health problems, including bacterial overgrowth in the small intestine. No other specific types of immune deficiencies have been reported in the GSD.

Autoimmune Diseases

Autoimmune diseases occur when the body's own immune system turns against parts of itself. Specific types include autoimmune hemolytic anemia, autoimmune thrombocytopenia, systemic lupus erythematosus, and discoid lupus erythematosus, among many others. No screening tests are available, and the hereditary component, if any, is not known. Some other GSD problems, such as perianal fistulas, pannus, and degenerative myelopathy, may have an autoimmune component. Treatment is with drugs to suppress the immune system.

187

In autoimmune hemolytic anemia, the body destroys its own red blood cells, leading to severe anemia. Affected dogs may be feverish and lethargic, and have whitish gums. In autoimmune thrombocytopenia, the body destroys its own platelets, leading to spontaneous bleeding. Signs may include petechia (small red spots on the surface of the gums and skin, and also within the eye). Autoimmune hemolytic anemia and thrombocytopenia often occur together. Symptoms can be confused with several other problems, including pyometra (infection of the uterus) and tick-borne diseases, such as erlichiosis.

In systemic lupus erythematosus, many organ systems may be affected. Symptoms may include a recurring fever as well as arthritis in several joints, small ulcers of the skin on the face or toes, bleeding beneath the skin, yellowish mucous membranes, and edema, as well as several changes in blood values. Lupus can mimic a variety of other chronic disorders, and in fact it is often called "the great imitator."

In discoid lupus erythematosus, ulcers arise on the nose and face. They are aggravated by exposure to ultraviolet light.

Pannus

Pannus (also known as chronic superficial keratitis or as German Shepherd Dog keratitis) is a chronic inflammation of the cornea, the eye's normally clear outer surface. It most often appears in young to middle-aged dogs, first appearing as a reddish area around the rim of the cornea, usually of both eyes. The pigmented area gradually expands toward the center of the cornea, leaving the affected areas covered with a brownish surface. Without treatment, the cornea becomes opaque and the dog goes blind. Pannus may be yet another autoimmune disease, in which a triggering factor (which seems to be ultraviolet light) causes the body to destroy its own corneal cells. Treatment consists of avoiding ultraviolet light (even fitting the dog with sunglasses) and instilling immunosuppressive drugs into the eyes.

Perianal Fistulas

Perianal fistulas (also known as anal furunculosis) are chronic draining tracts (small passageways leading into the body, often into the rectum) in the tissue around the anus. They occur more often in German Shepherds than in any other breed. The exact cause is not known, but it may be related to an autoimmune problem, the configuration of the tail in which the broad tail is seated snugly over the anal area, or an overabundance of apocrine sweat glands around the anus. Symptoms may include open sores around the anus, an offensive odor, constipation, painful defecation, weight loss, and lethargy. Affected dogs may lick their anal region more than is normal. Treatment can be involved and, often, unsatisfactory. Antibiotics won't cure the problem, but can help deal with secondary infections. Drugs to suppress the immune system are usually prescribed, too. Surgical excision of the affected tracts, and sometimes amputation of the tail, may be helpful, but a chance of fecal incontinence exists. Several types of surgical procedures are available, and owners of affected dogs should seek out the best surgical center to perform the operation. Left untreated (and sometimes even with the best of treatment), dogs with perianal fistulas can be in so much pain they must be euthanized.

Al Says

Research in humans has shown that phantom limb pain can be reduced by anesthetizing the part to be amputated the day before surgery. If your dog must have its tail amputated, ask your veterinarian to do this.

Cancers

Cancers occur relatively frequently in all breeds of dogs. Some breeds seem to be predisposed to certain types of cancers, and unfortunately the GSD is one of them.

For example, hemangiosarcoma, a malignant cancer of the circulatory system, is seen more often in GSDs than in any other breed. No screening tests are available, and the hereditary component, if any, is not known. Most often, hemangiosarcoma occurs as a tumor on the spleen or heart. As the tumor grows, internal bleeding can occur. Affected dogs may suddenly appear disoriented and collapse, and exhibit signs of hypovolemic shock. They may be extremely thirsty. Perhaps most noticeable, their gums may be almost white. If the tumor is on the spleen, the spleen can be removed. Not all tumors of the spleen are malignant, so it is a good idea to have a biopsy done and wait for results before making any decisions. If the tumor is malignant, or if it is on the heart, therapy is usually unrewarding. Unfortunately, most dogs with hemangiosarcoma succumb either to its primary effects (internal bleeding that cannot be stopped) or to cancer spread to other organs.

Osteosarcoma (bone cancer) occurs more frequently in large dog breeds, which includes the German Shepherd. Owners are faced with the terrible decision of amputation that must be made quickly, as time is of the essence to prevent the spread to other parts of the body. Dogs adjust to the loss of a limb fairly easily, but factors such as age, weight, arthritis, and other joint problems factor into how well the dog can cope with only three legs. The possibility of phantom limb pain can be reduced by having your veterinarian numb the leg for the day before it is to be removed. Unfortunately, even with the best of therapy, survival time for dogs with osteosarcoma is usually only a few months.

Mammary gland tumors are among the most common of cancers in the dog, occurring mostly in females that were not spayed early in life. Spaying after the age of 2 years doesn't impart the protection from mammary cancer that earlier spaying does. Approximately 50 percent of all mammary tumors are malignant. Therapy may include surgical excision and chemotherapy.

Lymphosarcoma is another of the more commonly seen cancers in dogs. This cancer affects the blood and lymph systems; symptoms may include swelling of the lymph nodes, especially those of the lower neck area and behind the "knees." Chemotherapy can extend the life of many affected dogs.

Parasites and Infectious Diseases

Some breeds of dogs are more prone to certain infections or parasites, perhaps because of immune system differences. Many breeds are predisposed to developing demodicosis, caused by mites. The German Shepherd is also more susceptible to a fungal infection (aspergillus) and a protozoan infection (erlichiosis).

190

Demodicosis

Demodicosis (also known as demodectic or red mange) is a type of mange caused by increased susceptibility to the demodex mite. Most dogs have some mites on them, but in some dogs the mites may proliferate and cause the hair to fall out. Localized cases, in which only a few spots or affected areas are seen, may clear on their own. Generalized cases, in which large areas of the dog are affected, can be difficult to cure. Left untreated, secondary infections can develop, and some dogs may even die. Treatment involves regular dips in a mitacidal solution, and in some resistant cases, long-term medication. Why some dogs develop generalized demodectic mange is unknown, but it may be associated with an immune deficiency. The condition often runs in families, and seems to be passed from dams to offspring, although the exact hereditary nature is unknown.

Aspergillus

When most people think of fungal diseases, they think of ringworm and problems that are relatively minor. Many fungal diseases are deadly, however, and aspergillus is one of them. Aspergillus is found in soil and decaying vegetation throughout the world. Dogs inhale the spores, and usually nothing happens. In some dogs, however, the fungus colonizes in the nasal passages, gradually causing the bone to deteriorate. These dogs have a nasal discharge, often tinged with blood. They may also sneeze, and the nose is painful. In some dogs the fungus spreads into internal organs, causing disseminated aspergillus. More cases of disseminated aspergillus are seen in German Shepherds (especially females) than in any other breed. Affected dogs may lose weight, appetite, and energy, and might also have fever, lameness, back pain, or paralysis. Treatment of nasal aspergillus is involved and expensive, but can be satisfactory. Treatment of disseminated aspergillus is, unfortunately, far less rewarding.

Erlichiosis

Erlichiosis (also called tick fever or tropical canine pancytopenia) is an underdiagnosed yet serious disease spread by ticks. Symptoms are diffuse, and may include listlessness, dull coat, occasional vomiting, and occasional loss of appetite. But aside from a fever in the initial

191

phases of the disease, no strong signs of disease are present. Owners may complain that the dog just doesn't seem as active or is just not quite right. Other symptoms may include coughing, arthritis, muscle wasting, seizures, spontaneous bleeding, anemia, and a host of others. The point is, no one or two symptoms would ever suggest erlichiosis as an initial diagnosis. A definitive diagnosis is made by means of a blood titer. Erlichiosis wreaks its havoc by parasitizing the white blood cells and crippling the immune system. If diagnosed early, it can be treated effectively; if not, it can be fatal. Erlichiosis was first diagnosed in German Shepherds returning from military duty in Vietnam; some reports contend that GSDs are more susceptible to it than other breeds. Regardless of breed, erlichiosis is a deadly disease that should be considered when a dog has a host of seemingly unrelated symptoms.

The Least You Need to Know

➤ German Shepherds are predisposed to several life-threatening disorders.

➤ Don't assume a limping dog has hip dysplasia, or that a non-limping dog does not.

➤ If your dog has symptoms of a GSD-predisposed disorder, bring it to the attention of your veterinarian.

➤ Early diagnosis may save your dog's life.

Canine
First Aid

In This Chapter

➤ How to be prepared for an emergency

➤ Administering artificial respiration and CPR

➤ Dealing with specific emergencies

Even experienced dog owners have a difficult time deciding what constitutes a true emergency; when in doubt, err on the side of caution and call the emergency clinic or your veterinarian for his opinion.

Because there are no paramedics for dogs, you must assume the role of paramedic and ambulance driver in case of an emergency. Now is the time to prepare for these lifesaving roles. Know the phone number and location of the emergency veterinarian in your area. Keep the number next to the phone; don't rely on your memory during an emergency situation. Study the emergency procedures described in this chapter, and keep this guide handy. Misplaced instructions can result in the loss of critical time. Always keep enough fuel in your car to make it to the emergency clinic without stopping for gas. Finally, stay calm. It helps you assist your dog, and helps your dog stay calm as well. A calm dog is less likely to go into shock.

In general:

➤ Make sure you and the dog are in a safe location.

➤ Make sure breathing passages are open. Remove the collar and check the dog's mouth and throat.

➤ Move the dog as little and as gently as possible.

➤ Control any bleeding.

➤ Check breathing, pulse, and consciousness.

➤ Check for signs of shock (very pale gums, weakness, unresponsiveness, faint pulse, shivering). Treat by keeping the dog warm and calm.

➤ Never use force or do anything that causes extreme discomfort.

➤ Never remove an impaled object (unless it is blocking the airway).

➤ If your dog is in pain, it might bite. You can make an emergency muzzle by tying a cloth or belt around its muzzle, tying it on the top and bottom, and then tying it behind the dog's ears.

ABCs of First Aid

In an emergency, first check to see if the dog is responsive by calling its name or tapping on its head. If it is not, quickly perform the ABCs of first aid:

A: Airway

B: Breathing

C: Circulation

➤ **Airway:** Make sure the airway is open. Extend the head and neck, open the mouth, and pull the tongue forward.

➤ **Breathing:** Make sure the dog is breathing. Is the chest rising and falling? Can you feel exhaled air against your cheek? If not, give two rapid breaths through the dog's nose before checking circulation.

➤ **Circulation:** Check gum color, capillary refill time, and pulse. Gum color should be pink. When you press your thumb on the gum, it should regain its color within 2 seconds. Check the pulse by feeling the heartbeat on the left side of the rib cage a couple of inches behind the elbow, or feeling the pulse on the inside of the thigh, near the groin.

If your dog has a pulse, but is not breathing, administer artificial respiration. If your dog does not have a pulse, administer cardiopulmonary resuscitation (CPR, see next page).

Artificial Respiration

1. Open the dog's mouth, and clear the passage of secretions and foreign bodies.

2. Pull the dog's tongue forward.

3. Seal your mouth over the dog's nose and mouth. Blow into the nose for 2 seconds, and then release.

4. You should see your dog's chest expand; if not, try blowing with more force, making a tighter seal around the lips, or checking for an obstruction (see step 8).

5. Repeat at a rate of one breath every 4 seconds.

6. Stop every minute to monitor breathing and pulse.

7. If air collects in the stomach, push down just behind the rib cage every few minutes.

8. Continue until the dog breathes on its own.

   ➤ For obstructions, wrap your hands around the abdomen, behind the rib cage, and compress briskly. Repeat if needed. If the dog loses consciousness, extend the head and neck forward, pull the tongue out fully, and explore the throat for any foreign objects.

   ➤ If drowning has occurred, turn the dog upside down, with a hold around its waist, and sway back and forth so that water

195

can run out of its mouth. Then administer mouth-to-nose respiration, with the dog's head positioned lower than its lungs.

CPR

1. Place your hands, one on top of the other, on the left side of the chest about 2 inches up from and behind the point of the elbow.

2. Press down quickly and release.

3. Compress at a rate of about 100 times per minute.

4. After every 15 compressions, give two breaths through the nose. If you have a partner, the partner can give breaths every two or three compressions.

Normal Values

Respiration: 10–30 breaths per minute at rest

Pulse: 60–120 beats per minute at rest

Temperature: 101.5°–102.5°F

Capillary refill time: Less than 2 seconds (checked by pressing on the gums)

Gum color: Pink (not white, red, bluish, yellowish, or with tiny red spots)

Hydration: Skin should pop back into position within 3 seconds of being lifted

Specific Emergencies

Most other types of emergencies give you a little more time to act, but not much. For the following situations, administer first aid and seek veterinary attention. Situations not described in this list can usually be treated with the same first aid as for humans. In all cases, the best advice is to seek the opinion of a veterinarian.

Poisoning

Signs of poisoning vary according to the type of poison, but commonly include vomiting, convulsions, staggering, and collapse. If you're in doubt about whether poison was ingested, call the veterinarian anyway. If possible, bring the poison and its container with you to the veterinarian. If the dog vomits, put the vomit in a plastic bag and bring it with you to the vet. In most cases, home treatment is not advisable.

Two of the most common and life-threatening poisons eaten by dogs are Warfarin (rodent poison) and especially ethylene glycol (antifreeze). Veterinary treatment must be obtained within 2 to 4 hours of ingestion of even tiny amounts if the dog's life is to be saved. *Do not wait for symptoms.* By the time symptoms of antifreeze poisoning are evident, it is usually too late to save the dog.

Al Says

You can reduce the risk of antifreeze poisoning by using a brand that does not contain ethylene glycol.

Call the veterinarian or poison control hot line and give as much information as possible. Induce vomiting (except in the cases outlined in the following paragraph) by giving either hydrogen peroxide (mixed 1:1 with water), salt water, or dry mustard and water. Treat for shock and get to the veterinarian at once. Be prepared for convulsions or respiratory distress.

Al Says

The Veterinary Poison Control hot line number is 1-900-680-0000. A charge will apply.

Do not induce vomiting if the poison was an acid, an alkali, a petroleum product, a solvent, a cleaner, or a tranquilizer, or if a sharp object was swallowed; also do not induce vomiting if the dog is severely depressed, convulsing, or comatose, or if over 2 hours have

passed since ingestion. If the dog is neither convulsing nor unconscious, dilute the poison by giving milk, vegetable oil, or egg whites.
Activated charcoal can absorb many toxins. Baking soda or milk of
magnesia can be given for ingested acids, and vinegar or lemon juice
for ingested alkalis.

Seizures

A dog undergoing a seizure may drool, become stiff, or have uncontrollable muscle spasms.

Wrap the dog securely in a blanket to prevent it from injuring itself
on furniture or stairs. Remove other dogs from the area (they may
attack the convulsing dog). Never put your hands (or anything) in a
convulsing dog's mouth. If it continues for more than 10 minutes or
repeats itself, you must try to get the dog to the emergency clinic.
More often, the seizure is over in a few minutes. Afterward, treat the
dog for shock. Call your veterinarian for advice, since some seizures
can result from poisoning, high fever, low blood sugar, liver or kidney disease, or other conditions that must be treated immediately.
More often, no specific cause is obvious. Such cases of *idiopathic
epilepsy* are often hereditary and have been reported in GSDs. Taking
careful note of all characteristics and sequences of seizure activity can
help to diagnose the cause.

Snakebite

Poisonous snakebites are characterized by swelling, discoloration,
pain, fang marks, restlessness, nausea, and weakness. Most bites are
to the head and are difficult to treat with first aid.

Restrain the dog and keep it quiet. Be able to describe the snake.
Only if you can't get to the veterinarian immediately, apply a pressure bandage (not a tourniquet, but a firm bandage) between the bite
and the heart. If on a leg, keep the limb lower than the rest of the
body.

Insect Stings and Allergic Reactions

Dogs are often stung by insects on their face or feet. Remove any visible stingers as quickly as possible. Administer a baking soda and
water paste to bee stings and vinegar to wasp stings. Clean the area

and apply antibacterial ointment. Keep an eye on the dog in case it has an allergic reaction, including swelling that could interfere with breathing or any change in consciousness. Call your veterinarian immediately if you think the dog may be having a severe reaction.

Insect stings are the most common cause of extreme allergic reactions. Swelling around the nose and throat can block the airway. Other possible reactions include restlessness, vomiting, diarrhea, seizures, and collapse. If any of these symptoms occur, immediate veterinary attention will probably be necessary.

Bleeding

Consider wounds to be an emergency if there is profuse bleeding, if they are extremely deep, or if they open to the chest cavity, abdominal cavity, or head.

Control massive bleeding first. Cover the wound with a clean dressing and apply pressure; apply more dressings over the others until bleeding stops. Also elevate the wound site, and apply a cold pack to it. If the wound is on an extremity, apply pressure to the closest pressure point as follows:

➤ For a front leg: inside of front leg just above the elbow

➤ For a rear leg: inside of thigh where the femoral artery crosses the thigh bone

➤ For the tail: underside of tail close to where it joins the body

Use a tourniquet only in life-threatening situations and only when all other attempts have failed. Check for signs of shock.

For sucking chest wounds, place a sheet of plastic or other nonporous material over the hole and bandage it to make as airtight a seal as possible. It probably won't work very well, but it may help.

For abdominal wounds, place a warm, wet sterile dressing over any protruding internal organs and cover with a bandage or towel. Do not attempt to push organs back into the dog.

For head wounds, apply gentle pressure to control bleeding. Monitor for loss of consciousness or shock and treat accordingly.

199

For animal bites, allow some bleeding, and then clean the area thoroughly and apply antibiotic ointment. A course of oral antibiotics will probably be necessary. It's best not to suture most animal bites, but a large one (over one-half inch in diameter), or one on the face or other prominent position, may need to be sutured.

Burns

Deep burns, characterized by charred or pearly white skin, with deeper layers of tissue exposed, are serious.

Cool burned areas with cool packs or towels soaked in water, or by immersing them in cold water. If over 50 percent of the dog is burned, do not immerse as this increases the likelihood of shock. Cover the area with a clean bandage or towel to avoid contamination. Do not apply pressure, and do not apply ointments. Monitor the dog for shock.

Electrical Shock

A dog that chews an electric cord may collapse and have burns inside its mouth. Before touching the dog, disconnect the plug or cut the power; if that cannot be done immediately, use a wooden stick to knock the cord away from the dog. Keep the dog warm and treat for shock. Monitor breathing and heartbeat.

Heat Stroke

Early signs of heat stroke include rapid, loud breathing, abundant thick saliva, bright red mucous membranes, and high rectal temperature. Later signs include unsteadiness, diarrhea, and coma.

Wet the dog down and place it in front of a fan. If this is not possible, immerse the dog in cool water. *Do not plunge the dog into ice water.* The resulting constriction of peripheral blood vessels can make the situation worse. Offer small amounts of water for drinking. You must lower your dog's body temperature quickly (but do not lower it below 100°F). Stop cooling the dog when the rectal temperature reaches 103°F because it will continue to fall.

Hypothermia

Shivering and sluggishness are signs that a dog has become excessively chilled. Later signs include a very low (under 95°F) body temperature, slow pulse and breathing rates, and coma.

Warm the dog gradually. Wrap it in a blanket (preferably one that has been warmed in the dryer). Place plastic bottles filled with hot water outside the blankets (not touching the dog). You can also place a plastic tarp over the blanket, making sure the dog's head is not covered. Monitor the temperature. Stop warming when its temperature reaches 101°F.

The Least You Need to Know

➤ Have a plan for getting your dog emergency veterinary help at all hours.

➤ Start by evaluating the ABCs: Airway, Breathing, and Circulation.

➤ Check the gum color; if very pale, treat for shock by warming the dog.

➤ The most common emergencies that are potential killers of GSDs are antifreeze poisoning, gastric torsion, heat prostration, and being hit by a car.

➤ When in doubt, err on the side of caution and get veterinary help.

Part 7

It *Is* How You Play the Game

So far, it's probably starting to sound like having a dog is all work and worry! Sometimes it may seem like that, but really, it's just so much fun we don't want to advertise it. Here's a secret, however: For all the work, for all the worry, the fun and satisfaction far outweigh it! Besides your everyday adventures playing, hiking, exploring the neighborhood, or just bumming around together, you can go totally insane and compete in dog shows, Obedience Trials, Tracking, Herding, Agility, and (shhhh...) Schutzhund, the latter being somewhat controversial in the United States. If you're more of a do-gooder, you and your trusty dog can save lives and help others in all sorts of ways. German Shepherds have helped people in more roles than any other breed, so even if you prefer adventures in an easy chair with your dog at your feet, you can read about this amazing breed's feats. Since most of these adventures do require travel away from home, however, we want you and your dog to arrive alive. So get ready for the adventures of a lifetime!

Chapter 19

Trials and Tribulations

In This Chapter

➤ Competing in AKC or SV conformation shows

➤ What your dog needs to know to earn Obedience titles

➤ Earning Tracking, Agility, and Herding titles

➤ Schutzhund requirements

Something about dogs in general, and maybe German Shepherds in particular, brings out the human need to proclaim "My dog's better than your dog." The crazier owners actually set out to prove it. But dog competitions are more than frivolous contests. At their best, they are a way of strengthening the human-dog bond, of developing a partnership to its fullest, and of allowing your dog to be all it can be (without even joining the army). Competitions are also a way of choosing which dogs have the right stuff to be the ancestors of tomorrow's German Shepherds. If you plan on breeding your dog, you owe it to its puppies of the future and their owners to prove your dog's mettle in some area of competition. Luckily, there are lots of choices.

Lord of the Rings

The German Shepherd's build reflects its athletic heritage and has always been an important consideration in the breed's development.

Early in the history of the breed, Max von Stephanitz personally judged the annual Sieger show in Germany. In America, shows are held every weekend, and a variety of judges make the choices (usually the wrong choices, according to most of the exhibitors except for the winners). At conformation shows, judges evaluate how well each dog conforms to the physical standard of perfection, both while standing and moving.

As long as your GSD doesn't have any disqualifying traits (see page 19), it is eligible to compete. Winning might be a little tougher. Don't think you can just show up with your dog on a rope and say, "I'm here fer my ribbons!" You need to train your dog and yourself before you start lugging home trophies. Both you and your dog must also be clean and well groomed—otherwise, your chances for success are as good as a Miss America candidate's if she shows up with food stuck in her teeth and doesn't even know she plans to work toward world peace.

The versatile German Shepherd affords the competition-minded owner a variety of exciting options for fun and sport with her dog. (Steven and Nancy Whitworth)

You might have guessed it: German Shepherds are shown unlike any other breed of dog. Other breeds are expected to pose four-square, but the German Shepherd has a distinctive show stance in which it looks more like an action figure ready to spring. The front legs are placed straight down and parallel, like most other breeds, and the left rear leg is placed so that the hock is perpendicular to the ground, like most other breeds. But it's that right rear leg that's crept up farther

206

and farther as the years have passed, so that now GSDs look like runners in their blocks, ready to go.

Al Says

If you think you might want to compete in AKC conformation shows, be sure to get a dog from AKC champion bloodlines. American GSD style differs from European GSD style, so even the best European champions often have difficulty competing in American shows, and vice versa.

Other breeds are expected to trot nicely at their handler's side without pulling. The German Shepherd is expected to run a full length in front of the handler and lead the way around the ring. Shepherd handlers have the longest leads ever seen in the show ring, and strong leads, too, since the dogs are often expected to practically pull their handler's behind them. Most dogs do one turn around the ring and are through; Shepherds may make many laps at all breed shows, and some specialty shows start to resemble the Daytona 500.

Other breeds are expected to look at their handler, perhaps focusing on a morsel of food the handler is holding. The German Shepherd is expected to look past its handler, out of the ring. Here's where it gets a little tricky. The AKC frowns on a practice known as "double-handling," in which people outside the ring attract the attention of a dog being shown. In fact, a judge can excuse a dog from the ring and refuse to judge it if it is being double-handled. Yet the German Shepherd ring is known as the Mecca of double-handlers, all trying (mostly unsuccessfully) to be subtle as they nonchalantly race from one side of the ring to the other, using all their ventriloquist training to make noises without any visible sign of their source. Just don't get in their way.

Most local kennel clubs offer handling classes where you can learn the fundamentals of presenting a dog in the ring. Many also have occasional match shows, where everybody is there for practice, including the judges. Don't take a match win or loss too seriously, and at any show, no matter how obviously feeble-minded the judge might seem, keep your opinion to yourself.

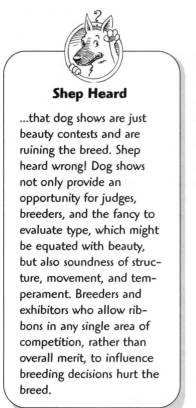

Shep Heard

...that dog shows are just beauty contests and are ruining the breed. Shep heard wrong! Dog shows not only provide an opportunity for judges, breeders, and the fancy to evaluate type, which might be equated with beauty, but also soundness of structure, movement, and temperament. Breeders and exhibitors who allow ribbons in any single area of competition, rather than overall merit, to influence breeding decisions hurt the breed.

If the idea of running around a ring leaves you cold, or if the idea of losing a lot isn't appealing, you can hire a professional handler to show your dog for you. Handlers are good at what they do and they know how to get the most out of a dog; Shepherds have a habit of being too mellow when shown by their owners, but look much more alert when seeking their owner ringside. As a result, your odds of winning at first are greater with a professional (as long as the professional is a GSD specialist). Nonetheless, it's your dog and there is nothing like the thrill of winning when you are on the other end of the lead!

You can enter any class for which your dog is eligible: Puppy (two divisions: 6 to 9 months and 9 to 12 months), 12 to 18 months, Novice, Bred by Exhibitor, American-bred, or Open. At a typical show, you enter the ring, pose your dog, trot around the ring, allow the judge to physically examine your dog while posed, trot in a straight line to and from the judge, pose again, trot again, and then (you hope) run to the first-place marker. All the first-place winners from each class within a sex are then called back into the ring to compete for Winners, with the dog selected Winners winning points toward its Championship title. The number of points can vary from 0 to 5, depending on how many dogs were in competition. To become an AKC Champion (Ch.), your GSD must win 15 points under at least three different judges, including two majors (defeating enough dogs to win 3, 4, or 5 points at a time under two different judges).

The Winners in each sex then return to the ring to compete for Best of Breed against all the German Shepherds in competition that are already Champions. The dog selected as the best GSD then goes on to represent the breed in the Herding Group competition. German

Shepherds have proved themselves to be formidable competitors in the Group, and those that do win the Herding Group go on to compete for Best in Show. The top Best in Show winner of all breeds in AKC history is (of course!) a German Shepherd bitch, Ch. Altana's Mystique.

Besides AKC shows, some GSD exhibitors prove their dogs at SV shows, which are held in the United States through the United Schutzhund Clubs of America (USA) and the Working Dog Alliance (WDA) section of the GSDCA. Classes are divided by age and sex, with no inter-age or inter-sex competition. Puppies are rated as very promising (VP), promising (P), or less promising (LP); older dogs are rated as very good (SG), good (G), or rarely, sufficient, insufficient, or excused. Working class entrants must have a working title (either Schutzhund or the SV Herding title) and certified hips. Only these dogs are eligible to receive a rating of excellent (V). The Excellent Select (VA) title is awarded only at prestigious national shows, and dogs must have slightly higher levels of working certification to be eligible.

Learnin' German

The top male and top female at the annual National Specialty show are called the Grand Victor and Grand Victrix, respectively.

The SV show ring is much larger than a conventional show ring at a normal conformation event, and a lot of running is involved. In all but the Puppy classes, a couple of gunshots are fired to evaluate temperament. Unlike AKC shows, double-handling is expected and has reached the level of an art form. The judge gives a critique of every dog.

Because GSDs are so much a true family member, it can hurt to have your noble dog placed last in its class. Just be sure your GSD doesn't catch on and always treat your dog like a champ whether it gets a blue ribbon or no ribbon at all. To survive as a GSD competitor, you must be able to separate your own ego and self-esteem from your dog's show potential. You must also not allow your dog's ability to win in competition cloud your perception of your dog's true worth in its primary role: that of friend and companion. A dog that is last in its class but first in its owner's heart is far better off than an unloved dog that is first in any competition.

H.I.T. or Miss

H.I.T. is Obedience lingo for High in Trial, the supreme award given to the top-winning dog at an Obedience Trial and an award that is no stranger to German Shepherd Dogs. Generations of attention to temperament, intelligence, and trainability have placed the German Shepherd among the top competitors at Obedience Trials everywhere.

Several organizations, including the AKC and United Kennel Club (UKC), sponsor Obedience Trials for all breeds, with progressively more difficult levels. The most basic level of AKC Companion Dog (CD) requires your dog to:

➤ Heel on lead, sitting automatically each time you stop; negotiating right, left, and about turns without guidance from you; and changing to a faster and slower pace.

➤ Heel in a figure eight around two people, still on lead.

➤ Stand still off lead 6 feet away from you and allow a judge to touch it.

➤ Repeat the heeling exercises at the start of this list, except off-lead.

➤ Come to you when called from 20 feet away, and then return to heel position on command.

➤ Stay in a sitting position with a group of other dogs, while you are 20 feet away, for 1 minute.

➤ Stay in a down position with the same group while you are 20 feet away, for 3 minutes.

As the degrees get higher, the exercises get more difficult, but also a lot more fun. To earn the Companion Dog Excellent (CDX) degree, your dog would have to:

➤ Heel off lead, including a figure eight.

➤ Come when called from 20 feet away, but dropping to a down position when told to do so partway to you, and then completing the recall when called again.

➤ Retrieve a thrown dumbbell when told to do so.

➤ Retrieve a thrown dumbbell, leaving and returning over a high jump.

➤ Jump over a broad jump when told to do so.

➤ Stay in a sitting position with a group of dogs, when you are out of sight, for 3 minutes.

➤ Stay in a down position with a group of dogs, when you are out of sight, for 5 minutes.

The Utility Dog (UD) degree is finally a chance for your canine Einstein to show off! It requires your dog to:

➤ Heel, stay, sit, down, and come in response to hand signals.

➤ Retrieve a leather article scented by the handler from among five other unscented leather articles.

➤ Retrieve a metal article scented by the handler from among five other unscented metal articles.

➤ Retrieve a glove designated by the handler from among three gloves placed in different locations.

➤ Stop and stand on command while heeling and allow the judge to physically examine it with the handler standing 10 feet away.

➤ Trot away from the handler for about 40 feet until told to stop, at which point it should turn and sit, until directed to jump one of two jumps (a solid or bar jump) and return to the handler.

➤ Repeat the previous exercise, but jumping the opposite jump as before.

Every exercise is scored, and to receive a passing score, the dog must pass each exercise with a score of at least half the available points and receive a minimum total score of 170 out of a possible 200 points. Each passing score is called a "leg," and it takes three legs to earn a title. Sound easy?

Then why stop there? How about trying for a Utility Dog Excellent degree, which requires your dog (which must already have its UD) to earn legs in both Open (CDX) and Utility classes at the same trials, not once but 10 times.

211

Or how about an Obedience Trial Championship (OTCH)? Not ouch, OTCH (and it really is pronounced "otch"). All that's required is for your dog (already a UD, of course) to place first or second in either Open or Utility classes, including three first places, until it earns 100 points. For each placement, the dog is awarded a certain amount of points depending on how many dogs were in competition. Few dogs of any breed have earned the OTCH degree, but German Shepherds are among them.

Al Says

Don't forget Obedience titles offered by the United Kennel Club (U–CD, U–CDX, and U–UD).

Dog obedience classes, often sponsored by obedience clubs, are a must if you plan to compete. They are a valuable source of training advice and encouragement from people who are experienced Obedience Trial competitors. They provide an environment filled with distractions similar to those you will encounter at an actual Obedience Trial. Perhaps most of all, they offer a ready source of shoulders to cry on for the all those Trials you should have passed.

If you enter competition with your GSD, remember this as your golden rule: Companion Dog means just that. Being upset at your dog because it makes a mistake defeats the purpose of Obedience as a way of promoting a harmonious partnership between trainer and dog. Failing a Trial, in the scope of life, is an insignificant event. Never let a ribbon or a few points become more important than a trusting relationship with your companion. Be sure you fulfill your responsibility as a Companion Human before demanding your Shepherd be a Companion Dog. Besides, your Shepherd will always forgive you for the times you mess up!

Powerful In-Scent-Ives

Of all the dog sports available to all the breeds, Tracking is the least popular. Why? Could it be that people don't enjoy sharing a quiet misty morning in the field with their dog? Don't they enjoy watching a dog do what humans can scarcely comprehend? Don't they want to teach their dog one of the most useful skills a dog could know? It seems unlikely.

Have no fear. Of all the breeds that can be found at a Tracking Trial, German Shepherds are among the most familiar. Could it be because German Shepherd people are a little different from other dog owners? Probably. Could it be because German Shepherds are good at tracking? Definitely.

The AKC Tracking Dog (TD) title is earned by following a 440- to 500-yard track with three to five turns laid down by a person 30 minutes to 2 hours before the trial.

The Tracking Dog Excellent (TDX) title is earned by following an "older" (3 to 5 hours) and longer (800- to 1,000-yard) track with five to seven turns, with some more challenging circumstances. One of these circumstances is the existence of cross tracks laid by another tracklayer about $1^{1}/2$ hours after the first track was laid. In addition, the actual track may cross different types of terrain and obstacles, including plowed land, woods, streams, bridges, and lightly traveled roads.

The Variable Surface Tracking (VST) title is earned by following a 3- to 5-hour track, 600 to 800 yards long, over a variety of surfaces that might be normally encountered when tracking in the real world. At least three different surface areas are included; at least one must include vegetation and at least two must be devoid of vegetation (for example, sand or concrete). Tracks might even go through buildings, and can be crossed by animal, pedestrian, or vehicular traffic.

The way to start training your dog depends on what motivates your dog. If your GSD is also a "chow hound," you can begin by walking a simple path and dropping little treats along the way. The dog will soon learn that it can find treats simply by following your trail. As training progresses, the treats get dropped farther

Learnin' German

The SV offers the FH and FH2 titles for Tracking.

and farther apart, until eventually only the mother lode of treats is left at the end of the trail.

If your dog is motivated more by the desire to be with you, you can have a helper hold your dog while you hide a very short distance away. Then the helper allows the dog to find you. Gradually increase the distance, and make sure the dog is using its nose to locate you.

Of course, the actual Tracking Tests require considerably more training than this, but once you have taught your dog to follow its nose, you're on the right track (pun intended!).

Overcoming Obstacles

German Shepherds set the standard for military and police dog work, and early on excelled in their ability to jump, sprint, climb, balance, and crawl, overcoming just about any obstacle in their path. For years, pet owners wondered why only service dogs got to have all the fun. Today the sport of Agility allows dogs of all breeds to hone their skills on an obstacle course made up of open and closed tunnels, an elevated walk-over, an A-frame climb over, a seesaw, weave poles, a pause table, and several types of jumps. Not surprisingly, German Shepherds take it all in stride.

The AKC titles, with an increasing level of difficulty, include Novice Agility Dog (NAD), Open Agility Dog (OAD), Agility Dog Excellent (ADE), and Master Agility Excellent (MAX). The United States Dog Agility Association (USDAA) and United Kennel Club (UKC) also sponsor trials and award titles.

Many obedience clubs are now sponsoring Agility training, but you can start some of the fundamentals at home. Entice your dog to walk through a tunnel made of sheets draped over chairs; guide it with treats to weave in and out of a series of poles made from several plumber's helpers placed in line; make it comfortable walking on a wide raised board; teach it to jump through a tire and over a hurdle. If you can't find a club to train with, you can make your own equipment. Contact the AKC, USDAA, or UKC for regulations. Agility is perhaps the fastest growing dog sport in America, and GSDs laid its foundation.

Agility is perhaps the fastest growing performance event now available. The components come naturally to German Shepherds, and the excitement is infectious. (Suzie Lucine)

Sheep Thrills

They're called German Shepherds. Get it? Then why do so many people seem surprised to see them acting like shepherds? Remember, they were shepherds first and then all the other great stuff developed later. Working with sheep is in the breed's genes. That's why the AKC has classified the German Shepherd in the Herding Group.

Working with livestock is one of the German Shepherd's original uses, and modern Herding trials demonstrate that today's dogs can still do the breed's work. (Dr. Zoë M. Backman)

215

Several organizations hold Herding Trials, with those sponsored by the AKC the most popular for GSDs in the United Sates. The AKC awards a series of Herding titles.

Herding Test (HT) and Pre-Trial (PT) are noncompetitive titles based on the display of basic herding instinct and ability.

Herding Started (HS), Herding Intermediate (HI), and Herding Excellent (HX) represent progressively more demanding titles. Three qualifying scores are required for each title.

Herding Championships (HCh) are acquired by earning placements in the most advanced level after completing the HX title.

The basic moves required in Herding are an outrun (in which the dog runs past the stock so that the stock is between the dog and handler), a lift (in which the dog begins to move the stock), a fetch (in which the dog brings the stock back toward the handler), a pen (in which the dog moves the stock into a small pen), and, for the HX title, a shed (in which the dog separates one or more head from the herd). Three types of courses are available: The "A" course requires working stock through obstacles and penning within an arena; the "B" course requires an outrun, lift, fetch, pen, and for an HX, a shed. The "C" course is performed with larger flocks in more open areas similar to the GSD's herding role.

Shep Heard

...that German Shepherds can't really herd. Shep heard wrong! It is true that their forte is in preventing stock from crossing certain boundaries, instead of bounding in and out and doing intricate stock han–dling, but that has never prevented them from bringing home the Herding titles!

The American Herding Breed Association (AHBA) also offers a variety of Herding titles. Tests are non-competitive events that evaluate dogs on a pass-fail basis. Trials are competitive events in which dogs compete for high scores.

Tests:

➤ Herding Capability test (HCT) consists of a test of basic instinct and of basic stock-moving abilities.

➤ Junior Herding Dog test (JHD) consists of a simple course ending in a fence-line pen.

To earn these titles requires two qualifying scores using sheep, goats, ducks, geese, or sometimes cattle.

Trials:

➤ Herding Trial Dog trials (HTD) include three successively more difficult levels (I, II, III), all of which include an outrun, lift, fetch, drive, and pen.

➤ Herding Ranch Dog trials (HRD) include a greater variety of elements and tasks more like those that a working stock dog might actually encounter.

To earn these titles requires two qualifying scores using sheep, goats, ducks (except for HRD), geese, or sometimes cattle. A small initial following the title signifies which species that title represents.

➤ Herding Trial Championship (HTCh) is awarded after earning ten additional qualifying scores after completing the HTD III or HRD III titles.

German Shepherds are known more for their expertise in handling very large flocks in open areas, where they act almost as "moving fences," constantly patrolling a boundary to prevent the sheep from crossing. In Germany and, more recently, America, German Shepherds can demonstrate their ability to control large flocks in *HGH* trials.

AKC Herding Trials usually make use of flocks of five to ten sheep, but SV trials use flocks of at least 200 sheep. The tasks faced by a Shepherd in these trials include:

➤ jumping into a pen of sheep and encouraging them to leave the pen calmly

Learnin' German

HGH stands for Herdengebrauchshund (Herding Utility Dog), and is a Herding title recognized by the SV and the USA. The German National Herding Trial is called the **Bundesleistungshueten.**

➤ keeping the sheep away from obstacles or passing cars when walking on a pathway

➤ keeping the sheep contained within a large grazing area by patrolling its boundaries

➤ circling the sheep and approaching them from the far side until the sheep move toward the handler

➤ keeping the sheep contained within a long, narrow grazing area by patrolling its boundaries

➤ keeping the sheep confined to the boundaries of a narrow road as they are moved along it

➤ preventing sheep from avoiding a bridge they are to cross

➤ on command, gripping a sheep by grabbing it on the thigh, nape, or ribs without tearing the skin

➤ re-penning the sheep

➤ in general, demonstrating obedience, diligence, and self-reliance

The best way to start herding is to find someone experienced in herding. Attend a Herding Trial and find out if someone in your area will show you the ropes. Besides profiting from their experience, you can use their stock that's already used to dogs and, best of all, you don't have to buy the farm to keep the stock.

Jumping is an essential aspect of Obedience, Agility, and Schutzhund competition. (Suzy Lucine)

Bite Me

Schutzhund—the epitome, the very title that says German Shepherd Dog. Actually, what the heck does Schutzhund mean, anyway? It's German for "protection dog." Schutzhund was developed specifically for German Shepherds (although other breeds also compete) to test a wide range of attributes necessary for a working dog. A Schutzhund Trial requires a dog to demonstrate its Tracking, Obedience, and Protection abilities all in the same day.

Schutzhund Trials have never been as popular in America as they are now, nor have they ever been as controversial. This is partly because of a public misconception that Schutzhund dogs are simply attack trained. Unfortunately, this public perception stems in part from some bad trainers who seem to share this idea. Attack or protection training without Obedience training is not Schutzhund! It is a dangerous imitation, and you are better off not to train your dog at all than to train it only partially in this area. The importance of finding a proper instructor cannot be overemphasized.

Even before competing in a Schutzhund Trial, a dog must pass the "Begleithunde" (or Companion Dog) test, which consists of a basic Obedience evaluation and a traffic safety exam. No, your GSD won't have to parallel park, but it will have to demonstrate it is under control around joggers, bicyclists, cars, strange dogs, and loud noises. The Schutzhund Trial itself begins with a brief temperament evaluation in which overly aggressive or uncontrollable dogs are weeded out of the competition even before it starts. Then let the games begin!

The first phase is the Tracking. Tracking for the SchH1 is actually a bit easier than the Tracking required for a TD. The track is somewhat shorter, about 20 minutes old, and laid by the handler. The track for the SchH2 is more difficult, being slightly longer, older, and laid by a stranger. The SchH3 track is even longer and older, and requires the dog to locate three dropped articles. It is comparable in difficulty to the track for the TD degree.

The second phase is Obedience. The basic exercises for SchH1 include:

➤ heeling on and off lead (including heeling into a group of people and executing a figure eight and ignoring two gunshots)

219

➤ sitting while the dog and handler are walking, with the dog remaining sitting while the handler continues to walk

➤ downing while the dog and handler are walking, with the dog remaining down while the handler continues to walk, and then coming to the handler when called

➤ retrieving a thrown dumbbell (weighing up to 650 grams, or about 23 ounces) on command, both on a flat surface and over a 1-meter jump

➤ going out ahead of the handler for 25 paces and downing on command

➤ remaining in the down position with the handler in view while another contestant performs the previous exercises

SchH2 exercises differ from SchH1 in adding a retrieve over a 5-foot wall, and substituting the flat retrieve article with a 1Kg (about 2.2 pound) dumbbell and the retrieves over obstacles with a 650 gram (about 23 ounces) dumbbell.

SchH3 exercises differ from SchH2 in adding a stand while dog and handler are walking, a stand while dog and handler are running (followed by a recall), substituting the flat retrieve article with a 2Kg (about 4.4-pound) dumbbell, and substituting the 5-foot wall with a 6-foot wall.

The third Schutzhund phase is protection.

For the SchH1 degree, the dog must search two blinds, and when it finds the "helper," must hold him in position by barking. When the helper attacks the handler, the dog must attack and hold the helper by biting, even when hit twice with a padded stick by the helper. The dog must pursue and attack a fleeing helper. In all cases, the dog must release the helper immediately when told to do so by the handler.

For the SchH2 degree, the dog must search six blinds. Upon finding the helper, the dog must bark but return to the handler when commanded. When the helper tries to escape, the dog must stop him by biting hard, and must release when the helper freezes. The dog must again bite the helper when the helper threatens the dog with a padded stick. The dog must watch the helper as the handler searches him. The dog must walk next to the handler as they escort the helper ahead of them; when the helper turns and tries to attack the handler, the dog must stop the helper by biting.

For the SchH3 degree, the dog performs similar exercises as for the SchH2, but does the whole thing off lead (in SchH2, parts of a couple of exercises are done on lead).

The Least You Need to Know

➤ Show dogs need to not only be good specimens of the breed, but also be trained to pose, trot, and "show" in a manner specific to German Shepherds.

➤ German Shepherds are naturals at Obedience Trials, Tracking Trials and Herding Trials. The number of successful GSD participants at all three is proof-positive of their proficiency.

➤ Agility Trials grew out of military and police dog obstacle courses. They are fun for dog and handler, and here GSDs are true naturals!

➤ Schutzhund Trials were developed specifically to test the German Shepherd's working ability. They combine Tracking, Obedience, and Protection work. Protection without Obedience is not Schutzhund and is dangerous!

➤ Competitions should be enjoyable for you and your dog and, on a more serious note, a means of proving which dogs are worthy of being bred.

Chapter 20

At Your Service

In This Chapter

➤ How you and your dog can be heroes in your spare time

➤ Shepherds that act as the eyes, ears, and hands for the disabled

➤ Shepherds that keep the peace

➤ What your dog sees, smells, and hears

GSDs are one of the most versatile breeds when it comes to competing successfully in a variety of fields. Despite this, most GSDs never enter a competition and never win a ribbon. They don't have to. They've already won the biggest prize of all—their owners' hearts. Some GSDs do even more, however, and win the hearts of others whose lives they touch or even save.

Early in their history, German Shepherds distinguished themselves as military and police dogs, roles they continue today. They have expanded their abilities to now serve as bomb- or narcotics-detection dogs or search-and-rescue dogs. Many GSDs have devoted their lives to helping disabled people. GSDs have proved themselves as capable guide dogs for the blind, hearing dogs for the deaf, and all-purpose assistants for the physically challenged. They have served as comforters and friends to the sick or lonely. No breed of dog has served so faithfully in so many roles.

In Search Of...

Dogs have long been known for their ability to follow scent trails and to locate hidden animals and people by scent. Although dogs have been used to hunt for lost people for decades, only recently has a concerted effort been made to produce educated search-and-rescue dog teams. National and local canine search-and-rescue teams are available for local emergencies, and can also be prepared to fly across country when disasters strike. They may search miles of wilderness for a lost child or through tons of rubble for a buried victim of an avalanche or earthquake.

So many dog training activities seem to have little relevance in society, but search and rescue is the exception. Your long hours of training just may save a life. Search-and-rescue dogs are the cream of the crop. If your GSD is capable of competing in Obedience, Agility, and Tracking, then it has the basics of a search-and-rescue (SAR) dog. But an SAR Shepherd is much more. These dogs must respond to commands reliably, negotiate precarious footing, follow a trail and find articles, and most of all, use air scenting to pinpoint the location of a hidden person. Well-trained dogs can search out a person from a quarter of a mile away, or one buried under snow, rubble, or even under water. Because they use air scenting rather than ground trailing, they don't need to follow a victim from a starting point to make a find.

Tall order, no doubt, but one that several heroic GSDs—and their equally heroic handlers—have already filled. German Shepherds remain the favored SAR dog breed. Their combination of hardiness, agility, endurance, ruggedness, intelligence, scenting ability, and tractability makes them ideal for the job. An SAR dog is only half of the team; handlers must also be trained in search technique, wilderness survival, first aid, and a variety of other skills, not to mention being pretty hardy and rugged themselves. Together, the development of an SAR team requires many hours of committed work—hours made worthwhile by joyful tears and saved lives.

Germane to Shepherds

The first search-and-rescue dogs were GSDs, finding victims from blitzkrieg bombings in WWII.

Contact the American Rescue Dog Association (see Appendix B) for more information. If you get started immediately, a year from now you might find yourself handing over a lost child to a grateful parent.

Cold Noses, Warm Hearts

Is the idea of trudging through wilderness in search of buried bodies a little too wild for you? You and your dog can still be lifesavers of a calmer kind. Therapy Dogs visit hospitals, nursing homes, mental health facilities, prisons, and other places where they can give people unconditional love, motivation to communicate, entertainment, and something warm and cuddly to hug.

Many German Shepherds proudly serve as Therapy Dogs—a natural outlet of their talents. (Dr. Zoë M. Backman)

Therapy Dogs must be meticulously well groomed and well mannered, but most of all, they must be friendly. If a person grabs them, yells at them, or hugs them until they can't breathe, they must be gentle and unflappable. The person half of the team is just as important. The handler needs to understand how to deal with people with a variety of disabilities. Local and national Therapy Dog groups can provide training and certification for you and your dog. The Certified Therapy Dog letters are among the proudest your dog can attain. The German Shepherd, with its uncanny knack for understanding human emotions, has warmed many hearts, dried many tears, and opened many arms, proving itself a true therapist in fur.

Hand and Foot

German Shepherds were one of the first breeds to provide assistance to people who were physically disabled. This assistance can take the form of pulling a person in a wheelchair, picking up dropped objects, getting objects off shelves the person can't reach, opening doors, and pushing a 911 button in case of emergency. Although Shepherds are used for this purpose, Golden and Labrador Retrievers are probably somewhat more popular because of the extensive retrieving that is often necessary. Sure, Shepherds are fine retrievers, but let's face it: The retrievers are great at what they do!

Other service dogs specialize in detecting when a person is about to have a seizure. Exactly how these dogs become aware of an impending seizure even before the person knows one is coming is unknown, but it is thought that the dog smells a change in body chemistry associated with changes in brain activity. These dogs supply a measure of safety and confidence for their people. Still other dogs provide safety once a seizure has ensued, lying next to the person until it has subsided. Seizure dogs must know the differences between friend and foe, allowing helpers to approach the victim while discouraging those with bad intentions. Seizure victims have been robbed as they lay defenseless; let's see them try that with a German Shepherd standing guard!

Eye for an Eye

The ravages of war don't end with the war. So it was that after World War I, many German soldiers were left blinded. Although dogs had been used sporadically to guide blind or visually disabled people for centuries, the efforts by the German government following WWI were the first concerted effort to train guide dogs for the blind. The breed, of course, was the German Shepherd. When a GSD breeder saw the program and reported on it in an American newspaper, a blind American contacted her and asked if he could go to Europe for training. Morris Frank and his German Shepherd, Buddy, became the first American guide dog team, and returned to the United States to promote the guide dog concept. Dorothy Eustis, the breeder who had trained him, came to America and founded The Seeing Eye in 1929. Since that time, thousands of German Shepherds have provided eyes and a link to the sighted world for their people.

Some guide dog facilities breed their own dogs; others accept donated puppies that pass certain stringent criteria. Most facilities rely on puppy raisers to provide a home environment, well-rounded socialization, and basic obedience to youngsters. The puppies then go to the school for formal training when they are from 12 to 18 months of age. It is tough relinquishing a puppy you have grown to love, but perhaps the most rewarding tough thing you will ever be asked to do. At the school, the dog receives intensive specialized training. Not all dogs graduate, but those that do have a full life ahead of them. Guide dogs usually retire when they are around eight years old. Many are then available for adoption to the family of their handler, puppy raiser, or the public.

The image of the German Shepherd guide dog is the most familiar of all service dogs.

The working guide dog is expected to take directional instructions from the handler; locate specified objects such as curbs, doors, and steps; stop at obstacles, changes in elevation, or dangerous traffic situations; and reasonably ignore distractions during its work and even commands from its handler if they would result in danger to the handler. They give their visually impaired handlers mobility, confidence, independence, and love—true friends in the dark.

All Ears

Dogs can also provide confidence for deaf or hearing impaired people. Although most dogs for the deaf are small dogs rescued from humane organizations, German Shepherds can also be trained to do the same job. At the lowest (novice) level, dogs are trained to alert the person to a smoke alarm, the person's name being called, and the alarm clock. A slightly more highly trained dog (home level) alerts the person to the doorbell, telephone, and oven timer. The certified hearing dog responds to these same sounds, but is also extensively socialized and obedience trained so that it is dependable in public as well as in the home. As such, it meets the Americans with Disabilities Act standard and is allowed in all public places.

Dog-Faces and Dog-Tags

One of the oldest jobs dogs have filled for centuries has been that of warrior, fighting side by side with their human partners in the fiercest of battles. In the 20th century the role of dog warrior changed from primarily hand-to-tooth combat to jack-of-all-trades. This change came about largely because of the multi-faceted talents of the German Shepherd. Soldiers discovered the dogs could serve not as only as warriors, but also as sentries, patrols, scouts, mine detectors, tunnel detectors, and messengers. Training is rigorous, consisting of obedience and attack training as well as super-canine obstacle course maneuvers. Military dogs, specifically German Shepherds, have proved to be a weapon that has often made the difference between winning or losing, the world's first (and best) "smart missile."

Taking a Bite Out of Crime

So much has the German Shepherd become identified with police work that many people know it only as the "Police Dog." The GSD remains one of the most popular all-around police dogs in the world, challenged only by the Belgian Malinois. The police dog, or K-9, has proved one of the most valuable officers on the force. Who else can pursue (and catch) a fleeing suspect, locate crime scene evidence, sniff out contraband, and control a crowd? And it does this without ever drawing a weapon (except for those glistening choppers). Besides its official duties, police dogs act as ambassadors for the police department, canines that add a humanizing dimension to the people half of their teams. They get the attention of bad guys, too. Criminals who wouldn't think twice about challenging a human officer wouldn't think of challenging a canine cop. Many K-9s have literally saved the lives of their handlers; regrettably, many have given their own lives in the effort. Despite the risks, the life of a K-9 is good. They get to go to work with their special person, part of a team on the lookout for an adventure.

I Smell a Rat!

Most police dogs are trained for drug detection, and some are also trained for explosives detection. Many are specialists, used exclusively for bomb detection at airports or for drug detection in building and automobile searches. The Federal Aviation Administration makes extensive use of dogs, including German Shepherds. No machine has ever been found that can compete with the dog's sense of smell, and studies have shown the GSD to be among the best of scenters. Dogs have been used to find all sorts of contraband, termites and other insect pests, gas leaks, cows in estrus—if it can be smelled, a German Shepherd can smell it.

Shep Heard

...that drug detection dogs are made addicted to drugs so they will seek them out. Shep heard wrong! Dogs can be taught to seek out explosives, bugs, dead people, or anything that has a scent. The most common reward? A chance to chase a ball or play tug-of-war.

More than any other dog breed, the German Shepherd has served in many capacities to help people and save lives as well as property. (Christine Alderson)

229

On Guard!

Dogs have a natural tendency to protect their own territory, and guard dogs have this tendency encouraged. German Shepherds are naturally protective and courageous, and have long been a favorite breed for guard duty. They may accompany their handlers on patrol, run loose within the confines of a secured area, or even perform their guard duties from the foot of your bed at night. The GSD's superior senses of smell and hearing, as well as night vision, make it adept at detecting the creepiest of creeps. Even without training, most German Shepherds can deter intruders simply by barking. Trained dogs, and even some untrained ones, will detain an intruder by barking and grasping the person if the person tries to escape. As a general rule, it is unwise to have a guard dog trained to attack an intruder because of the possibility of an "innocent" intruder (such as children or mentally unsound people) being hurt.

Good Sense, Good Senses

What do the guide dog, hearing dog, and search-and-rescue dog all have in common? They have to rely on both their good sense and good senses.

Vision of Perfection

The canine eye is superior to the human eye at seeing in very dim light. This ability comes in part from a reflective structure (the tapetum lucidum) in the back of the eye that reflects light back into the retina's light-sensitive cells, in essence magnifying the light. The reflected light is the eyeshine you may see from your dog's eyes when you shine a light into them at night. The dog's ability to see in dim light is also partly due to having a much higher proportion of the type of retinal cells (rods) that are highly sensitive to dim light than humans possess. The price the dog pays for this night vision is sacrificing keen detail and color vision. The dog's sense of color is like that of what is commonly called a "color-blind" person, which is not really blind to color at all. That is, they confuse similar shades of yellow-green, yellow, orange, and red, but can readily see and discriminate blue, indigo, and violet from all other colors and each other.

Hi-Fido

Your GSD can hear much higher frequencies than you can, and so can be irritated by high hums from your TV or from those ultrasonic flea collars. The high-pitched "dog whistles" so popular years ago emit a tone higher than humans can hear, but well within the dog's range. Dogs need to be trained to respond to these whistles just as they would any other command or signal. The problem is that owners can't tell when the whistle malfunctions. Ultrasonic training devices now available emit a high-frequency sound inaudible to us, but irritating and distracting to dogs. They can be a useful training aid for disrupting unwanted behavior, but only if accompanied by rewarding the dog for correct behavior.

Good Scents

The German Shepherd, like all dogs, has a powerful sense of smell. The Shepherd's scenting ability is so vastly superior to ours that it is as though we were blind in comparison. No machine has been developed that can outperform the dog's nose in olfactory detection. German Shepherds have trailed people after snow has covered their tracks, or after gasoline has been poured over them and set afire. Some evidence exists that dogs with more olfactory area, which corresponds to a long, deep, muzzle, have better scenting powers, but this has never been proved. Certainly GSDs have proved themselves on the trail, and are especially adept at jobs requiring them to search out hidden people and contraband.

The Least You Need to Know

➤ Search-and-rescue dogs use air-scenting to find lost people or bodies buried in rubble, snow, dirt, and even under water. GSDs are the most popular dog for the job.

➤ Certified Therapy Dogs provide comfort and stimulation for elderly, ill, or confined people. Dogs must be friendly, tolerant, and obedient to be good at the job.

➤ The first guide dogs were GSDs, and they still excel at the job. Puppy raisers are always needed to provide early socialization, training, and love.

➤ Dogs for the deaf alert hearing-impaired people to smoke alarms, alarm clocks, the person's name, doorbells, and telephones.

➤ Your dog lives in a different sensory world from yours. It smells more, hears more, and sees better at night than you do.

The Travails
of Travels

In This Chapter

➤ The pros and cons of traveling with your dog

➤ Traveling the right way by land, sea, and air

➤ Stay-at-home options

➤ Finding a lost dog

Hitting the road with your Shepherd pal might seem like a good idea, but all roads that lead to Rome are paved with good intentions (or something like that). Anyway, taking your dog with you on a trip without any forethought can lead to a miserable time for both of you, and maybe even a dangerous time. With some planning, though, you might find your Shepherd to be the best traveling companion you could choose. After all, German Shepherds seldom argue about what radio station to listen to.

A Vacation with Your Alsatian

German Shepherds make excellent road buddies. They agree with everything you say, they are always up for a side trip, they give you a good excuse to stop and enjoy the scenery up close, and they scare away any bad guys you might come across. With proper planning, a GSD copilot can steer you to destinations you might otherwise have missed.

Without proper planning, sharing your trip with any dog can be a nightmare, as you are turned away from motels, parks, attractions, and beaches. It's no fun trying to sneak a dog into a motel room (German Shepherds are just a tad too big to fit under your coat; besides, even the mutest dog will find plenty to bark at once it discovers you're trying to keep it quiet). Several books are available listing establishments that accept pets, and they are well worth consulting.

If the weather is warm, plan on driving past all the attractions (they cost too much anyway—see how your dog is already saving you money?). If you must play tourist, call ahead to attractions to see if they have safe boarding arrangements for pets. Safe means a secure locked kennel run, not a chain next to the parking lot. Plan on driving past all those shopping places, too. See how your dog is saving you even more money! With all the money you save, you might even be able to take another vacation—this time without your dog, so you can actually do something.

If you're crazy with the urge to spend money on local color, and the conditions are unsafe for leaving your dog in your car, there's one possible compromise: a local boarding kennel. Call around and see if you can arrange doggy day care at a safe facility.

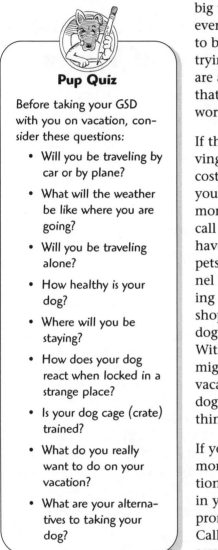

Pup Quiz

Before taking your GSD with you on vacation, consider these questions:

- Will you be traveling by car or by plane?
- What will the weather be like where you are going?
- Will you be traveling alone?
- How healthy is your dog?
- Where will you be staying?
- How does your dog react when locked in a strange place?
- Is your dog cage (crate) trained?
- What do you really want to do on your vacation?
- What are your alternatives to taking your dog?

You might be tempted to leave your dog in your car with the windows down. If your dog is sufficiently protective and tough looking this might work, but even the toughest dog can be a target for

234

dognappers or weirdos. If you have a cage, you can place your dog in it, padlock the cage door, and padlock the cage to the car for security. Never leave your dog tied in or to your car. Many a dead dog has been found hanging out the car window after being tied inside. One other warning: In this litigation-crazed society, it's not unheard of for somebody whose own dog has bitten or scratched them to seek out unsupervised dogs and claim "dog bite!" when your dog did nothing but hang its head out the window.

You may also be tempted to leave your dog in your motel room during the day. Do so only if you can afford to have the room redone after your dog has redecorated it. The dog's perception is that you have left it in a strange place and forgotten it; it either barks or tries to dig its way out through the doors and windows in an effort to find you, or becomes upset and relieves itself on the carpet.

The number of establishments that accept pets decreases yearly. You can thank dog owners who seem to think their wonderful "Poopsie" is above the law, owners who let Poopsie poop on sidewalks, beaches, and playgrounds, bark herself hoarse in the motel room, and leave behind wet spots on the carpet, chew marks on the chairs, and hair everywhere. Miraculously, there are still some places where pets are welcome. Please do everything you can to convince motel managers that dogs can be civilized guests.

Al Says

Bring sheets from home to place on the carpet or bed if you allow your Shepherd loose in a motel room.

If you are staying at a campground, keep your dog on a leash or in an exercise pen at all times. Other campers could have tiny dogs that your dog might chase, and many campgrounds have wildlife wandering through that could prove too tempting for your Shepherd to ignore. Walk your dog away from campsites, and always clean up after it.

If you plan to stay with friends, ask beforehand if it's okay for you to bring your GSD. Have your dog clean and parasite free. Bring your dog's own clean blanket or bed, or better yet, its cage. Your GSD will appreciate the familiar place to sleep, and your friends will breathe sighs of relief. Do not allow your dog to run helter-skelter through their home. Even though your dog may be accustomed to sleeping on furniture at home, a proper canine guest stays off the furniture when visiting. If your hosts have pets of their own, be sure your dog does not chase or fight with them. Walk your dog (and clean up after it) to make sure no accidents happen inside. If they do, clean them immediately. Don't leave any surprises for your hosts! Changes in water or food, or simply stress, can often result in diarrhea, so be particularly attentive to taking your dog out often. Always remember that anyone who allows your dog to spend the night is doing so with a certain amount of trepidation; make sure they have every reason to invite both of you back.

Al Says

Always keep a couple of plastic baggies in your pocket. Dogs can decide to relieve themselves when and where you least expect it!

Always walk your GSD on lead when you're away from home. If frightened or distracted, your dog could become disoriented and lost. The long retractable leads are perfect for traveling. Keep an eye out for little nature excursions, which are wonderful for refreshing both dog and owner. But always do so with a cautious eye; never risk your or your dog's safety by stopping in totally desolate locales, no matter how breathtaking the view.

Ready, Shep, Go!

You might think that packing for your dog would be a cinch; after all, your Shepherd is wearing its entire wardrobe on its back! But unlike you, your dog needs almost all of its food packed, as well as a lot of other things you don't want to have to hunt down in a strange place. Most of all, you need to pack with your dog's health and safety in mind.

Place all your dog's belongings in a separate bag. It makes things easier to find and keeps your own stuff from being covered by your dog's stuff. Consider packing:

➤ medications, especially anti-diarrhea and heartworm preventive

➤ food and water bowls

➤ food and dog biscuits

➤ chewies and toys

➤ bottled water or water from home—many dogs are very sensitive to changes in water and can develop diarrhea much easier than you might think.

➤ flea comb and brush

➤ bug spray or flea spray

➤ moist towelettes, paper towels, and self-rinse shampoo

➤ bedding

➤ short and long leashes

➤ flashlight for night walks

➤ plastic baggies or other poop disposal means

➤ current health and rabies certificates

➤ recent color photo in case your GSD somehow gets lost

➤ its own cage from home

Your dog should be wearing a collar with license tags, including a tag indicating where you could be reached while on your trip or including the address of someone you know will be at home.

No Crash Test Doggies!

Bliss for a dog is a ride in the car with the wind in its coat and bugs in its teeth as it hangs its head out the window and enjoys! Sure, that would be fun while it lasted, but it might not last long before your dog is thrown from the car, gets its nose stung by a bee, or gets its eye put out by a rock. Kids would love to run around inside the car and hang out the windows, but there are laws for their safety (and yours) that prevent them from doing so. And people who let their dogs ride in the back of a pickup truck might think they are looking cool, but they might as well have a Shepherd-sized bumper sticker that reads "Moron at the Wheel."

We hope you wear a seatbelt when you drive your car (you don't want to chance leaving your dog an orphan, now do you?). Your dog has a higher center of gravity than you do when riding in the car and far less ability to grab onto something. It doesn't take much to send your German Shepherd flying into the dashboard, windshield, or you, or out of the vehicle altogether. Dogs have been killed, and people have been killed by their flying dogs, as a result of relatively small accidents. Dogs have been killed by airbags. Dogs have been killed by being run over after being thrown from vehicles. Dogs have also caused deadly accidents by getting a leg caught in the steering wheel, bumping the car out of gear, or jumping in the driver's lap.

Including your German Shepherd in travel or vacation plans can be either wonderful or disastrous, depending on the effectiveness of your planning. (Barbara McGuire)

But you can't exactly teach your Shepherd to buckle up for safety. You can, however, use a doggie seatbelt and buckle your dog up for its own safety. They are available at pet stores and through pet catalogs, and many GSDs have learned to wear them. Don't think tying your dog in place by its collar will do just as well—that's a good way for your dog to get a broken neck. You can improvise by fitting your dog with a harness and attaching that to the seatbelt. The back seat is safer than the front, and the front seat is absolutely off limits if your car has passenger-side airbags.

You can keep a sturdy cage in your car, which has saved many a dog's life. Cages can go flying, too, so remember they should be securely fastened in the car for human as well as canine safety. On the cage affix a sticker or tag that reads "In case of an accident, take this dog to a veterinarian, and then contact the following persons (list names and phone numbers), who have guaranteed payment of all expenses incurred." Remember that you might not be able to speak for your dog in the event of a serious accident.

There's a time and place for your Shepherd to run amok and be a free spirit. A ride in the car is not one of them.

Up in the Air

Modern air travel is fairly safe, but should not be undertaken frivolously. Chances are your Shepherd can't fit under the seat, so unless it is a service dog, it will be riding in the baggage compartment. Although baggage compartments are heated, they are not air-conditioned, and in hot weather dogs have been known to overheat while the plane was still on the runway. Never ship in the heat of day or the middle of the summer. If airline personnel say it's too hot, believe them. If they say it's not too hot, doubt them. Don't ship on Fridays or the day before holidays. Dogs do occasionally get misrouted and have been found on Mondays after spending a weekend alone in a closed freight office. It's best if your dog can fly as excess baggage, but if you must ship it by itself, it is usually better to ship "counter to counter" than to ship as air freight.

Buy an airline-approved cage, which meets certain specifications for size, strength, and ventilation. If your dog is not cage-trained, set it up in your house and get your dog used to eating and sleeping in it.

Ready the cage for the trip by securing its fasteners super-tight, adding bedding that could be thrown away if need be at your destination, and finding a water bowl or bucket that won't spill and that your dog's head can't get caught in. You can also hang a bucket from the cage door with an eyebolt snap. Plaster your name and address and the words "LIVE ANIMAL" all over the outside.

The night before the trip, fill the water bowl with water and freeze it. Take it out of the cooler just before the flight and attach it to the inside of the cage. As it melts during the flight, the dog will have water that otherwise might have spilled out during the loading process. You might want to include a large chew toy to occupy your jet-setter, as long as it's one you already know is safe for your dog. Most people feel it is safer to ship without a collar on their dog. As a last measure, put an elastic bungee cord around the cage door.

Al Says

Don't feed your dog before an airplane trip. There's no place to answer nature's call at cruising altitude.

When you make your airline reservations, you must mention that you are flying with a dog. It will cost you extra money, but more important, most flights restrict the number of dogs they can carry because they don't have unlimited room. You have to show up for the flight early. Be sure to walk your dog one last time, and stay with it as long as possible before loading. Note that it is against the rules to place any live animal on a conveyor belt or to leave it on the tarmac for more than a few minutes in warm weather. Once on the plane, request that the flight attendant check to make sure the dog has been loaded before taking off. If the weather is hot and you

Shep Heard

...that dogs are welcome on trains. Shep heard wrong! In the United States, dogs are not allowed on trains unless they are service dogs.

sit on the runway, make your concerns known and demand action be taken.

Then sit back and anticipate your joyous reunion when you get to your destination!

The German and the Sea

Sorry. With very few exceptions, you can't take your dog on a cruise. You can take it on your own boat, of course, and if you do, be sure to practice good canine nautical safety.

Teach your dog the rules of the sea. Your dog should never jump overboard unless told to do so. Hold your dog on leash if you have doubts or if you are in a fast-moving boat. Dogs are not equipped with boat shoes and they could slip off the deck easily. Dogs can't dog paddle indefinitely—certainly not for long in rough seas, and not at all if they're knocked unconscious. Get a doggy life vest (really) that fits your Shepherd and use it.

Groom and Board

You may have gathered that sometimes you and your dog will both be better off if you take your trip alone. Should you just leave your dog with a giant pile of food, hire a dog-sitter, or use a boarding kennel?

If you are only going to be gone overnight, have a doggy door and an Alcatraz-escape-proof yard or kennel, and a healthy dog that doesn't gorge itself, then—and only then—can you simply leave a good supply of food and water. Too many dogs will eat the entire supply as soon as you step out the door, which could even bring on a case of gastric torsion (or at least discomfort), so it's not a good idea. You can get a feeder that's on a timer, but a determined dog might just break into it.

No doubt your dog will be more comfortable in its own home, so you can arrange for a pet-sitter to visit twice a day. Again, this works best with a dog door and secure fence. You also need to have a dog that will accept a stranger in the home. Good pet-sitters want to make friends with the dog before you leave home. Hire a bonded, professional pet-sitter. The kid next door is seldom a good choice for this important responsibility. It is too easy for the dog to slip out the door, or for signs of illness to go unnoticed, unless the sitter is an experienced dog person. Your dog's life is a heavy responsibility for any child.

Your GSD may be safer (if not quite as contented) if you board it at a kennel. The ideal kennel is approved by the American Boarding Kennel Association, has climate-controlled accommodations, and keeps your GSD either indoors or in a combination indoor/outdoor run. The run should be covered so that a climbing or jumping dog cannot escape, an extra security fence should surround the entire kennel area, and someone should be on the grounds 24 hours a day. Make an unannounced visit to the kennel and ask to see the facilities. While you can't expect spotlessness and a perfumed atmosphere, most runs should be clean and any odor should not be overwhelming. All dogs should have clean water and bedding or a raised area for sleeping. A solid divider should prevent dogs in adjoining runs from direct contact with one another. Strange dogs should not be allowed to mingle. Good kennels require proof of current immunizations and an incoming check for fleas. The staff will demand to bathe your dog if it has fleas, and offer to bathe it again before you pick it up (most dogs smell pretty doggy after a stay in a kennel). You will be allowed to bring toys and bedding, and the staff will administer prescribed medication. There will also be arrangements for emergency veterinary care.

Whatever means you choose, always leave emergency numbers and your veterinarian's name. Make arrangements with your veterinarian to treat your dog for any problems that may arise. This means leaving a written agreement stating that you give permission for treatment and accept responsibility for charges.

Accidents Happen

Shepherds usually stick pretty close, but sometimes the unforeseeable happens and you and your dog are suddenly separated. If so, you need to act quickly. Don't rely on the dog's fabled ability to find its way home; it happens a lot more in movies than in real life.

➤ Start your search at the worst place you could imagine your dog, usually the nearest road. If you are in your car, don't drive so recklessly that you endanger your own dog's life should it run across the road.

➤ If you must leave the area where your dog was lost, try to leave its cage, blanket, some of your personal belongings, or even your open car in case the dog returns while you are gone.

➤ Get pictures of your dog and go door to door.

➤ Post large posters with a picture of your dog or a similar-looking GSD.

➤ Distribute fliers at the local animal control organization, the police department, parking lots, and all veterinary clinics.

Shep Heard

...that dogs can navigate home using mysterious powers. Shep heard wrong! Most "incredible journeys" are undocumented. Even if they were true, the other 99 percent of dogs apparently have no such powers and get lost a block away from home.

➤ Take out an ad in the local paper.

➤ Mention a reward, but do not specify an amount. Some scam artists answer lost dog ads and ask for money to ship the dog back to you from a distance or to pay vet bills, when they don't really have your dog. If your dog is tattooed, you can have the person read the tattoo to you to positively identify it. Never give out your dog's tattoo number or divulge secret identifying marks. Some dognappers steal dogs so they can collect large rewards, but you should never give anyone reward money before seeing your dog.

➤ Mention whether your dog is likely to run away if approached. Some well-meaning or reward-hungry people have run dogs away trying to catch them.

Losing a dog is a heartbreaking experience, a loss without closure or explanations. The best time to find a dog is right after it is lost. Too many people take too long to realize their dog is really not coming back on its own, time in which they probably could have found their dog. This is one instance in which it pays to be an alarmist.

Better to cry wolf than to cry tears over a friend you never got to say goodbye to.

Give Your Dog a Chip on Its Shoulder

Every dog should have an up-to-date license tag on its collar. The flat tags are better than the hanging ones because they are less likely to be caught in a playmate's tooth. But they don't work too well if you are left holding the tag as your dog runs down the street after a bath or after slipping its collar, and dognappers laugh at them. You need at least two forms of identity.

One form is a tattoo. While you could have a skull and crossbones or "Mom" tattooed on your dog, it's easier to trace your Social Security number or your dog's registration number. Tattoos are usually placed on the inside of the dog's thigh and provide a relatively permanent means of identification (sometimes they fade or are hard to read on a dog with dark skin or a thick coat). The tattoo numbers can be registered with one of the several lost-pet recovery agencies that contact you if the dog is reported. They can be obscured by subsequent tattooing, however.

Shep Heard

...that microchips can migrate throughout the dog's body. Shep heard wrong! Some early microchips could migrate several inches from their original site, but changes in their design have made them fairly immobile.

The most permanent and informative identification is the microchip. It contains information about the dog and is placed under the dog's skin with a simple injection. The shortcoming of microchips is that they require a special scanner (owned by most animal shelters, but few veterinarians) to be read. The number is registered with one of the microchip dog-recovery agencies, which contact you if your dog is reported missing.

The best solution is all three: license tag, tattoo, and microchip. Of course, the best solution is to never chance getting separated from your companion.

The Least You Need to Know

➤ Before you take your dog on a trip, consider the weather, accommodations, and where your dog will stay if you go sightseeing or shopping.

➤ Thoughtless dog owners have made it increasingly difficult to find motels and recreation areas that allow dogs. Please don't add to the problem.

➤ Don't let your dog run loose in your car. It's a deadly form of permissiveness. Use a doggy seatbelt or a cage.

➤ If your dog gets lost, as soon as your dog is missing, take action—lots of action.

Part 8

If You're Not Part of the Solution...

Unless you've been skipping ahead, you are now almost to the end of the book and, therefore, far smarter than the average dog owner. What will you do with your newfound knowledge? Will you scoff at my pearls of wisdom and just do whatever you want? Will you keep your great bounty of knowledge to yourself? Owning a dog in the United States isn't getting any easier, and if you really love your dog, and dogs (and especially GSDs) in general, then you should do your best to set a good example and to educate others. Of course, the number one way in which you should educate is to buy boxes of this book and pass them out. If you don't want to do that, then at least tell everyone with a GSD they need it.

Have you ever dreamed of breeding a litter? Those cute little pupsters nipping at your heels, and the money just rolling in? Read on for a rude awakening. If you can breed a litter, look into those trusting puppy-dog eyes, and not flinch at the futures they have in store, you are one hardhearted person. Don't be part of the problem...

Finally, if you've done everything the way you should, congratulations— you can read the last chapter. Being a responsible dog owner means more than enjoying the fun years. Now it is time to pay your dog back for a lifetime of love and devotion.

To the Rescue

One of the most unfortunate aspects of owning a dog is that so many people feel the compulsion to breed them. It seems like a neat idea at the time. Puppies are so cute, all your friends say they wouldn't mind having one, you love your dog and want another just like her, and you may just pick up a little extra spending money. If only it were so. The problem is that too many people have this idea. So many, in fact, breed their pets that millions of dogs are abandoned and euthanized every year. Please don't be part of this nationwide problem. Even better, be part of the solution.

Too Much of a Good Thing

Most dog breed books contain a chapter about breeding. This one does not, for a very good reason. In 1997, 23,424 German Shepherd litters, resulting in 75,177 individuals, were registered with the AKC.

Do you really think 75,177 good new homes were waiting for these puppies? How many do you think are still in whatever homes they found? How many do you think are still alive? This doesn't even count the GSDs that were registered with other organizations or not registered at all. Please don't add to the problem. Unfortunately, people seem to take the term "litter" seriously and treat breeding with about as much thought as producing any other household litter. Keep in mind:

➤ Being a popular breed does not mean that good homes are waiting for every puppy. Many more good GSDs are born than there are good homes available. The puppy you sell to a less-than-perfect home could end up neglected, abused, discarded, or returned.

➤ Unless your GSD has proved itself by earning titles and awards in competitions, or by being an outstanding working dog, you may have a difficult time finding buyers for its puppies.

➤ The average litter size for GSDs is seven puppies. Breeding so you can keep one pup ignores the fact that six others may not get a good home, or may be ransacking your home for the next 10 years.

➤ Selling puppies will not come close to reimbursing you for the stud fee, prenatal care, potential whelping complications, Caesarean sections, supplemental feeding, puppy food, vaccinations, advertising, and a staggering investment of time and energy.

Recipe for fun: A boy and his dog—just add water. And the need for breeding does not enter this picture.

➤ There is definite discomfort and some danger to the bitch when whelping a litter. Watching a litter being born is not a good way to show children the miracle of life; there are too many things that can go wrong.

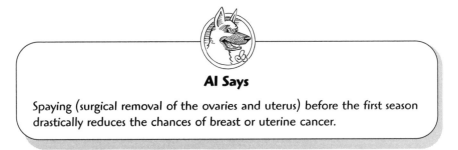

Al Says

Spaying (surgical removal of the ovaries and uterus) before the first season drastically reduces the chances of breast or uterine cancer.

➤ Responsible breeders have spent years researching genetics and the breed, breed only the best specimens, and screen for hereditary defects to produce superior puppies. Unless you have done the same, you are doing yourself, your dog, the puppies, any buyers, and the breed a great disservice.

Note: If you must breed your GSD, please invest in a book about the mechanics of breeding. Too many uninformed breeders allow their dogs to suffer and even die because they don't have proper information.

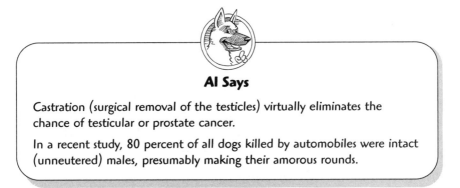

Al Says

Castration (surgical removal of the testicles) virtually eliminates the chance of testicular or prostate cancer.

In a recent study, 80 percent of all dogs killed by automobiles were intact (unneutered) males, presumably making their amorous rounds.

Pup-Quiz!

- Does your GSD have an OFA elbow clearance and OFA, PennHIP, OVC, or "a" hip clearance?
- Do you know the complete medical history of your dog's ancestors, particularly for hereditary disorders?
- Is your GSD titled in Conformation, Obedience, or Schutzhund competition?
- Is your GSD really a physically and temperamentally superior specimen of the breed?
- Is your GSD healthy and in good weight and condition?
- Do you know anything about whelping a litter and are you prepared for life-threatening developments?
- Can you afford to pay for a Caesarean section?
- Can you afford to take time off work to bottle-feed puppies?
- Can you cope emotionally with the sale or death of puppies?
- Do you have proper facilities in which to raise puppies?
- Do you have at least five homes waiting for puppies, with deposits?
- Can you check out each prospective home and guarantee it really is a good one?
- Can you provide health guarantees for your puppies and afford to stand behind them?
- Can you field questions from new owners of your puppies at all hours of the day and night?
- Can you accept each and every puppy back into your home should its new owners not be able to keep it, for as long as that puppy is alive?

How many of those 23,000-plus litters bred in a year do you think were bred by people who could answer yes to these questions? What happens to the more than 75,000 GSDs bred in the United States every year? Some die of natural causes. Many, many more die of unnatural causes. Of these, most are struck by cars. Many are poisoned or shot for being nuisances. A few are tortured and killed for the sheer sick fun of it. Of the survivors, many are "lost" and become feral and usually starve. Others are given away, and then given away by their next owners, and so on. Some end up in the pound or in German Shepherd rescue. Some are simply driven to the country, an interstate, or the other side of town and dumped. Of those that are kept, some go to puppy mills or backyard breeders where they are bred as often as possible, perhaps producing hundreds of puppies in their lifetime, until they cease to produce and are dumped or euthanized. Some are tied to a chain or stuck in a pen in the backyard where they will sit without companionship, activity, or shelter for the next 10 years. Some do find good homes, mostly with people who cared enough to do their homework and find good, responsible breeders. Do you see how lucky your breeder was to find you? Do you think you would be so lucky?

A Friend in Need Is a Friend Indeed

You have the precious ability to save a life. You can't save every German Shepherd, but what if the breeders of those 75,000 Shepherds all did their part to support German Shepherds in need, many of which they themselves created. Unfortunately, people aren't like that, and it will always be the case that good people pick up after bad people. Be a good one.

Support German Shepherd Dog Rescue. If you can find room in your home and heart, consider adopting a rescue GSD as your next family member. Even if you cannot add a new permanent member, by volunteering as a foster home, you can help nurse a homeless GSD back to physical or emotional health while it awaits a new permanent family. If you have reached your dog or emotional limit, you can still do your part with financial contributions or by joining the network of hardworking people who match dogs and people or who canvass animal shelters for German Shepherds. Even if you are not up to a full-fledged commitment, you can at least register with your local animal shelter and ask to be contacted whenever a GSD comes through the door.

It's easy to love a German Shepherd when everything is going well. The true test of your love for the breed is your ability to help when the chips are down.

When Divorce Is the Best Course

What if you get your German Shepherd and it doesn't work out? The only thing worse than getting a dog and then not keeping it for its entire life is getting a dog and keeping it against your will for its entire life. If you have reached the conclusion that dog ownership is not for you, then try to find a home for your dog while it is still a cute puppy. You can contact your dog's breeders and ask if they want it back. This is one of the major advantages of buying from a reputable breeder. They should always take the dog back, no matter what the dog's age, although you should not necessarily expect your purchase price to be returned. You can try to find a new owner through a newspaper ad. Never advertise your dog as being free; vile people exist who collect free animals for horrific purposes. You can contact the German Shepherd Dog Club of America Rescue, who may provide a foster home and do their best to find the best new owner. As a last resort, you can take your dog to an animal shelter, where they will take over the responsibility of finding it a home. If you have a cute puppy or if your dog is obviously a purebred German Shepherd, its chances of being adopted are fairly high. Never take your dog to the country and let it go to fend for itself. Such dogs are routinely shot, killed by cars, or starve.

You are allowed to make one such mistake in your life. Do not think things will go better with another dog. In 99 percent of the cases, it is the owner who is the problem. Try an aquarium next time.

We hope, though, that you and your Shepherd share a lifetime of happy adventures. Your life may change dramatically in the years to come: marriage, divorce, new baby, new home—for better or worse, your dog will still depend on you and still love you. Always remember the promise you made to yourself and your future puppy before you made the commitment to share your life: to keep your interest in your dog and care for it every day of its life with as much love and enthusiasm as you did the first day it arrived home. Remember, too, that your Shepherd will change through the years, and an aging Shepherd requires an even greater measure of care, dedication, and love from you.

The Least You Need to Know

➤ Many thousands of GSD litters are bred each year and only a small percentage of the puppies produced find permanent loving homes.

➤ You will most likely be doing yourself, your dog, your buyers (if any), and the breed a grave disservice by breeding your GSD.

➤ You can do your part for the GSD by working to save GSDs in trouble instead of producing more.

➤ If you can't keep your dog as a beloved family member, consider giving it up for adoption through GSD Rescue.

Chapter 23

Shepherding in the Years

One day you will look at your Shepherd companion and be shocked to realize its face has silvered and its gait has stiffened. It sleeps longer and more soundly than it did as a youngster and is slower to get going. It may be less eager to play and more content to lie in the sun. Congratulations! You own a geriatric German Shepherd. It's only natural to feel a bit sad, but getting your dog to healthy old age is a worthy accomplishment. Just make sure you appreciate all the stages along the way.

You can't turn the clock back, and besides, as you share the years with your dog, you will learn to appreciate the different stages of its life. Puppies are so full of curiosity and mischief, who could resist them? Adolescents begin to blossom into adults, sometimes doing the goofiest things, and just when you think the dog is hopeless, it astounds you with a feat of loyalty and intelligence. Adults mature into true dependable companions, dogs that you can trust with your life. Anyone who has had a GSD for its entire life, however, would probably assert it is the senior GSD that's really the best. With the wisdom of years, the GSD becomes almost humanlike in its ability to tune in to your emotions. The older GSD, its eyes often hazy because of cataracts, its gait stiff, and its face gray, is in the opinion of many GSD fanciers, the most beautiful GSD of all.

Germane to Shepherds

All dogs age at different rates, but by 8 years of age, most German Shepherds can be considered in their golden years. The average life span for a German Shepherd is about 10 or 11 years, although rare individuals have lived past 12 years of age.

Eat and Run

Both physical activity and metabolic rates decrease in older animals, meaning that they require fewer calories to maintain the same weight. Older dogs that continue being fed the same diet they ate as young dogs are at risk for obesity; such dogs also have a greater risk of developing cardiovascular and joint problems. Some German Shepherds lose weight with age, which can be equally bad. Your dog needs a little fat so it has something to fall back on if it gets sick. Other GSDs lose weight and may need to eat puppy food to keep the pounds on. High-quality (not quantity) protein is especially important for older dogs. Most older dogs do not require a special diet unless they have a particular medical need for it.

Older dogs should be fed several small meals instead of one large meal, and should be fed on time. Moistening dry food or feeding canned food can help a dog with dental problems enjoy its meal. They may enjoy eating while lying down or eating off a raised platform.

Many people have this macho idea that their dog will never slow down with age. Dogs do age at different rates, but staying in a state of denial about your dog's increasing age or decreasing abilities is not doing it any favors. Tone down your hiking trips, and instead, just camp in one spot. Older German Shepherds that may have had joint problems in youth can now really begin to suffer with them. It is important to keep your older GSD relatively active, without putting too much stress on its joints. If your dog is sore following a day of unaccustomed activity, you have probably asked too much. You may have to walk with your dog and do your marathon running by yourself. Swimming is an excellent low-impact exercise as long as the dog doesn't get chilled and is never put in a dangerous situation. Exercise is essential in keeping your dog healthy and happy, but it should be exercise the dog can handle.

Act Your Age

A new puppy or pet may be welcomed and encourage your dog to play, but if your dog is not used to other dogs, the newcomer will more likely be resented and be a source of irritation. Some older dogs become cranky and impatient, especially when dealing with puppies or boisterous children. But don't just excuse behavioral changes, especially if they're sudden, as simply caused by aging. They could be symptoms of pain or disease.

Older dogs tend to like a simpler life, and although they are still up for adventure, that adventure may have to be tempered a bit, or at least not last quite so long. Long trips can be grueling for an older dog, and boarding in a kennel may be extremely upsetting. Consider getting a house-sitter who your dog knows if you want to go on vacation.

Older dogs may experience hearing or visual loss. Be careful not to startle a dog with impaired senses, as a startled dog could snap in self-defense. The slight haziness that appears in the older dog's pupils is normal and has a minimal effect on vision, but some dogs, especially those with diabetes, may develop cataracts. These can be seen as almost white through the dog's pupils. The lens can be removed by a veterinary ophthalmologist if the cataract is severe.

Dogs with gradual vision loss can cope well as long as they are kept in familiar surroundings and extra safety precautions are followed. For example, don't move furniture, and place sound or scent beacons throughout the house or yard to help the dog locate specific landmarks. Also lay pathways in the yard, such as gravel or brick walkways, and even in the house with carpet runners. Block open stairways or pools. Dogs with hearing loss can learn hand gestures and also respond to vibrations.

Even in the healthiest dogs, something has to give way first, and often it is the hindquarters. Your dog may need some help getting up and need some steadying when it walks. You can wrap a big towel under its belly and steady it by using the towel as a sling. Hind-quarter harnesses are also available. Of course, especially in a German Shepherd, any rear weakness needs to be checked thoroughly by a veterinarian.

You may have depended on your dog for years when it was younger. Now it is your turn to let your dog lean on you.

Your German Shepherd and you will travel a long way together. As it ages, be sure to make every step meaningful. (Dr. Zoë M. Backman)

Staying Well Up in Years

The immune system might be less effective in older dogs, so it is increasingly important to shield your dog from infectious disease, chilling, overheating, and any stressful conditions. At the same time, an older dog that is never exposed to other dogs may not need to be vaccinated as often or for as many diseases as a younger dog. Discuss this with your veterinarian.

Vomiting and diarrhea in an old dog can signal many different problems; keep in mind that an older dog cannot tolerate the dehydration that results from continued vomiting or diarrhea, so never let it continue unchecked.

Al Says

The older dog should see its veterinarian at least twice a year. Blood tests can detect early stages of diseases that respond well to treatment.

Older dogs present a somewhat greater anesthesia risk. Most of this increased risk can be negated, however, by first screening dogs with a complete medical workup. Many older dogs need tooth cleaning under anesthesia, and this is generally safe as long as your dog is otherwise healthy.

Older dogs tend to have a stronger body odor, but don't just ignore increased odors. They could indicate specific problems, such as periodontal disease, impacted anal sacs, seborrhea, ear infections, or even kidney disease. Any strong odor should be checked by your veterinarian. Like people, dogs lose skin moisture as they age, and although dogs don't have to worry about wrinkles, their skin can become dry and itchy. Regular brushing can help by stimulating oil production.

While GSDs of any age enjoy a soft warm bed, it is an absolute necessity for older GSDs. Arthritis is a common cause of intermittent stiffness and lameness, and it can be helped with heat, a soft bed, moderate exercise, and possibly drug therapy. New arthritis medications have made a huge difference in the quality of life for many older German Shepherds, but not every dog can use them. Ask your veterinarian to evaluate your dog.

In general, any ailment that an older dog has is magnified in severity compared to the same problems in a younger dog. Some of the more common symptoms and their possible cause in older GSDs include:

➤ **diarrhea:** kidney or liver disease, pancreatitis

➤ **coughing:** heart disease, tracheal collapse, lung cancer

➤ **difficulty eating:** periodontal disease, oral tumors

➤ **decreased appetite:** kidney, liver, or heart disease, pancreatitis, cancer

261

➤ **increased appetite:** diabetes, Cushing's syndrome

➤ **weight loss:** heart, liver, or kidney disease, diabetes, cancer

➤ **abdominal distention:** heart or kidney disease, Cushing's syndrome, tumor

➤ **increased urination:** diabetes, kidney or liver disease, cystitis, Cushing's syndrome

➤ **limping:** arthritis, hip or elbow dysplasia, degenerative myelopathy

➤ **nasal discharge:** tumor, periodontal disease

If you are lucky enough to have an old GSD, you still must accept that an end will come. Heart disease, kidney failure, and cancer eventually claim most of these senior citizens. Early detection can help delay their effects, but unfortunately, can seldom prevent them ultimately.

When You've Done Everything

Despite the best of care, the time will come when neither you nor your veterinarian can prevent your dear friend from succumbing to the ravages of old age or an incurable illness. It seems hard to believe that you will have to say good-bye to one who has been such a focal point of your life—in truth, a real member of your family. That dogs live such a short time compared to humans is a cruel fact, but one you must ultimately face.

You should realize that both of you have been fortunate to have shared so many good times, but make sure your GSD's remaining time is still pleasurable. Many terminal illnesses make your dog feel very ill, and there comes a point where your desire to keep your friend with you as long as possible may not be the kindest thing for either of you. If your dog no longer eats its dinner or treats, this is a sign that it does not feel well and you must face the prospect of doing what is best for your beloved friend. For every person, the ultimate point is different. Most people probably put off doing something for longer than is really best for the dog because they don't want to act in haste and be haunted by thoughts that maybe it was just a temporary setback. And of course, they put it off because they can't stand the thought.

Euthanasia is always a difficult and very personal decision that no one wants to make, and no one can make for you. Ask your veterinarian if there is a reasonable chance of your dog getting better and if it is likely that your dog is suffering. Ask yourself if your dog is getting pleasure out of life and if it enjoys most of its days. Financial considerations can be a factor if it means going into debt in exchange for just a little while longer. Your own emotional state must also be considered.

We all wish that if our dog has to go, it would fall asleep and never wake up. This, unfortunately, almost never happens. Even when it does, you are left with the regret that you never got to say good-bye. The closest way you can simulate this is with euthanasia. Euthanasia, which is painless, involves giving an overdose of an anesthetic. Essentially the dog falls asleep and dies almost instantly. In a very sick dog, because the circulation is compromised, this may take slightly longer, but the dog is unconscious.

If you do decide that euthanasia is the kindest farewell gesture for your beloved friend, discuss with your veterinarian beforehand what will happen. You may ask about giving your dog a tranquilizer beforehand if it is afraid of the vet's office. You might feel better having the doctor meet you at home or come out to your car. Although it won't be easy, try to remain with your dog so that its last moments will be filled with your love; otherwise, have a friend that your dog knows stay with it. Try to recall the wonderful times you have shared and realize that however painful losing such a once-in-a-lifetime dog is, it is better than never having had such a partner at all.

Eternal in Your Heart

Many people who regarded their German Shepherd as a member of the family nonetheless feel embarrassed at the grief they feel at its loss. Yet this dog has often functioned as a surrogate child, best friend, and confidant. Partnership with a pet can be one of the closest and most stable relationships in many people's lives. Because people are often closer to their pets than they are to distant family members, it is not uncommon to feel far more grief at the loss of the pet. Unfortunately, the support from friends that comes with human loss is too often absent with pet loss. Such well-meaning but ill-informed statements as "He was just a dog" or "Just get another one" do little to ease the pain, but the truth is that many people simply don't know how to react and probably aren't really as callous as they might sound. Many people share and understand your feelings, however, and pet bereavement counselors are available at many veterinary schools.

After losing such a cherished friend, many people say they will never get another dog. True, no dog will ever take the place of your dog. But you will find that another GSD is a welcome diversion and helps keep you from dwelling on the loss of your first pet, as long as you don't keep comparing the new dog to the old. True also, by getting another dog you are sentencing yourself to the same grief in another ten years or so, but wouldn't you rather have that than miss out on a second once-in-a-lifetime dog?

The loss of a companion may mark the end of an era for you, a time when you and your GSD grew up or grew old together. But one could scarcely ask for a better life partner than a special German Shepherd—perhaps the most magnificent being ever created.

The Least You Need To Know

➤ Older dogs may have changed metabolism. Special care must be taken to prevent obesity or wasting.

➤ Older dogs need more frequent veterinary attention and are more prone to several serious disorders.

➤ You will probably eventually have to evaluate your dog's quality of life and may have to consider euthanasia, if the quality is very poor.

➤ The grief of losing a pet is very real and can be debilitating. Help is available.

Bark Like a Dog-Person

Alsatian: At one time, the name for the German Shepherd Dog in England. *Or: The drool that comes out of your dog's mouth when it imitates Pavlov's dogs (that's* salivation*!).*

American-Canadian White Shepherd: Name for white German Shepherds in Europe.

Angulation: Angles between bones, typically between the shoulder blade and upper arm and between the upper and lower thigh. *Or: The emotion with which your GSD gazes upon you (that's* adulation*!).*

Aspergillus: Fungal infection, either of the nose or entire body, to which GSDs seem predisposed.

Autoimmune disease: Disorder in which the dog's immune system treats part of the dog's own body as though it were a foreign invader. *Or: Perception of many dogs and their owners that they are immune from harm by automobiles.*

Backyard breeder: Uninformed person who breeds dogs irresponsibly. *Or: Person who breeds backyards.*

B.A.R.F.: Acronym for Bones and Raw Food diet described in the text. *Or: What you may want to do when you have to feed bones and a raw food diet.*

Bitch: A female dog. *Or: What you do if your dog doesn't win.*

Bite: Occlusion. Also refers to how hard a dog bites in protection work.

Bloat: See **Gastric torsion.**

Breed Warden: Local representatives of the SV who evaluate prospective breedings and inspect litters. *Or: What a breed prison guard aspires to become.*

Bundesleistungshueten: German national Herding trial. *Or: Huh? Speak American!*

Castration: Removal of the testicles. *Or: What you do when you dress your GSD up in cute outfits.*

Cauda equina syndrome: Group of neurological signs resulting from the compression of spinal nerves.

CBC: Complete blood count; counts or estimates red blood cells, white blood cells, and platelets. *Or: Place in Atlanta where they keep diseases.*

Chem panel: Blood chemistry panel; measures various elements in bloodstream. *Or: Paneling derived from the Asian Chem tree.*

Coarse: Large-boned, lacking in refinement. *Or: Rough-talking dog, particularly a female.*

Conformation: Structure of a dog. Conformation shows evaluate how well a dog conforms to the breed Standard. *Or: When your dog gets accepted into church (that's* confirmation*!).*

Cushing's syndrome: Hyperadrenocorticism, a hormonal imbalance seen mostly in older dogs. *Or: When your dog can't sleep on hard surfaces.*

Degenerative myelopathy: Progressive disease in which the dog gradually loses control of first its hind limbs and then its forelimbs.

Demodicosis: Demodectic mange, also called red mange. *Or: Type of mange that votes on everything (that's* democratic*!).*

Deutsche Schaferhunde: German for German Shepherd Dog. *Or: Foreign name for an all-American breed.*

Disqualification: Trait that renders a dog ineligible to compete in AKC conformation shows. *Or: A dog with either dis quality or dat quality.*

Distemper: Extremely contagious and serious viral disease that all dogs should be inoculated against. *Or: What you have got to get control of when you see what your dog has done to your house.*

Dogma: Beliefs held in the absence of evidence. *Or: Dam of a litter.*

Dominance aggression: Aggressive behavior aimed at being top dog, even over the owner. *Or: Yes, sir! Whatever my dog wants, he gets.*

Double-handling: Also doubling. Having a second person attract a dog's attention from outside the show ring so the dog looks alert. *Or: Showing two dogs at once, with one for posing and the other for stunts.*

Drive: Strong thrust from the hindquarters. Also, strong desire to chase or protect. *Or: What your GSD is trying to figure out how to do as soon as you leave the keys within reach.*

Elbow dysplasia: Malformation of the elbow joint, often resulting in lameness.

Erlichiosis: A tick-borne disease. *Or: When your dog won't quit licking you.*

Flea allergy dermatitis (FAD): Allergic reaction to the bite of a flea. *Or: A passing fashion like those colorful bandanas all the dogs are wearing.*

Flooding: Misguided attempt to cure a dog's fear by overwhelming it. *Or: What your overwhelmed dog will likely do on your floor.*

Flying trot: Trot in which all four feet are suspended off the ground at full extension. *Or: Type of flying fish (that's* trout*!).*

Furunculosis: See **Perianal fistula.**

Gastric torsion: Life-threatening condition in which gasses become entrapped in the stomach, often caused by the stomach twisting.

Grand Victor: Best male at the GSDCA annual National Specialty show. *Or: Does that mean the Best Puppy is a Baby Grand?*

Grand Victrix: Best female at the GSDCA annual National Specialty show.

GSD pyoderma: Skin infection to which German Shepherds are predisposed.

Guard hairs: Longer coarser hairs making up the outer coat. *Or: Collection of shed hair formed into the shape of a life-size GSD on alert so that burglars think your dog is actually awake.*

Heartworms: Potentially deadly parasites that live in the heart and are spread by mosquitoes. *Or: All GSD puppies because they worm they way into your heart.*

Hemophilia: Deficiency in a specific blood-clotting factor.

Herdengebrauchshund: Herding Utility Dog title recognized by the SV. *Or: What your dog does when it chases a Brittany/Dachshund crossbreed.*

Hip dysplasia: Abnormal hip joint in which the ball and socket do not make a snug fit, often resulting in debilitating lameness.

Hot spot (pyotraumatic dermatitis): Moist reddened area caused by the dog chewing on itself, often in response to an allergic reaction. *Or: Where all the dogs in the neighborhood like to hang out.*

Hypothyroidism: Decreased production of thyroid hormone, resulting in a wide spectrum of symptoms.

Kennel cough: Tracheobronchitis, a highly infectious respiratory disease. *Or: What you do when you take a deep breath in a kennel of wet dogs.*

Körung: Survey system of the SV that recommends whether or not a specific dog should be bred.

Maldigestion: Inability to digest food properly because of pancreatic exocrine insufficiency.

OFA: Orthopedic Foundation for Animals, a registry of dogs for hip and elbow dysplasia, among some other disorders. *Or: Group devoted to providing corrective shoes to animals.*

Osteochondrosis dissecans: Degeneration of bone underlying the cartilage of joint areas, usually seen in young dogs.

Osteosarcoma: Malignant bone cancer.

Overshot: Occlusion in which the top incisors are in front of the bottom incisors, with a gap between them. *Or: When you throw something at your dog and it goes over its back.*

Pannus: Autoimmune problem in which the cornea of the eye becomes opaque.

Panosteitis: Excessive formation of bone growth around some joints, resulting in intermittent lameness in growing dogs.

Parvovirus: Extremely contagious gastrointestinal disease, especially life-threatening in puppies.

Patent ductus arteriosis: Congenital heart problem.

Perianal fistula: Draining tract in the area around the anus.

Pink papers: SV registration papers designating that both parents were recommended for breeding. *Or: What some people might use to housebreak girl puppies.*

Pituitary dwarfism: Type of hereditary dwarfism in GSDs caused by lack of growth hormone.

Puppy mill: Large-scale breeding operation dealing in many different breeds, usually in substandard conditions.

Reach: Length of forward stride. *Or: What your dog will stay just beyond when you are in a hurry and it has your car keys in its mouth.*

Rescue: Taking responsibility for an unwanted dog. Also, any such unwanted dog. *Or: What YOU will need if you try to rescue all the dogs that need it.*

Roach: An overly arched back. *Or: What you will have after your dog has dribbled crumbs all over the place.*

Sable: Black-tipped outer hairs in which the undercoat is lighter. *Or: "Hmm, the wife always said she wanted a sable..."*

Saddle: Dark patch over the back. *Or: What some oversized GSDs need.*

269

Schutzhund: German for protection dog, a title entailing Tracking, Obedience, and Protection tests. *Or: Breed of dog that continues to mess on your floor.*

Scissors bite: Occlusion in which the top incisors fit snugly in front of the bottom incisors. *Or: What your dog's teeth will do to any papers you have lying around.*

Set up: To pose a dog by hand in the show ring. *Or: To play a trick on your dog.*

Sieger: Best male at the annual SV show. *Or: Something you smoke.*

Siegerin: Best female at the annual SV show. *Or: Shouldn't that be Sieger-ette?*

Separation anxiety: Abnormal stress in response to the owner's absence. *Or: Fear that the owner will want to separate the dog's head from its body after seeing the damage the dog has just done in the owner's absence.*

Sound: A dog that is built and moves correctly, particularly referring to movement when viewed from the front and rear. *Or: What you hear from the other room when your dog is getting into trouble.*

Spay: Removal of the uterus and ovaries. *Or: Type of shovel (that's spade!).*

Specialty: Prestigious show in which only one breed is shown (in this case, a show for GSDs only). *Or: Whatever your dog is good at, such as digging holes in the furniture, taking up the entire bed, or puking in front of guests.*

Stop: Transition point from muzzle to backskull, as viewed in profile. *Or: What you keep yelling at your puppy.*

Subvalvular aortic stenosis: Congenital heart problem.

Type: Essential characteristics of the breed. *Or: What your GSD could probably do if only its paws weren't so big.*

Undershot: Occlusion in which the top incisors are behind the bottom incisors. *Or: When you throw something at your dog and it goes under the dog instead of over it.*

Verein für Deutsche Schaferhunde (SV): The German national parent club for German Shepherds and the largest breed club in the world.

Veteran: Older dog, usually over seven years of age. *Or: Dog that was in the war.*

Von Willebrand's disease: Defective blood platelet function, resulting in excessive bleeding.

Weedy: Lacking sufficient bone and musculature. *Or: What's left in the part of the yard the dog hasn't finished digging up.*

Withers: Highest point of shoulders, where a dog's height is normally measured. *Or: The owner's idea of where the dog will follow, as in "Whither thou goest..."*

WUSV: World Union of SV clubs. *Or: That's those wrestlers on TV, right?*

X-pen: Small portable wire enclosure. *Or: What your writing pen will be if you leave it within your dog's reach.*

Can't Get Enough?

Organizations

Agility Association of Canada (AAC)
RR#2
Lucan, Ontario N0N 2J0
519/657-7636

America GSD Working Dogs Group
3810 Paule Ave.
St. Louis, MO 63125-1718
314/638-9686
fax: 314/638-0609
E-mail address: USASchutzhund@worldnet.att.net.
http://www.germanshepherddog.com/

American Kennel Club (AKC)
5580 Centerview Drive
Raleigh, NC 27606-3390
919/233-9767
E-mail: info@akc.org
http://www.akc.org/

American Rescue Dog Association
P.O. Box 151
Chester, NY 10918
http://www.ardainc.org/

The American White Shepherd Association
http://www.onewaits.com/awsa/framedead.htm

Assistance Dogs International
c/o Freedom Service Dogs
P.O. Box 150217
Lakewood, CO 80215-0217
http://www.assistance-dogs-intl.org/

**Canine Companions for Independence
(Service, Signal, Social, and Therapy Dogs)**
P.O. Box 446
Santa Rosa, CA 95402-0446
707/577-1780
707/577-1756 (TTY)
fax: 707/577-1711
E-mail: info@caninecompanions.org
http://www.caninecompanions.org/

Canine Performance Events (CPE)
P.O. Box 445
Walled Lake, MI 48390
E-mail: cpe-agility@juno.com

Delta Society National Service Dog Center
289 Perimeter Rd. E.
Renton, WA 98055
800/869-6898
800/809-2714 (TDD)
http://www2.deltasociety.org/deltasociety/

Deutscher Verband der Gebrauchshundsportvereine (DVG)
Sandi Purdy, Secretary
5718 Watson Circle
Dallas, TX 75225
214/361-0183
E-mail: SPurdy5718@aol.com
http://webusers.anet-stl.com/~dvgamer/

German Shepherd Dog Club of America
Membership: Gail Hardcastle
4120 Douglas Blvd. #306-102
Granite Bay, CA 95746-9437
Phone: 916/791-5642

fax/message: 916/791-0530
E-mail: hardcg@aol.com
http://www.gsdca.org/Noframes/GSDCA.html

German Shepherd Dog Club of America, Inc., Rescue

Linda Kury, Rescue Committee National Chair
369 Drake Court
Santa Clara, CA 95051
408/247-1272
http://www.gsd-rescue.com/rescue_usa.html

German Shepherd Dog Club of America Working Dog Association

http://www.gsdca-wda.com/

German Shepherd Dog Club of Canada

Membership: Jim Randall
RR 3
Fergus, ON N1M 2W4
E-mail: gsdcc@albedo.net
http://juliet.albedo.net/~gsdcc/

The Kennel Club

1–5 Clarges Street
London, W1Y 8AB
England
http://www.the-kennel-club.org.uk/

North American Dog Agility Council (NADAC)

HCR 2, Box 277
St. Maries, Idaho 83861
208/689-3803
E-mail: nelsonk9@iea.com

North American Police Work Dog Association

4222 Manchester Ave.
Perry, OH 44081
888/4CANINE
http://www.napwda.com/

North American Ring Association (French Ring Sport)
Roxanne Allen, Treas.
113 Brook Rd.
Falmouth, ME 04105
http://www.cybertours.com/~pettrain/narahome.htm

Orthopedic Foundation for Animals
2300 E. Nifong Blvd.
Columbia, MO 65201
573/442-0418
fax: 573/875-5073
E-mail: ofa@offa.org
http://www.offa.org/

Paws With a Cause
4646 South Division
Wayland, MI 49348
616/877-PAWS (TDD/VOICE)
800/253-PAWS (TDD/VOICE)
616/877-0248
E-mail: paws@alliance.net
http://www.ismi.net/paws/

PennHIP
271 Great Valley Parkway
Malvern, PA 19355
800/248-8099

Rin Tin Tin Canine Ambassador Club
Daphne Hereford
P.O. Box 1505
Rosenberg, TX 77471
281/239-7106
fax: 281/232-3365
E-mail: oRinTinTin@aol.com

United Kennel Club (UKC)
100 East Kilgore Road
Kalamazoo, MI 49001-5593
616/343-9020
http://www.ukcdogs.com/whats_new.htm

United Schutzhund Clubs of America (USA)
3810 Paule Ave.
St. Louis, MO 63125-1718
314/638-9686
fax: 314/638-0609
E-mail: USA Schutzhund@worldnet.att.net.
http://www.germanshepherddog.com/INDEX.HTML

United States Dog Agility Association (USDAA)
P.O. Box 850995
Richardson, Texas 75085-0955
972/231-9700
E-mail: info@usdaa.com

Verein für Deutsche Schaferhunde (SV)
Steinerne Furt 71/71a
D-86167 Augsburg
Germany

White German Shepherd Dog Club International, Inc.
P.O. Box 70222
Salt Lake City, UT 84170-0222
http://www2.aros.net/~wgsdcii//clubinfo.htm

Magazines

Canadian GSD Gazette
Available through the GSD Club of Canada

Clean Run (Agility)
35 Walnut Street
Turners Falls, MA 01376
800/311-6503
fax: 413/863-8303
E-mail: info@cleanrun.com
http://www.cleanrun.com/

Dog Sports magazine (covers protection, Schutzhund,
   search and rescue, and so forth)
Cheryl Carlson, Editor
231 Orin Way
Douglas, WY 82633-9232
307/358-3487
fax: 307/358-4752
E-mail: DSM@coffey.com
http://www.cyberpet.com/cyberdog/products/pubmag/dgsptmag.htm

Dog World Magazine
P.O. Box 56240
Boulder, CO 80322-6240
800/361-8506
http://www.dogworldmag.com/

DVG America
Available through Deutscher Verband der
   Gebrauchshundsportvereine (DVG)

German Shepherd Dog Review
30 Far View Road
Chalfont, PA 18914
gsprock@azstarnet.com

German Shepherd Quarterly
Hoflin Publishing
4401 Zephyr St.
Wheat Ridge, CO 80033
303/420-2222
http://web.hoflin.com/Magazines/The%20German%20Shepherd-
   %20Qrtly.html

Pure Bred Dogs/AKC Gazette
Available through the AKC

Ring Sport News (French protection ring sport)
Available through International Ring Sport Association

Schutzhund USA
Available through United Schutzhund Clubs of America

The Shepherd's Din (for White GSDs)
Available through White German Shepherd Dog Club
  International, Inc.

Books

Ackerman, Lowell J. *Dr. Ackerman's Book of the German Shepherd.*
TFH Publications, 1996.

Allan, Roy and Clarissa. *The Essential German Shepherd Dog.* Ringpress
Books, Ltd., 1996.

Antesberger, Helmut. *The German Shepherd Dog: A Complete Owner's
Manual.* Hauppauge, NY: Barron's Educational Series, Inc., 1985.

Barwig, Susan (ed.). *The German Shepherd.* Wheat Ridge, CO: Hoflin
Publishing, 1994.

Barwig, Susan and Stewart Hilliard. *Schutzhund: Theory and Training
Methods.* New York: Howell Book House, 1991.

Bennett, Jane. *The New Complete German Shepherd Dog.* New York:
Howell Book House, 1987.

Coile, D. Caroline. *Show Me! A Dog-Showing Primer.* Hauppauge, NY:
Barron's Educational Series, Inc., 1997.

Cree, John. *Training the German Shepherd Dog.* Trafalgar Square, 1997.

Dunbar, Ian. *The Essential German Shepherd Dog.* New York: Howell
Book House, 1998.

Freund, Jan L. *German Shepherd Champions 1952–80.* Camino
Publications, 1986.

Freund, Jan L. *German Shepherd Champions 1981–86.* D. Johnson
Enterprises, 1985.

Hart, Ernest H. and William F. Goldbecker. *The German Shepherd Dog.*
TFH Publications, 1985.

Hegewald-Kawich, Horst and Vriends, Matthew. *The German Shepherd Dog: Expert Advice on Training, Care, and Nutrition.* Hauppauge, NY: Barron's Educational Series, Inc., 1996.

Kerstiens, Cindy (ed.). *The Best of the First Ten Years of the German Shepherd Quarterly.* Wheat Ridge, CO: Hoflin Publishing, 1992.

Lanting, Fred L. *The Total German Shepherd Dog.* Loveland, CO: Alpine Publications, 1990.

Nicholas, Anna Katherine. *The Book of the German Shepherd Dog.* TFH Publications, 1983.

Palika, Liz. *The German Shepherd Dog: An Owner's Guide to a Happy Healthy Pet.* New York: Howell Book House, 1995.

Rankin, Sheila. *The Ultimate German Shepherd Dog.* New York: Howell Book House, 1998.

Seigal, Mordicai and Matthew Margolis. *The Good Shepherd: A Pet Owner's Guide to the German Shepherd.* Little, Brown, and Company, 1996.

Strickland, Winifred Gibson and James A. Moses. *The German Shepherd Today.* New York: Howell Book House, 1998.

Von Stephanitz, Max. *The German Shepherd Dog In Word and Picture.* Wheat Ridge, CO: Hoflin Publishing, 1994 (reprint of 1925 edition).

Walkowicz, Chris. *The German Shepherd Dog.* Wilsonville, OR: Doral Publications, 1991.

Willis, Malcolm B. *The German Shepherd Dog: A Genetic History.* New York: Howell Book House, 1991.

Willis, Malcolm B. *Pet Owner's Guide to the German Shepherd Dog.* New York: Howell Book House, 1993.

Willis, Malcolm B. *Best Friend's Guide to the German Shepherd Dog.* New York: Howell Book House, 1993.

Videos

The AKC German Shepherd Standard
Video #VVT 812
AKC, Attn: Video fulfillment
5580 Centerview Drive
Raleigh, NC 27606-3390
919/233-9767

Complete line of GSD training videos and equipment, including Obedience, Tracking, Schutzhund, and police work:

Leerburg Video
P.O. Box 218
Menomonie, WI 54751
715/235-6502
fax: 715/235-8868
E-mail: frawley@leerburg.com
http://leerburg.com/table.htm

German Shepherd: Structure

German Shepherd: Gait and Locomotion

German Shepherd: Handling and Judging

All three videos produced by Center for Studies in College, 1997.

Web Sites

Working Dogs (extensive links dealing with GSD performance and work)
http://workingdogs.com/doc0007.htm

The GSD Ring of GSD sites on the Web
http://dbirtwis.interspeed.net/gsdring.html

GSD Infoline
http://www.gsd-infoline.com/index-e.htm

GSD Web Site
http://www.gdconsulting.com.au/GSD/

281

The Real GSD (extensive information about the history of the
Working GSD, emphasizing SV)
http://www3.sympatico.ca/realgsd/

WUSV information
http://www.tp-hundeguide.dk/index/wusv/index.htm

WUSV GSD breed Standard
http://sentex.net/~sirius/breed_standard.htm

Conformation Showing Auf Deutshe! Describes the SV conformation
show system.
http://www.ultranet.com/~reiher/conformat.html

German Shepherds in Herding
http://www.geocities.com/Heartland/Ranch/5093/

Working Dogs International Cyberzine
http://www.workingdogs.com/

List of GSD e:mail discussion lists
http://dbirtwis.interspeed.net/lists.html

List of local GSD clubs
http://www.cheta.net/connect/canine/Clubs/germshep.htm

The Dog Agility Page
http://www.dogpatch.org/agility/

French Ring Sport
http://members.aol.com/malndobe/frring.htm

National Association for Search and Rescue (NASAR) Dog/Handler
Guidelines
http://www.nasar.org/prod/members/canine/caninegd.htm

The Tracking Page
http://personal.cfw.com/~dtratnac/

The Obedience Home Page (for the sport of dog obedience)
http://www.princeton.edu/~nadelman/obed/obed.html

Careers in Dogs links
http://www.uwsp.edu/acad/psych/dog/misc.htm#career

Information about responsible breeding
http://www.dog-play.com/ethics.html

Canine Diversity Project (genetics and health)
http://www.magma.ca/~kaitlin/diverse.html

World Wide Web Virtual Library of Veterinary Medicine
http://netvet.wustl.edu/vetmed.htm

Encyclopedia of Canine Medical Information
http://www.vetinfo.com/dencyclopedia/deindex.html

Information on degenerative myelopathy in GSDs
http://www.vetmed.ufl.edu/sacs/index.htm

Canine Sports Medicine Update online magazine
http://www.concentric.net/~Dovervet/csmu/

Rainbow Bridge Tribute Page (dealing with the loss of a pet)
http://rainbowbridge.tierranet.com/bridge.htm

Emergencies

National Animal Poison Control Center
800/548-2423 or
888/4ANIHELP (888/426-4435)
$30 per case—credit card
900/680-0000
$30 per case—phone bill
http://www.napcc.aspca.org/

Index

285